HARVARD MIDDLE EASTERN STUDIES 12

TRIPOLI
A MODERN
ARAB CITY

TRIPOLI
A MODERN ARAB CITY

JOHN GULICK

HARVARD UNIVERSITY PRESS

CAMBRIDGE, MASSACHUSETTS

1967

In

Remembrance

of

My Father

MILLARD BURR GULICK

Master of Architecture

1892–1956

and

My Great-Uncle

CHARLES BURTON GULICK

Professor of the Classical Culture of Greece

1868–1962

PREFACE

THE SUBJECT OF this book is the present-day city of Tripoli, Lebanon. As a social anthropologist interested in Arab culture and also in urban cultures generally, I chose to study a Lebanese city because of the already existing mass of information on Lebanese culture to which I myself had contributed a village study. Some of this information, I knew, could be applied in my work on Tripoli. I chose Tripoli itself for three primary reasons. First, it is large enough to qualify in anyone's mind as being "urban," but it is not so large that a single investigator's work cannot, in a limited time, encompass at least some of its aspects. Second, Tripoli's population is mostly Sunni Muslim, and in this respect the city is not "typically Lebanese" but is representative of non-Lebanese Arab cities. Third, Tripoli is not one of the great and famous Arab cities. If its name sounds familiar, it is probably only because it is confused with North African Tripoli on whose shores the U.S. Marines fought. Unlike that other Tripoli, and unlike Aleppo, Baghdad, Cairo, Damascus, Jerusalem, and others, it has neither an illustrious history nor is it a "special case" of some sort in the world of today. It is the kind of "ordinary" city which needs more attention by serious investigators.

Urban growth is one of the major phenomena of the twentieth century, and much of it is taking place in "ordinary" cities like Tripoli, whose population has increased sixfold in the past fifty years. This rate of growth is not unusual for a city in one of the technologically underdeveloped nations, of which Lebanon, despite its relative westernization and prosperity, is certainly one.

Urban growth is probably as important an aspect of the development of these nations as village aid and agricultural reforms. Yet the only concepts available for its elucidation are wholly inadequate. The word "urbanization" is widely used not only to mean urban growth as it is

PREFACE

indicated in census materials, but also with an acquired overload of connotations which are treated as if they were established facts. The word is constantly used to imply growth of impersonal relations, loss of roots, increase of social disorganization, loss of meaningful symbols, the general spread of anomie, and other dire but impalpable ills. In vain, it seems, a number of observers have pointed out in recent years that, although such phenomena may have been among the birth pangs of the industrial metropolises of the West, they are not the only diagnostic criteria of western urban life today. True, they may serve to highlight some of the difficulties in contemporary western urban life, but they ignore its satisfactions and attractions, and therefore do not typify it.

Yet social scientists, including some anthropologists studying technologically developing peasant cultures like Lebanon's, persist in using these words as if they represented characteristic urban realities which, in turn, supposedly are the opposite of rural ones. "The rural-urban dichotomy may not conform to reality very closely, but it is a good heuristic device" — this is the argument. It may be a good heuristic device, but it is also assumed to be a model, which is not quite the same thing. A good model, like a good map, oversimplifies certain aspects of reality in order to facilitate initial comprehension of it, but its oversimplifications do not create miscomprehensions. To insist, for example, that impersonal relationships, as opposed to personal ones, typify modern urban life, despite numerous studies showing the importance of urban neighborhood and family relationships, is to insist on miscomprehension of urban realities. At best, this is a perversely heuristic procedure, for it leads most students into unnecessary error rather than to the discovery of reality. It is probably nearer the truth to say that the city dweller has to deal with more impersonal relationships than does the villager, in addition to his personal ones, but the clichés of the rural-urban dichotomy do not adequately convey this observation.

The research on Tripoli which I conducted from September 1961 to July 1962 was based on the belief that the conventional conception of urban life as a set of undesirable opposites to rural life is deceptive. However, an adequate model has not yet been developed as a substitute. This book does not pretend to work out such a model, but it does constitute, I hope, a step in the right direction. I conceive of the city as an environment which the inhabitants can and do alter but to which they must also continually adapt themselves. The inhabitants are described from various anthropological, sociological, and psychological points of view, combined with an awareness of the various problems which in general accompany high-density urban living. I try to specify what are statements of fact (and their sources) and to distinguish them from suppositions and generalizations. In discussing both facts and generalizations, I avoid loaded or ambiguous terms, such as those of conventional urban "theory," or else give them precise definitions and use them consistently. I agree with C. Wright Mills that much "significant" social science literature consists of pretentious verbosity which not only obscures quite simple meanings but also can foster an erroneous impression of new insights. This is certainly true in the area of urban theory, and if we are to improve it, we must divest ourselves of the old platitudes before we can develop any new wisdom.

All field studies suffer from limitations. Students of urban ecology and demography will find this book deficient in the kind of statistics they value. Few such statistics exist for Tripoli, and those figures I do use were obtained in bits and pieces, from many sources, often only after long negotiation or by indirect means. Urban sociologists will decry the lack of survey data in this book. Such a survey would require the services of a trained corps of Lebanese, and preferably Tripolitan, interviewers. This I did not have the time or facilities to develop, although I did conduct a survey among Tripolitan students at the American University of Beirut. Social anthropologists will miss extended and intimate details on such things as kinship behavior. The people in Tripoli to whom I had introductions, and with whom I became best acquainted, belonged to a minority group. They included some sharp observers of the city, but those details of their lives of which I became aware were not necessarily typical of it. Nevertheless, problems of kinship and marriage, of neighborhood behavior, of village ties and social class, are by no means neglected herein.

Among Lebanese residents of Beirut whom I know, Tripoli has the reputation of being "closed" and "fanatical." This opinion is not easy to evaluate. It is true that the leaders of Tripoli in the 1920's did not want their city to be included in the new state of Lebanon and that there has been, ever since, resentment of the powers-that-be in Beirut. It is true that a prominent Tripolitan was one of the leaders of the "insurgents" in the crisis of 1958, a conflict which might easily have crystallized into one of the worst fears of the Lebanese: large-scale, open warfare between Muslims and Christians. It is true that the degree of westernized emancipation of women evident in Beirut is not so great in Tripoli, where young ladies in ski pants seeking refreshment after a day of sport in the mountains have been publicly insulted. Such elements make up the reputation. Yet I have no evidence that the Tripolitans are any more wary of the motives of strangers than are the Lebanese generally, nor that their sectarianism is any more intense. These feelings do not make social science research easy in Lebanon, but I am not sure that the Tripolitans are especially difficult in this regard.

Two political events during the period of study exacerbated the normal feeling of general unrest in the area. Early in the fall of 1961 Syria declared its independence of the United Arab Republic. In Tripoli, many people would like to belong to Syria but also have openly pro-Nasser sentiments. This event created a mood of confusion and disappointment in the city; as one of my informants said, "You couldn't have started your study at a worse time."

On December 31, 1961, an attempted coup by members of the Partie Populaire Syrienne was quelled in Beirut. Its aftermath colored Lebanese public affairs for the remainder of the period of study. This was an affair in which Americans were not, for once, considered to be involved, but the Lebanese — in an atmosphere of mass detentions, military roadblocks, and searches — became, I think, more than usually circumspect with each other, and this did not make communication easier.

With all these circumstances in mind, I owe much gratitude to a number of people in Tripoli who helped me in so many ways and, in their fashion, shared their lives and city with me. First, I would like to acknowledge the courtesies extended to me by the Honorable Muhammad Misqawi and the Honorable Elias Nahhas, president and vice president, respectively, of the Tripoli Municipal Council.

Secondly, I would like to thank the Reverend and Mrs. George E. Khuri for their great helpfulness and hospitality. The many other people who contributed to my knowledge of Tripoli and assisted my study of it in so many ways are too numerous to mention by name. But I want them to know that I have not forgotten them. I hope that those of them who read this book will find it interesting. Undoubtedly it is not without errors, but its intention is to contribute to greater knowledge and wisdom.

As usual in such studies as this, a number of friends and scholarly colleagues provided suggestions, inspiration, and help: Samir G. Khalaf, Derwood W. Lockard, Levon Melikian, Karen and Gene Petersen, E. Terry Prothro, and Afif Tannous.

My research in Tripoli in 1961–62 was made possible by a grant from the Near and Middle East Joint Program of the American Council of Learned Societies and the Social Science Research Council, supplemented by a smaller grant from the University Research Council of the University of North Carolina. The American University of Beirut made all of its facilities for faculty available to me and my family during our stay in Lebanon. While in Lebanon, I was very much assisted in the translation of Arabic books, magazines, and newspapers by Miss Nada Ghandour.

The University of North Carolina granted me a leave of absence in 1961–62 and soon again in 1964–65. During this latter period I had the privilege of enjoying a Research Fellowship in the Center for Middle Eastern Studies, Harvard University, providing time and freedom from routine academic chores to facilitate the writing of this book. I am particularly grateful to Sir Hamilton A. R. Gibb, Director of the Center; and to Carolyn Cross, Elizabeth Randolph, Brenda Sens, and Martha Smith, for their assistance and their careful work in the preparation of the manuscript of this book.

During 1961–62, my Harvard fellowship was supplemented by a Special Fellowship from the National Institute of Mental Health.

My wife, Margaret E. Gulick, has been constant in her companionship, patience, encouragement, and very thorough and helpful comments on and criticisms of the manuscript of this book.

To all these individuals and institutions, as well as to many other people too numerous to name individually, I wish to express my thanks.

There are two matters concerning the reading of this book about which the reader should be warned. The first has to do with the transliteration of Arabic names and words. The method used herein is very much simplified — so much so that it fails to make a number of important phonemic distinctions. I personally would have much preferred a more precise transliteration. However, since technical linguistic issues are not involved in this book, this imprecision should not affect those readers who are not familiar with Arabic. Those who do know Arabic need to be assured that I am fully aware that the system of transliteration used here does not make any discrimination between the long and short vowels, between the frontal and palatalized consonants, or between the fortis pharyngeal aspiration and the lenis aspiration. Readers interested in technical details of the Tripoli dialect are referred to the monograph by Hassan el-Hajjé.

The second warning is this: in most of my discussions of Tripoli I use the present tense because it is simpler and more realistic. However, it is important that readers keep in mind that the present in terms of which I write is that of 1961–62 and not that of the time when the book was written (1964–65) or of whenever it is read. This warning is perhaps particularly important for those readers whose interest in this book is primarily in the contemporay life of the city, its institutions, and the behavioral patterns of its people.

Chapter II is a history of Tripoli, necessarily alluding to epochs and events in Middle Eastern history, and many people are not familiar with

PREFACE

that history. The later parts of Chapter II, however, describe recent developments in the city, and these developments bear directly on its contemporary life. A much more detailed physical description of Tripoli will be found in Appendix A. It was written to be read in conjunction with the maps and is intended especially for readers who can visualize buildings, streets, and urban topography from verbal descriptions of them.

J. G.

October 1966
Chapel Hill, North Carolina

CONTENTS

Tables

Maps

Photographs

following p. 206

TRIPOLI
A MODERN
ARAB CITY

MAP 1

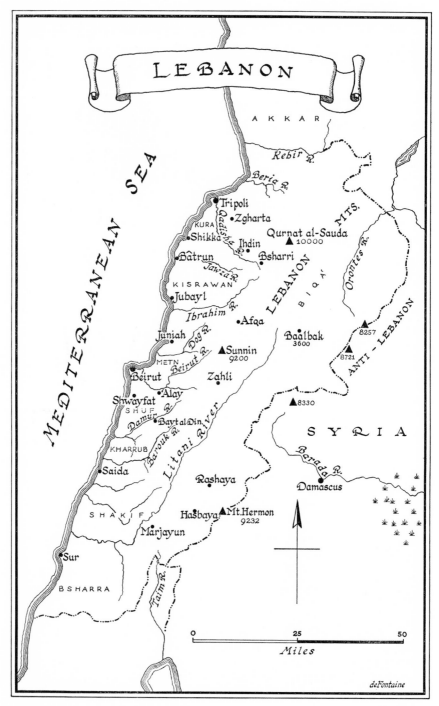

LEBANON

MEDITERRANEAN SEA

AKKAR

Kebir R.

Beria R.

•Tripoli
•Zgharta

KURA
•Shikka
Qadisha R.
Ihdin
Qurnat al-Sauda
▲ 10000

•Bâtrun
Jawza R.
•Bsharri

KISRAWAN

L E B A N O N   M T S.

B I Q A '

Orontes R.

•Jubayl

Ibrahim R.
•Afqa

Baalbak
3600

Juniah
Dog R.
▲Sunnin
9200

METN
Beirut R.

Beirut

Zahli

Shwayfat
•Alay
SHUF
Damur R.
•Bayt al Din.

KHARRUB
Barouk R.
Litani River

•Saida

Rashaya

▲8330

▲8257

▲8721

A N T I - L E B A N O N

S Y R I A

Barada R.

•Damascus

SHAKIF
Hasbaya ▲Mt.Hermon
9232

•Sur
Marjayun

B S H A R R A

Taim R.

0   25   50

Miles

deFontaine

Chapter I

SIGHTS AND SOUNDS

ALLAAAAHU AKBAR!"

At an hour before dawn, the call to prayer begins to reverberate through the streets. First one and then another mosque takes up its chant. Quickly others follow, and in a few moments it is as if they were singing a sort of round in which the different parts complement and echo against each other. After about five minutes, the electrically amplified voices fall silent, and the city is as hushed as before.

Slowly life stirs. The buildings, some under fluorescent tubes curving over the main streets, some heavily shadowed, are mostly dark, but here and there a window is bright. In the middle of a whole block of shuttered storefronts, sleepy passengers board a country bus in front of a lighted doorway. An old man with a broom of twigs sweeps yesterday's debris into piles in the gutter. A coffee vendor, his tall tin decanters gleaming beside him, squats against a wall. Apparently dozing, he is ready for his first customer, and so are many of his competitors.

In the Tal, all the shops are dark and deserted, but from behind the iron grilles barring the entries of the cinemas, Steve Reeves and Gina Lollobrigida mutely proclaim their horrendous epics. The last to close at night, the movies will not reopen until afternoon.

Beyond the silent workshops of Zahriyyah, the day is already further advanced in Bab al-Tibbani. Beneath glaring lights, trucks from north, east, and south are being unloaded. Crates of cabbages, grapes, and other produce are checked off and opened. A score of two-wheeled carts, their horses or mules bedecked with ornaments and talismans, stand ready for the loads they will distribute to various parts of the city. While none of the groceries is open yet, the butcher shops are bright, bloody, and ready for business, for the slaughterhouse in the Mina has done its night's work.

At dawn, the call to prayer is no longer the predominant voice of the city, and if more people heed it, more people are also busy in other activities. Sheet-metal storefront shutters begin to rattle open. Carts, automobiles, trucks, and buses are more numerous. In the small, cavernous cafés of Bab Hadid, 'Attarin and Sagha laborers eat bread and hot milk from steaming bowls. When the streetlights go out, the city is temporarily darker, but it is vibrating with activity.

Soon, schoolchildren in twos and threes are making their way in every direction. Even the smallest ones carry briefcases or book bags, and the small boys and nearly all of the girls wear uniform smocks — black for the government schools and a wide assortment of gingham designs for the private ones. At seven o'clock, one of the latter seems barricaded behind the high wall which protects its yard from the sidewalk. Its solid, iron gate, which rolls horizontally on tracks, is closed. A young peasant woman, with a small child on her hip, strides purposefully along the wall and sits down with her back against it. While the child sucks its thumb, plays in the gutter, or seeks its mother's breasts, the young woman greets each passerby with open hand. Another entrepreneur appears with a pushcart and takes his station beside the gate. He is selling cookies, candies, and nosegays.

The children begin to arrive on foot and by car and enter the school through a postern in the gate. The street becomes the ultimate in traffic bedlam when a school bus incredibly forces its way through the cars and enters the gate which has been rolled open for it, the jostled peddler continuing to do business all the while. Inside, the children are dragooned into lines awaiting the march to their classrooms. The gate is closed again, and traffic abates to its normal daytime flow. A latecomer, her head completely enveloped in a transparent black veil, quickly approaches the postern, sweeping off the veil with one hand as she enters. The peddler moves away, and the young woman walks off with her child as briskly as she came. The postern clangs shut, and the school, from which chanted recitations can now be heard, again presents to the world its closed front —

yellow stuccoed wall and black gate, blank except for posters advertising movies and stenciled notices which mean "Post no bills."

Bent double, a barefoot servant girl sweeps water over the tiled floor, using a broom with no handle. The water gushes through spouts in the balcony wall and splashes onto the pavement below. Carpets hang over the walls of other balconies. Whacking thumps resound against the concrete buildings across the street as other servants, or men hired for the purpose, beat the carpets, charging the air with dust which settles upon balconies below. And sitting in pajamas on one of these a young man peels an orange, tossing the coils of skin into the street. It is his Jaguar, perhaps, which is parked on the sidewalk next to an open ditch in the street. A round basket full of vegetables rises from the hands of a pushcart vendor, lifted by a string to an apartment above. Voices call from building to building as the clotheslines of the apartment house, on roof and balconies, are filled with white laundry.

Behind the ticket counter at the bus station in the Tal, the agent's heavy blue jowls quiver as he shouts into the telephone, checking off reservations against seat numbers scrawled in a book before him. Hanging up, he turns again to the dozen arms and hands outstretched to him. With a look of resigned despair he serves first one and then another, at random. Customers with tickets extricate themselves from the tangle and board the bus, searching for their numbered seats and arguing with anyone who has been disorderly enough to take the wrong one. The bus is of German make, but painted outside on its front is a life-sized pink hand with an open eye in its palm, both transfixed by an arrow. Painted inside above the windshield is a sign asking God for his blessings, and from the mirror dangle metal and leather talismans. "Ruh!" cries the attendant, slamming the rear door shut, when he has taken the last ticket. "Go!" And the bus swings into the boulevard, headed for Beirut. Taxis and other cars dodge behind and in front of it, their horns blowing wildly, a quiet send-off compared to the reception it will have in the capital.

Pedestrians crowd the sidewalks of the Tal and overflow into the streets. Gendarmes lounge around the discolored yellow walls of the old Saraya in front of which Syrians in *kuffiyah* and *gumbaz* pace back and forth offering rugs for sale. Some they carry on their shoulders; some are rolled out on the sidewalk. Newsboys (actually young men) shout the headlines, carrying an assortment of Beirut papers extended on a wooden framework. Newspapers and magazines from Beirut and Cairo festoon the fence enclosing an outdoor coffee-house, and here men sit at small tables smoking water pipes and playing cards, backgammon, or dominoes.

Chickens, carried along by their feet, stare beady-eyed at the pavement on which, soon, they will expire in a flurry of blood and feathers.

Cloths snap between the hands of shoeshine boys as they put on a high polish, and books of national lottery tickets flutter in the hands of youths who shout that one's luck may never turn if one does not take a chance right now. From posters in shop windows, President Nasser, President Shihab, Premier Karami, and other politicians as well, variously smile and smile. From radios in cars, cafés, and shops, the news is broadcast in staccato cadences, and Arabic love songs quaver and wail.

And all is permeated by sharp odors: cinnamon, cleaning fluid, coffee, diesel and gasoline fumes, kerosene, roasting mutton, sesame seeds, tobacco smoke, and urine.

"Al 'ibbi -'ibbi -'ibbi -'ibbi - hawn!" shouts a *service* driver, anxious for his fifth fare to complete his payload for the Qubbah. Cars for the Qubbah wait in one place. Cars for the Mina wait in another, outside the park. The spearlike tops of the iron pickets of the park's fence have been bent over or twisted off, and many of the supporting stone piers lack part or all of their conical ornamental tops. One of these is embedded in the ground inside the park, and the grass around it is carefully trimmed. Seated on a bench, a young man and a very old one converse quietly. *Cling-cling*: a passing coffee seller announces himself. The young man beckons to him, and he dextrously pours water into two small porcelain cups, dashes the water on the ground, and replaces it with pungent coffee which the two customers sip noisily. At the park gate a man carefully selects a ka'k from a push-cart. It is shaped like a large, eccentric doughnut. Holding it by the narrow part, he tears a hole in the widest part, sprinkles dried thyme into its hollow interior and begins to munch. Waiters carry plates of bread and hummus or filafil among the pedestrians to merchants who prefer to eat in their shops rather than go home or to a restaurant.

If many people take an early afternoon siesta, it is not apparent in the streets, for traffic and business continue with unabated intensity.

4

The din of the iron workers' shops in Zahriyyah, of the furniture makers in Tirbi'a, and the copper and brass artisans in Nahhasiyyin betoken no more and no less activity than does the murmuring of Bazarkan, where it is as if the bargaining voices were muffled in the bolts of cloth which fill the little shops. Cross-legged, a goldsmith hammers out a bangle on a steel cone. It will join the others which hang from padlocked rods in the window of his shop — a shop so small that it seems like little more than an enlarged display case. A huddled crone feeds chips into the roaring oven of the hammam; over its arched doorway a red flag with a white mitt-like hand on it signifies that the steam bath is at the moment being used by women only.

White carcasses of sheep hang stiffly by the hind feet outside the butcher shops. Each has been stamped all over by the meat inspector, and each has a bunch of herbs sprouting from its anus. Modesty? Obscenity? Folk hygiene? A shaykh from the Muslim kulliyyah steps along fastidiously in his elegant long coat, neatly trimmed beard, and immaculate white turban carefully wrapped around his tarbush. An old woman raises her opaque veil with the back of her hand, peers into a small café, and shouts severely to a man within. Two young women in high heels, nylons, and tightly fitting dresses buy tickets for the first afternoon movie. Gold earrings and teeth sparkle through their thin veils. As soon as the lights go off inside the theater, they throw their veils back away from their faces and light up cigarettes; but as the intermission starts, they quickly cover their faces again.

The day reaches its crescendo shortly after the middle of the afternoon. All businesses are open and traffic is heavy, but to the shoppers now are added strollers who are out to watch the throng, to visit sweet shops, sit in cafés, or go to the movies; and then the streets are thronged with thousands of schoolchildren — homeward bound on foot, in buses and cars. The last call to prayer may be heard by those who are close to a mosque, but not by others.

By early evening, most of the stores and workshops are closed or closing, and lights begin to shine from the windows of private homes. Public bustle is reduced in intensity and confined to such places as the Tal and the waterfront of the Mina, where it is limited for the most part to restaurants, coffeehouses, and cinemas. Then, one by one, these begin to close. Late revelers are rarely heard after about 11 o'clock, for by now most of the city is asleep. But already trucks

5

are moving toward Tripoli with foodstuffs which will feed it next day.

LANDSCAPE AND WEATHER

This concentration of daily life is located on the shore of the eastern Mediterranean near the mouth of the river which originates high in Mount Lebanon just below the famous cedars. High upstream, where it flows through a spectacular canyon cut into the limestone, the river is called Qadisha. Downstream, and north of the canyon, it flows across a plateau which, where it is not broken by foothills, is covered by olive groves. At an altitude of about two hundred feet above sea level the plateau drops sharply down to a triangular plain whose surface is no higher than about fifteen feet. The base of the triangle is formed by the escarpment of the plateau, runs in a northeast-southwest direction, and is five and a half miles long. The river, now called Abu 'Ali, has cut a deep notch in the escarpment at about its midpoint, and it empties into the sea a mile and a half north of this. The apex of the triangular plain is a rocky point about two and a half miles northwest of the notch. The plain itself is composed of alluvial deposits of the river and sandy deposits of the currents of the sea.

Al-Mina, the port of Tripoli, is built on the rocky point, the apex of the triangle; the center of Tripoli is at the midpoint of the base. Al-Qubbah is the northeastern face of the escarpment at the notch and Abu Samra is the opposite, southwestern face. The citadel of Tripoli is built on a northern spur of Abu Samra, and the old parts of the city adjoin the citadel, west and north of it, in the plain. In other words, the old parts of the city were built in the plain at the foot of the escarpment where the Abu 'Ali cuts through it. Subsequently, and especially recently, the city has grown out into the plain, along the escarpment in both directions, up the escarpment, and even onto the plateau on both sides of the river.

Southwest of Tripoli, the olive groves extend down into the plain, but most of the latter is planted in citrus orchards. Deep green all year and crisscrossed by drainage ditches, the plain looks very lush in contrast to the escarpment, where olives are interspersed with naked, rocky outcrops, and particularly in contrast to Mount Turbul, a 2,200-foot coastal foothill which, from the Mina, appears to be northeast, or to the left, of Tripoli. Also seen from the Mina, the 10,000-foot climax of Mount Lebanon, a great white loaf whether covered with snow or not, fills the southeastern horizon and appears to loom over Tripoli. The same view from al-Qubbah or Abu Samra is no less magnificent, but from these vantage points it is obvious that Mount Lebanon is actually quite distant. From Mount Lebanon, in turn, one sees Tripoli beyond the olive plantations of the plateau. The Mina, glistening white, appears to float in the blue sea from which the citrus plain is hardly distinguishable, and Abu Samra and al-Qubbah, also apparently white, are about all one can make out of Tripoli. Approaching Tripoli from the southwest, along the coastal highway from Beirut, one is impressed by the Mina, projecting far out to the left, then the low dark green line of the plain here and there relieved by white, eight-story apartment houses, and then by the city itself; much of it appears to be on a slope, which is actually Abu Samra with some of the buildings of al-Qubbah behind it.

Study of the map (or better still, acquaintance with Tripoli itself) reveals that all of these views involve distortions of the actual lay of the land. From the streets of the European-style commercial parts of the city, notably the Tal, this distortion is complete. Mount Lebanon is hidden behind the escarpment, the dramatic cut of the river is hidden by Abu Samra, and most of Abu Samra is obscured by buildings. The name Tal itself is perplexing on first encounter. Meaning "hill," it does not refer to the escarpment but to a low sandhill in the plain. At the turn of the century, this was doubtless a prominent landmark on the edge of town. Now it is surrounded and covered by buildings, and is easy to miss.

Tripoli's climate is essentially the same as that of Beirut, fifty miles to the south. There is almost no rain from April to October, but the summer atmosphere is humid as well as hot, and many Tripolitans take refuge in the mountains. Especially on the outskirts of the city, many flat-roofed dwellings have grape arbors on their roofs, making them more attractive for outdoor sleeping in summer. The arbors are rooted in the ground, and the trunks are trained up the sides of the buildings. This is a traditional practice, widespread in villages, but it has been carried over to modern concrete buildings which absorb a tremendous amount of heat during the daytime and therefore re-

7

MAP 2

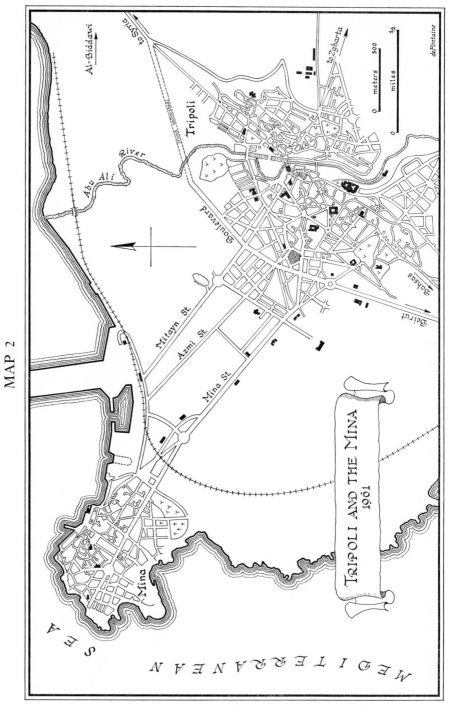

TRIPOLI AND THE MINA
1961

Al-Biddawi

to Syria

to Zgharta

meters 500

miles ½

deFontaine

Tripoli

Abu Ali River

TRIPOLI HIGHWAY

Boulevard

Bahsas

Beirut

Mitayn St.

Azmi St.

Mina St.

Mina

MEDITERRANEAN

SEA

main very hot inside long after sunset. Some of the older houses with hipped tile roofs have an additional structure on top which has large windows on all four sides to admit the cool night breezes for summer-time sleeping.

Winter is the rainy season, but the season's rainfall varies greatly from year to year. It is also spasmodic during any one winter. Completely overcast days are infrequent; there is usually at least some sun, and completely clear winter days are common. The rain is apt to come in rather violent squalls, and after a few minutes the gutters may overflow and the long flights of steps up to the Qubbah and Abu Samra become waterfalls. Rubber boots and all sorts of plastic raincoats are very popular articles of clothing. Thunderstorms are frequent, occasionally accompanied by hail, but it rarely, if ever, freezes or snows in Tripoli. Nevertheless, it is chilly in winter, especially at night or in the shade. Charcoal braziers or various types of kerosene heaters are standard household equipment, and heavy sweaters, scarves, and knitted woolen caps (all European style) are worn by almost everyone. The level of the Abu 'Ali is higher in winter and spring than in summer and fall. It often threatens to flood, and sometimes does, as in December of 1955. This was a major disaster, drowning many people and making many more homeless by destroying old buildings near the river's banks. Straightening and widening the bed of the river is part of Tripoli's long-range renewal program, some of which has already been done.

Except for the alluvial plain, the surroundings of Tripoli seem basically denuded and desiccated. Wild flowers bloom briefly in spring, and the olive trees are gray-green all year, but these do not hide the fact that the soil is thin and stony. Nor can they hide the crumbling, weathered limestone crags and outcrops where thorny shrubs are the main natural growth. During the past fifty years or so, the eucalyptus and a splendid shade tree related to the banyan (*Ficus nabita*) have been imported into Lebanon, but they are found mostly along roads or in densely inhabited areas like the Tripoli park, and so they do not very much relieve the bleakness of the landscape. That bleakness is augmented by the white dust which pours from the two cement factories at Shikka, a few miles south of the city, and by the white expanses of salt in the evaporation pans all along the coast.

One need not go into the desert to appreciate why green is a sacred

color to the Arabs, why gardens and groves of trees are a special de-
light to them, and why travelers over several centuries have described
how pleasant is the sight of Tripoli and its orange groves.

HINTERLAND

Tripoli is the capital of the Muhafazat of the North, one of the
five provinces of the Lebanese Republic. It is sometimes referred to
as the "second capital" of the republic. It is second in size to Beirut,
and one of its citizens, Rashid Karami, has been premier of Lebanon
several times (including the period of my study), as his father had
been.

Yet despite these possible indications of integration, there is, as I
have mentioned earlier, a sense of estrangement between Tripoli on
the one hand and Beirut and Mount Lebanon on the other. Nor is
this feeling a superficial one. The cultural factors involved, considered
more fully later, are epitomized in the two names of the river.
Qadisha is an Aramaic word meaning "holy" and is cherished by the
Christian Maronites, whose ancestors first took refuge high in the
mountains near its source, who retained the Aramaic language long
after Arabic-speaking Muslims had occupied the coast and plains, and
who in recent times have developed strong affiliations with Christian
France rather than the Arab Middle East. Abu 'Ali, by contrast, is an
Arabic and specifically Muslim name.

Tripoli's geographical relationships to its hinterland can be stated
very briefly. To the south, there is often no coastal plain at all, and
the coastal plateau is rough and at several places dissected by small
rivers which have cut steep canyons. The present coastal highway and
railroad are twentieth century developments, and until recently, overland travel to the south was difficult and dangerous. The inland
plateaus immediately east and south of Tripoli are themselves blocked
in by Mount Lebanon to the east and various foothills to the south.
But to the northeast there is a coastal plain, and it opens out into the
Plain of Akkar; this in turn provides a pass through the mountains to
the east. Thus Tripoli has relatively easy access to the inland plains
of Syria, and until very recently it was the major port serving them.
Significantly, one of the names which has traditionally been used
to differentiate it from North African Tripoli is Trablus al-Sham
(Tripoli of Damascus).

Chapter II

THE GROWTH OF TRIPOLI

THE PRESENT CITY, with its separate port, dates from the year 1289 A.D. However, the site had been occupied for at least 1,500 years previously, and there are some continuities between the earlier settlements and the present one.

PHOENICIAN AND HELLENISTIC SETTLEMENTS

In regard to Tripoli's beginnings, Hitti says:

Originally consisting of three separate settlements of Sidonians, Tyrians and Aradians, this triple city coalesced into one in the first year of the reign of Artaxerxes III Ochus (359–338 B.C.) and was given a Semitic name, "Athar" or the like, as the name appears on a native coin of 189–188 B.C. . . . In this newly created town the four Phoenician city-states held an annual council in which some three hundred delegates participated. The council discussed problems of common interest. It was at one of these meetings in 351 that the decision was made to proclaim full independence [from the Persian Empire].[1]

Tripoli apparently began as part of a reaction to foreign influence, a reaction repeated in much of its subsequent history.

Alexander the Great's defeat of the Persians relieved the Phoenicians of Persian domination but subjected them to strong Hellenistic influences for several centuries. Tripolis is a Greek word meaning triple city, and it was presumably given to the city as its name during the Hellenistic period, but sometime after 188 B.C. The most obvious

11

explanation is that it refers to the original triple settlement, but this derivation is not certain.

Under the Hellenistic Seleucid rulers, Tripoli enjoyed some measure of local autonomy and was one of the coastal towns which issued coins inscribed in both Semitic and Greek.[2] During the same period, it was a port of embarkation for lumber taken from Mount Lebanon.[3] Under the Romans, it had some privileges of self-government, but it was not of any particular importance.[4]

At the present time, there is one possible remnant of the pre-Muslim life of Tripoli. It is a curious one. Al-Biddawi is a small town outside the city, about a mile north of Bab al-Tibbani, on the road to Syria. The mosque there is part of a compound of buildings once the zawiya of a religious brotherhood. Adjoining this compound is an outdoor café in the middle of which is a large pool containing a school of gray fish. Apparently a type of carp, they are called the "sacred" fish of al-Biddawi. Whether they are actually venerated by anyone is a question, but they are protected from molestation, an extraordinary privilege for any Lebanese animal, and visitors are expected to feed them dried chickpeas, available for a small sum. The tradition is that there have been such fish here since Phoenician times. Burckhardt saw them in 1812,[5] but they are not mentioned in any earlier accounts. The Phoenicians did have a fish cult; the early Christians used the fish as a symbol of Jesus, and if the Biddawi fish are surviving the tender mercies of the current era, perhaps their ancestors were also able to survive the intervening Fatimid, Crusader, Mamluk, and Ottoman eras.

THE FIRST MUSLIM TOWN, 636–1109 A.D.

In 635 A.D., three years after the death of Muhammad, Muslim armies laid siege to Tripoli, which was located on the site of the present Mina and was protected by high walls. The Muslims captured it in 636 and developed their own town on the same site. Subsequently, in the tenth century, a traveler recorded his admiration of the fertility of its land and the low prices of its produce. Later, in 1047, Nasir-i-Khosrau, a Persian pilgrim, visited Tripoli. Thanks to him we know, for example, that at that time the city was producing citrus fruits, as well as sugar cane, bananas, and dates. Khosrau admired the mosques, bazaars, and paper factory, and the cleanliness of the streets and buildings, some of them four to six stories high. He estimated the population at 20,000, mostly Shi'ite Muslims. The harbor was busy and full of ships from many ports, including Greek, Sicilian, and other western ones. The military garrison was loyal to the Fatimid rulers of Egypt.[6]

Shortly after Khosrau's visit, in 1069, a local amir of the Banu Ammar clan declared Tripoli's independence of the Fatimids and embarked on a building program which gave the city a fine library and schools.[7]

THE CRUSADERS' TOWN, 1109–1289 A.D.

This period of prosperity was, however, accompanied by political chaos in the whole Levantine area, and the Crusaders took full advantage of it at the end of the century. In 1099, Raymond of Toulouse began what would be a ten-year siege of Tripoli. To facilitate it, he initiated construction of the present citadel in 1103. He died in 1105, but the siege continued until 1109, when the Crusaders finally took the city. They destroyed it — schools, library, and all — but they soon built their city where the Muslim one had been. In addition, they developed a settlement in the vicinity of the citadel. Almost nothing is known about this, except that it included at least three churches, remnants of which still exist, incorporated into newer structures. This is the first evidence of a settlement elsewhere than at the present Mina, but under the Crusaders it was apparently always secondary to the port city.

Tripoli was a Crusader town for 180 years. Unlike Jerusalem, it was not recaptured by the Muslims only to be captured a second time by the Crusaders. Despite earthquakes, it prospered during the period of the Crusades and was the chief town of one of the Latin states of the Levant, the County of Tripoli. This state encompassed the coastal territory from Jubayl (halfway between Tripoli and Beirut) to Latakia in Syria. It included the Plain of Akkar, and eastern access to this was guarded by the famous castle, Krak des Chevaliers. Under the Crusaders, Tripoli was, as before, a busy port with a heterogeneous population including western Europeans, Greeks, Armenians, Maronites, Nestorians, Jews, and even Muslims.[8] It also continued to be a producer of lemons, oranges, and sugar cane, and it became a major center of silk weaving, having at one point about 4,000 weavers.[9]

It was the seat of a bishopric and had convents, schools, and hospitals.[10]

THE MAMLUK TOWN: FOURTEENTH CENTURY

As the thirteenth century advanced, the Muslims steadily increased their pressure on the Crusaders. One by one the towns fell to them, and the Latin states disintegrated. Tripoli was one of the last to hold out, a haven for refugees from other places. But in 1289 it was captured by the Egyptian Mamluk sultan, Qalawun, and again destroyed. This time, it was not rebuilt on the same site. Rather, Qalawun centered the new city around the inland citadel.[11] This was the beginning of modern Tripoli.

Whether the Mamluks' razing of what is now the Mina was any more thorough than the Crusaders' had been is not known. The important point is that the successive occupants of the place have obliterated almost all evidence of previous settlements. Today there is no trace even of the massive Fatimid and Crusader fortifications mentioned by contemporary travelers. In fact, some granite column drums dumped in shallow water are the only visible remains of pre-Mamluk occupations, nor are there in the Mina any structures belonging to the Mamluk period, although in Tripoli there are.

Although the Mamluks did not block up Tripoli's harbor, as they did many other Levantine ports for fear of a return of the Europeans,[12] their initial interest in the port seems to have been mainly defensive. During the first part of the fourteenth century, while the new city was prospering, the port barely survived commercially, partly due to lack of trade with Europe.[13]

The Mamluks divided Syria and Lebanon into six provinces, one of which was Tripoli.[14] Its borders appear to have been very similar to those of the Latin County. As early as 1294, the town was linked up with the network of fire-signal towers the Mamluks had been developing throughout the Levant.[15] There still are several of these towers along the coast between Beirut and Tripoli. They were also fortifications, and the Mamluks' defenses of Tripoli itself consisted of the inland citadel and seven towers along the shore, but no walls. One of the towers (building 7, Map 3) still stands near the railroad station at the port and is admired by experts for its architectural features.[16]

As a provincial capital, Tripoli outranked any of the Lebanese

MAP 3

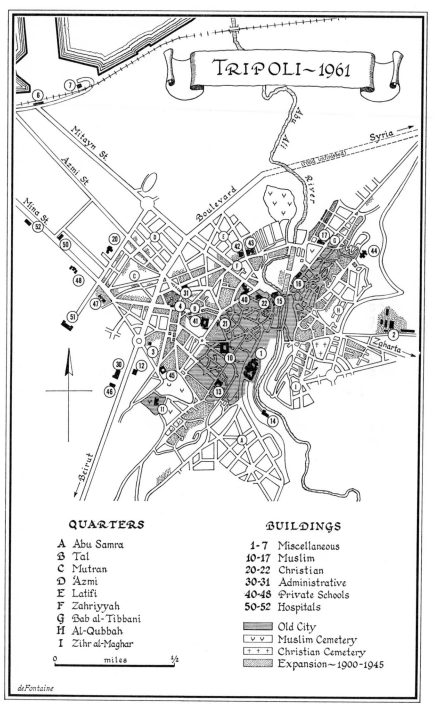

TRIPOLI ~ 1961

Syria →

(road unfinished)

Abu Ali River

Mitayn St.

Azmi St.

Mina St.

Boulevard

Beirut

Zgharta →

QUARTERS

A Abu Samra
B Tal
C Mutran
D ʿAzmi
E Latifi
F Zahriyyah
G Bab al-Tibbani
H Al-Qubbah
I Zihr al-Maghar

0   miles   ½

deFontaine

BUILDINGS

1- 7 Miscellaneous
10-17 Muslim
20-22 Christian
30-31 Administrative
40-48 Private Schools
50-52 Hospitals

▤ Old City
∨∨ Muslim Cemetery
+++ Christian Cemetery
▨ Expansion ~ 1900-1945

[15]

towns, but it was itself overshadowed by Aleppo and Damascus. Ziadeh estimates that in the fourteenth century it had 20,000 people, as contrasted with 100,000 each in Aleppo and Damascus; however, Antioch, Beirut, Gaza, and Jerusalem had only 10,000 each.[17]

The Mamluks greatly embellished Damascus and Aleppo with fine buildings — particularly mosques, *hammams* ("Turkish" baths), and *madrasahs* (Koranic schools) — and Tripoli to some extent shared in this architectural renaissance.[18] Hitti remarks that Tripoli was, in fact, the only Lebanese city to benefit from the Mamluk madrasah system.[19] It was certainly in the orbit of the two great interior cities and was connected with them (rather than with towns to the south) by post roads.[20]

Remnants of the Mamluks in 1961–62

In 1954, there were 35 structures in Tripoli dating from the Mamluk period.[21] In 1961–62, most of them were still there, but two or three small ones had been sacrificed to street widening, an aspect of the renewal program discussed later. Most of these are in the Old City (al-madini al-'adimi), the part of Tripoli in existence before about 1900. Map 5 (see Chapter V) shows their locations, plus those of half a dozen early Ottoman buildings. An appreciative description of them, with photographs, can be found in the UNESCO volume already cited.

Three of these buildings demonstrate that the Mamluks did not indulge in total destruction of the Crusaders' work. Some of the walls of the citadel (building 1, Map 3) are pre-Mamluk; the main portion of the minaret of the Mansuri mosque (the grand mosque, building 10, Map 3) was the belfry of a cathedral; and the main hall of the Taylan mosque (building 11, Map 3) was originally the nave of a church. Sixteen of the Mamluk buildings were originally madrasahs, but none is now used as such. Some are used as mosques, others as storerooms, and the remainder are deserted. The seven Mamluk mosques are all in use, as are the four *khans*, two of the three hammams, and two small covered *suqs* (streets of small shops). The khans are large, rectangular buildings with arcaded courts. They were originally built to serve caravans as combinations of inn, stable, and warehouse. Three are now used as warehouses, and one (Khan al-Askar) is the very much overcrowded tenement of families made homeless by the 1955 flood.

These buildings go back to Tripoli's beginnings as a Sunni Muslim city, and the latter is an identification very important at present. Yet most of the structures themselves are in bad repair, and the only spontaneous sentiment likely to save at least some of them is unwillingness to demolish religious edifices. There are also legal deterrents. Not many Tripolitans seem to care anything about them architecturally or historically.

PRE-OTTOMAN FLORESCENCE: FOURTEENTH AND FIFTEENTH CENTURIES

The buildings were appreciated when they were new. Al-Qalqashandi, reporting on Tripoli about the year 1390, describes it as a well-organized city with a hospital, schools, baths, and fine bazaars, all built of whitewashed, wet-laid limestone. He also speaks of the houses being on steep slopes so that fresh water ran into them from their roofs. Another author of the same period, cited by Ziadeh, mentions that water was available on the upper floors of Tripoli's houses.[22] The most likely location of the houses described by al-Qalqashandi would have been the lower slopes of al-Qubbah and possibly of Abu Samra. He also writes admiringly of the surrounding orchards, which had been recently expanded by a marsh drainage program, and of the busy harbor.[23] Somewhat earlier, in 1355, Ibn Battuta, the famous traveler, commented on Tripoli's rich land and sea resources.[24]

In addition to its fine new schools, baths, mosques, suqs, and zawiyas, Mamluk Tripoli also had the residence of the provincial governor. Somewhat simpler than the provincial administrations of Aleppo and Damascus, Tripoli's lacked a vizier, and the governor himself, rather than a special officer, was in charge of the citadel.[25] The *wali* of the city was responsible to the governor and appointed the chief police officer.[26] Other officials, certainly not unique to Tripoli, were the *qadi* (theocratic magistrate) and the *muhtasib* (market commissioner, who also supervised teachers, healers, and other practitioners).[27]

The port seems to have revived gradually during the latter part of the fourteenth century, by the end of which there was a resident Venetian consul in Tripoli. Citrus fruits, sugar cane, and textiles continued to be the main products. Tripoli was a major supplier to Europe of candy and loaf and powdered sugar. Other exports were olive oil, soap (made from olive oil), and Syrian cotton.[28] General conditions in the fourteenth and fifteenth centuries were of course very different from what they are at present. Yet, as will become clear later on, there have been some administrative and economic continuities from then to now.

Tripoli was spared the devastation of the Mongol invasions of the fifteenth century, but it witnessed the displacement of the Mamluks by the Seljuqs. And then, early in the sixteenth century, along with Egypt and all of the Levant, Tripoli was conquered by the Ottoman Turks; under their rule it remained until the end of World War I.

EARLY OTTOMAN TRIPOLI: DECLINE

In 1520, the Ottomans divided the Levant into three vilayets: Aleppo, Damascus (including Beirut and Saida), and Tripoli (including the coast from Jubayl to Tartus and the inland Syrian towns of Homs and Hama). Now the chief town of an Ottoman pashalik, Tripoli continued in its role of provincial capital, but secondary to greater cities in the region. Economically dependent on the interior Syrian cities, it was, to the Christian Lebanese mountaineers, the headquarters of predatory Ottoman exactions. The various pashas of Tripoli made many tax collecting forays into the hinterland and the Ma'ni and Shihabi amirs of Lebanon (sixteenth to nineteenth centuries) were tax farmers for them. Yet the literature gives the impression that Tripoli itself declined during this period.

Until 1612 it was the port of Aleppo,[29] but thereafter Aleppo began to use northern ports. One reason for the shift was the overzealousness of the pasha of Tripoli, who carried his efforts in extortion to the point of having the French merchants in the town buried alive. D'Arvieux, the French consular merchant who is the source of this story, visited Tripoli about 1679 and noted its "ruined harbor," although he admired the baths, the khans, the fine houses with courtyards and running water on the ground floors, and the "rich" and "clean" inhabitants.[30]

In the seventeenth and eighteenth centuries, there were French and other mercantile residents in Tripoli, and intra-European competition for trade became intense. But in the second half of the eighteenth century various factors, including the Turkish-Russian wars and Tripoli's midposition between Aleppo-Alexandretta and Saida-Jaffa, contributed to a further decline.[31] Concurrently, the Ottoman pashas, when not raiding the countryside for taxes, were intriguing among themselves and against each other. The Tripolitans even rebelled against their pashas on more than one occasion, but to no avail.[32]

LATER OTTOMAN TRIPOLI: WESTERNIZATION BEGINS

It is at this point of low ebb, the last quarter of the eighteenth century, that the modern history of Tripoli begins. This was the time when European influences in the Middle East began the series of unremitting changes which continue today to characterize the culture of the whole area.

In January and February of 1784, a Frenchman who wrote under the nom de plume of Volney visited Tripoli and described it in some detail. He reported that it had a population of 4,000 or 5,000 people, about the same as Latakia and only slightly smaller than Beirut, with 6,000. The seven fortified towers served only as roosts for birds; the town was defenseless and could have been captured by "any pirate." In addition to producing oranges, Tripoli's main business was exporting silk whose quality was inferior to what it had been. The silk was traded mainly to the French in return for cloth, coffee, and sugar — the last having formerly been an export of Tripoli. The people were hesitant to invest in new orchards because they feared that such evidence of free capital would only invite the pasha's extortions.[33]

The pasha annually paid to the Ottoman Sultan the equivalent of 937,500 French livres and equipped the yearly caravan to Mecca. The money, in addition to tribute from the Nusayri and Maronite mountaineers in Syria and Lebanon respectively, came from rents, estates, customs duties, and "casual extortions." The people were in a generally rebellious mood as far as the pasha was concerned.[34] There were orchards all around, but the climate was unhealthful, especially at the end of summer, when fevers were epidemic.[35] French consuls had reported that 4,000 people had died in 1760 of "pestilence." [36] In the winter, however, mountain people came down to Tripoli to live.[37]

This general feeling of depression and decay is consistent with what we know of general conditions at the time. It is also reflected in an eighteenth-century gouache of a market in Tripoli.[38] Pipe-smoking merchants sit or sprawl in their tiny one-story shops on waist-high platforms. Projecting wooden awnings are rotting away. A dome and minaret in the background bear some resemblance to those of the Tawbat mosque in the Dibbagha section of the present Old City, still a section of small shops, many of them only one story high. The platforms, however, no longest exist. Women in the picture, incidentally, are wearing veils which do not cover their eyes, a style no longer seen in Tripoli. Another contemporary print [39] shows the Mina viewed from the north. Three of the towers are conspicuous, as is the rather sparse distribution of buildings near the point. This indicates that a considerable portion of the present old section of the Mina was built up later than the eighteenth century. The same is suggested in a third eighteenth-century picture [40] of Tripoli seen from the present Zahriyyah section, which was then open country. The picture emphasizes the buildings on the slopes of al-Qubbah, but it gives the impression of a smaller town around the citadel than is the present Old City. As we shall see, subsequent sources present a picture of steady increase in population.

During the first third of the nineteenth century, Tripoli was often caught in the midst of political rivalries centered elsewhere, all exacerbated by the weakness of the Ottoman central government. Pressures and counterpressures from such personages as Ahmad al-Jazzar (the infamous pasha of Acre) and Bashir II (the great Shihabi amir of Lebanon), and, finally, various reactions to the invasion of Ibrahim Pasha of Egypt affected the succession of Tripoli's pashas. The most notable of these, Mustapha Barbar, was a man of very humble origins who is reputed to have contributed to the welfare of the city during his several, discontinuous tenures in office. In 1807, for instance, he donated two buildings as an endowment (*waqf*) for the grand mosque,[41] and in 1813 he made water available at the Taylan mosque and donated two houses as waqf for it. They were near Barbar's palace, which was located somewhere between the citadel and the grand mosque.[42]

Yet during the six intervening years, the city was attacked and damaged, and Barbar was forced to flee it; he was later reinstated. The following account of these incidents is typical of the whole Ottoman political history of Tripoli:

In 1808 Kinj Yusif Pasha was appointed by the central government in Istanbul to supervise Syria. He issued orders for Barbar to give up the citadel but keep on ruling the city. Barbar refused to obey. The pasha sent an army to Tripoli. Most of the residents evacuated the city while Barbar took refuge in the citadel. The army entered the city and severely damaged it. The citadel was besieged for eleven months until it could no longer hold out. Barbar escaped and journeyed to Saida where he was received by Sulayman Pasha. Later on, orders were issued from the capital condemning Kinj Yusif to death for the great harm he had inflicted on the city. Sulayman replaced him, and Barbar again took over the city.[43]

Barbar would be forced out of office and reinstated twice more before his career came to an end. In 1824, while he was out of office, the incumbent pasha was killed during a tax-collecting expedition (essentially a military raid) in Syria. His successor had such a bad reputation that many Tripolitans fled on hearing of his appointment. He set about destroying the fine houses of two of the most prominent Christian families and was paid to desist, but later his brother Husayn, who succeeded him, resumed the protection racket. The people finally rebelled and surrounded Husayn in the Saraya (administrative building), but he managed to escape by being hidden in garbage. By playing one faction off against another, he was able to reinstate himself and tried to arrange the death of Barbar, who was living in Beirut. Barbar fled to Egypt, and when he returned to Tripoli in 1830 it was with the conquering armies of Ibrahim Pasha. Barbar was forced out of office for the last time in 1832 when he refused to collect any more taxes for the Egyptians. The city was under direct Egyptian control from then until 1840, when Ottoman rule was reestablished.[44]

Despite all this turmoil and damage, the city was evidently prospering to some extent. Burckhardt visited it in 1812. He estimated its population to be 15,000, of whom a third were "Greek Christians." He was impressed by the well-built quality of the houses, the beauty of the orchards and gardens, the arched-over streets, and the Khan al-Sabun (building 3, Map 5), but he reported that the Saraya had been destroyed during the troubles of 1808. Evidently it had not yet been replaced by a new one. The people of the Mina were chiefly "Greek sailors," either fishermen or shipwrights. The principal exports were silk, sponges, and soap.[45] John Carne, saying that Tripoli had better gardens than Beirut and was more healthful than Saida (Sidon) and Sur (Tyre), described it as follows: "Tripoli is the best looking town in Syria, the houses being built of stone, and neatly constructed within. It is surrounded and embellished with luxuriant gardens, which not only intermingle with the houses in the town, but extend over the whole plain lying between it and the sea."[46]

Carne also felt that Beirut was "dirty and disagreeable" compared to Tripoli, but he observed that it was a more congenial residence for Europeans than the other Levantine towns.[47] And, in fact, it was at this period that Beirut was beginning to grow more rapidly in size and prosperity than its neighbors, very largely because of its attractiveness to westerners.[48] If we can believe Volney's and Burckhardt's population estimates, Tripoli had a spurt of growth between 1784 and 1812, but it thereafter grew more slowly for some time, partly due to the competition of Beirut.

Missionary Schools

On July 4–5, 1850, James L. Patterson passed through Tripoli and said it was "the most picturesque and hottest of towns," with "narrow, ill-paved bazaars." He also mentioned that Roman Catholic schools under European management were in operation there.[49] These Roman Catholic schools were soon to be joined by American Protestant ones. This was the very beginning of westernized educational enterprises which were not long in adding great impetus to cultural change in the direction of "modernization." Lebanon as a whole was affected by this particularly early, and Tripoli, despite its traditional links with the Syrian interior, shared in these developments. The mid-nineteenth century will serve as a sufficient base-line from which to begin an analysis of recent and continuing cultural change in Tripoli, and therefore as a foundation for some understanding of the nature of the present-day city.

Franciscan monks had been received in Tripoli as early as the seventeenth century,[50] but their interests were probably more with the Maronite mountaineers than in Tripoli itself. Despite the fact that it had Christian residents, Tripoli had had its Christian martyrs, such as the Maronite patriarch who was burned at the stake in 1365 and Shaykh Kin'an al-Zahrir who was tortured and beheaded in 1741 because he would not become a Muslim.[51] Moreover, from 1840 to

1860 Lebanon was convulsed by a series of outbreaks, including the massacre of Christians by Muslims and Druze. While these troubles did not touch Tripoli directly, the sectarian situation there was described as follows by an American eyewitness, Henry H. Jessup:

It is a Moslem city whose aristocratic families and Ulema look with disdain on the small population of Greeks and Maronites dwelling among them. But, as is generally the case, where the Christians are in a small minority, there had never been any attack by the Muslims on the Christians, but the chief reason was probably the existence of a powerful Maronite population in Lebanon nearby on the east, who often, out of mere bravado, threatened to attack the Moslems of Tripoli should they injure their Maronite and Greek fellow citizens.[52]

In 1855, Muslim mobs threatened to murder "Greek Christians" for siding with Russia against Turkey, and in 1858 ten cannons were sent to Tripoli to help protect it against possible attack by the Maronites in Zgharta, a large village in the plateau east of Tripoli.[53]

The "foreign colony" into which Jessup and other American educational missionaries moved in the mid-nineteenth century was very small. In addition to a few European ecclesiastical teachers, there were French and British consular officials. Other western nations were represented by Middle Easterners. In Tripoli and elsewhere:

France and England were represented by foreigners, but Russia, Austria, the United States, Belgium, Denmark and Switzerland by Oriental Greeks and Catholics. On feast days . . . they marched with stately tread through the narrow streets, preceded by armed, gaily caparisoned Moslem kavasses or janizaries, with their tall, silver-headed staves rattling on the pavement, the pompous dragoman or interpreter in the rear, a fringe of small boys all around.[54]

American Presbyterian missionaries established a boys' day school in Tripoli in 1854, and one for girls in 1856. A girls' boarding school was added in 1873, and a boys' boarding school in 1900.[55] Today, these schools are among the most prominent in the city, as they have been all along. The same group of missionaries established many other schools in Syria and Lebanon, together with the Syrian Protestant College (now the American University) in Beirut. In 1871, a medical mission was established in Tripoli, and its major achievement was what is now the Kennedy Memorial Hospital in the Mina, the first, and now the oldest, modern hospital in Tripoli.

Jessup says that Tripoli at this time had a "reputation for the aristocratic pride of its people, both Moslems and Greek Christians."[56] He also was pleased by shady walks among the orange trees and by the splendid view of the mountains; but he says that the roofs and walls of houses tended to absorb moisture and that window glass was rare.[57] In summary:

Tripoli was a quaint old city with its snow-white houses, surrounded on three sides with green olive and orange groves, and above it the brown sandstone castle of Raymond of Toulouse, on a range of low hills which is cut through by the dashing river Kadisha. . . . The people were three-quarters Moslems and one-quarter Orthodox Greeks and a few Maronites and Papal Greeks, and about fifteen Jews.[58]

MID-NINETEENTH CENTURY TRIPOLI RECONSTRUCTED

If we make certain allowances, we can further visualize Tripoli as it was one hundred years ago in terms of the present Old City (see Map 3). If the newer parts of Tripoli were magically to vanish, the remainder, the Old City, would not, of course, be identical with mid-nineteenth century Tripoli. Among the differences would be electricity and newer buildings. Many old ones have been demolished by nature (e.g., by flood) or by man (e.g., to make way for new streets). On the other hand, the extent of the Old City probably coincides fairly closely with the edges of the city as it was, and many of the buildings, streets, alleys, and arches are the same as they were a century ago. Traces of the whitewash which impressed observers, from Qalqashandi's time to Jessup's, are even discernible in some cases.

Map 5 shows the portion of the Old City which lies west of the river, the more important portion. I will, as far as my information allows, reconstruct mid-nineteenth century Tripoli in terms of this map. The aristocratic Muslim families for the most part apparently lived in the area generally between the citadel and the grand mosque. The section called Rifa'iyyah was quite possibly named for the Rifa'i family; one member told me that they used to live there. In the nineteenth century (but not now) there was a Beni Baraka section in this general location, named for a family no longer prominent. Jessup mentions a "city gate," apparently on the west side of the city.[59]

If he meant this literally, it must have been a gate across one of the narrow streets, for there was definitely no separate wall of the sort Beirut had, which can still be seen in Jerusalem. Buildings 9, 10, and 11 (Map 5) did not then exist. Their present sites were orange groves; considerable remnants survived until quite recently and after the initial build-up of the Tal section. Sahit Saraya 'Adimi (Old Saraya Square) is the site of the Ottoman administrative building and governor's residence, the one which eventually replaced the Saraya destroyed in 1808. This *past* Old Saraya was torn down and replaced as an administrative building by the *present* Old Saraya, which the Ottomans built in the Tal in the 1890's or early 1900's. The *present* New Saraya (building 30, Map 3) was receiving finishing touches inside at the time of my study. In the space of a hundred years, Tripoli has had three major administrative buildings, each, in its time, on the edge of the city.

After World War II, Shari' Kinayis (Churches Street) was cut along an edge of the Old City, destroying some old buildings. It is appropriately named: in addition to the church and cathedral noted on Map 5, there are three other churches along Shari' Kinayis, or near it, on both sides. This is the largest concentration of churches in the city, and the name Hayy Nasara (Christian Quarter) is still used to some extent for the adjacent section, although this is no longer primarily a Christian residential area. One hundred years ago, however, the Christians of Tripoli lived either in this quarter or in the Mina, then predominantly Christian, and when Christian women went outdoors they were veiled like Muslims so as to avoid abuse. The small Jewish community lived in or near a large, heavy-walled compound of buildings (Har Yihud) near the Orthodox Cathedral. Animals used to be slaughtered somewhere along the banks of the river, rather than in the Mina as at present. It could well have been at Dibbagha, traditionally a section of tanneries. Goat and sheep hides are still stretched out to dry on the walls of the mosque there. Until the devastation of the 1955 flood, the area north of Dibbagha, across the river, was orange groves. At present it is a wasteland, partially dissected by a new river channel with concrete sides and bottom, awaiting other new developments.

As Yanni and Jessup indicate, there were, one hundred years ago, Christian as well as Muslim aristocrats in Tripoli. The Christian aristocrats were primarily merchants, while the wealth of the Muslim ones was based primarily on income from estates in the hinterland and from the orchards surrounding the city. In their works Yanni and Jessup mention by name three of the then prominent Christian families. Unfortunately, they do not specify any of the Muslim ones, possibly a reflection of some Christian bias on their part. At any rate, the names of the three Christian families are ones present-day Tripolitans may mention as being those of fine old families which have lost their preeminent position. Since today's most important Christian families have ramified connections and ties in places like Antioch, Latakia, and Alexandria, it is safe to assume that their forebears were forming them, or already had them, one hundred years ago.

Terms like "Greek Christian" and "Oriental Greek" were used by nineteenth-century authors. When Jessup referred to aristocratic Greek Christians, he was almost certainly referring to Tripolitan Arabs whose religion was, and is today, Greek Orthodox, and not to people of Greek nationality. This is also the most likely meaning of the various other references to "Greeks." However, there are some probable exceptions. For example, throughout the nineteenth century and into the early twentieth, members of a family obviously Greek in name, and presumably in culture, served as consuls for the United States and various European countries in Tripoli. Also, the "Greek sailors" in the Mina, mentioned by Burckhardt, could well have included people of Hellenic culture as well as Greek Orthodox Arabs. Hereafter, when referring to the Greek Orthodox Arabs of Tripoli, I shall use the term Eastern Orthodox so as to avoid any misconception that they are nationally or culturally Greek. Jessup's term "Papal Greeks" probably refers to members of the Greek Catholic sect which split away from Eastern Orthodoxy in the eighteenth century to become a Roman Catholic Uniate church. The Maronites are also Roman Catholic. Their sect began as a schismatic offshoot of the Byzantine Church, and its early members took refuge in Mount Lebanon not later than the seventh century.

To recapitulate: Tripoli's mid-nineteenth century population consisted of a large majority of Sunni Muslims, the wealth of whose aristocratic families was based primarily on land ownership. The Christian minority consisted mostly of Eastern Orthodox Arabs, living in their own quarter and in the Mina. The aristocratic families were primarily merchants. Maronite peasants occupied the plateau and mountains east of Tripoli, Eastern Orthodox peasants occupied the inland plain of Kura immediately south, while Sunni peasants occupied the coastal and Akkar plains to the northeast. Beyond the Akkar, in the coastal mountains of northwestern Syria, lived Nusayris (or 'Alawites, members of one of the several sects which deviated from Shi'ite Islam) and Shi'ite Isma'ilis. Today, this sectarian distribution is roughly the same, but there have been some important modifications.

INITIATION OF MODERN GROWTH: LATE NINETEENTH CENTURY

In 1881, Yanni estimated that Tripoli had about 20,000 people, but he did not say whether or not the Mina was included in this total. He remarked also on the great interest in learning among the people, specifying Islamic jurisprudence and theology and, among the Christians, an increasing interest in literature and mathematics. He expressed the general hope for a railroad connection for the city, and reported that a horse tramway between the Mina and the city had just been completed. This development was encouraged by the Ottoman governor.

Another visitor, at about this time, quoted Burckhardt and Carne on Tripoli's orchards and said they were still the same. He reported also that of the seven original fortified towers, one had disappeared entirely and only one other was in reasonably good condition. He, too, estimated the population to be 20,000, but said that 6,000 of these were in the Mina. Tripoli's main exports were silk, soap, olive oil, tobacco, oranges, lemons, and sponges. There was currently a slump in commercial activity, and a railroad connection to the interior, he said, was badly needed.[60]

The city grew little, if at all, between 1812 and the 1880's. During this period, Tripoli was demoted in the Ottoman administrative structure. Previously it had been the chief town of a vilayet which bore its name. In the nineteenth century it became the chief town of a *liwa*, or subdistrict, of the vilayet of Beirut. But between the 1880's and the beginning of World War I, it not only grew in population but also began to expand beyond the confines of the Old City. In 1909, the carriage road connecting Beirut and Tripoli was completed, as was, in 1911, the railroad from Aleppo to the new Tripoli station (building 6, Map 3). These are the only events during the period which can be dated specifically. The discussion from here on is based on the memories of older informants, deductions from architectural styles, some old photographs, and a few maps, beginning with Baedeker's.[61]

The tramway ran from the eastern edge of the Mina (the section called Buwwabi, "Gates") to the western edge of Tripoli, to what is now Sahit Saraya 'Adimi. (This was, in any case, its terminus in the late 1930's, at about which time the tramway was torn up.) The line ran southeast from the Mina along the present Shari' al-Mina for about three-quarters of the way; then it turned almost due east, skirting the southern edge of the Tal, to its destination (see Map 2). "New" Tripoli began to grow out along this route. Initially, the growth consisted of the building by several aristocratic families of fine new houses. At first some people thought it foolhardy to build houses outside of town, for fear of robbers and cutthroats who might lurk in the orchards. Such fears obviously did not prevail, however. Sometime before 1909, the Ottomans built the stone clocktower (building 4, Map 3) just west of the Tal and (as mentioned earlier) a new Saraya across the road and the tramway from the tower. The latter is 15 to 20 feet square at the base and about 100 feet high. It is divided into six distinct sections including the pyramidal top. There is a clock face in each of the four sides just below the top and an ornamental window in each side of each of the other sections. Vaguely baroque in style, it is definitely not Middle Eastern in appearance. At first it stood in complete isolation and was presumably considered the last word in modernity.

The Saraya has a sloping tile roof, with an interior court and a multiple-arched portico, and has two very high stories. It is more congruent than the clocktower with the style of many of the mansions built near it at about the same time; these were also two stories high, had hipped roofs, and featured the classic Lebanese arcades of pointed arches and slender round columns. Another style favored by the aristocrats at the turn of the century is what might be called Turkish Victorian. Often more than two stories high, such buildings have cornices and balconies bristling with gingerbread and "keyhole" windows whose circular tops are embellished with lacy, geometric mullion work and bits of stained glass. The most conspicuous example of the style is the mansion of the Karami family (building 3, Map 3), but it can also be seen in two of the old five-story hotels built near the Tal before World War I.

Baedeker's 1912 map indicates an extension of separate buildings out along the road toward the Mina, but no buildings on or surrounding the Tal or in the area now occupied by the park. The latter area was then vacant and used for casual athletic contests. An airplane landed on it during the war — according to an informant who knew it then. Perhaps the Ottomans had plans for a park here; it is not unlikely that they did, for they obviously had in mind a modern civic center of which the New Saraya and clocktower were parts. Also, one of the last Ottoman governors (Azmi Bey) had the perfectly straight street which bears his name built from the new port facilities east of the Mina to the Tal. The other two avenues between the city and the Mina were then, and for a long time to come, narrow, crooked roads.

In typical fashion, the name Tal began to be expanded from its original, literal referent and applied to the whole new section of public buildings, up-to-date hotels, and fine mansions. From this new section, in turn, roads were extended to connect with those already coming out of the Old City toward Beirut in one direction and toward Syria in the other; before the war began, fashionable houses were being built along these new roads also. For some time, orange groves continued to grow between these new developments and the Old City.

At the same time, Bab al-Tibbani (Hay Gate) was beginning to grow out to and around the cemetery which it now completely surrounds. This was then as now the wholesale vegetable distribution center, not fashionable, but very busy. The foreign schools still had their buildings in the Mina or in the Old City (building 12, Map 5, for instance), but before long they moved to larger quarters on the outskirts of the city.

In 1912 Tripoli had 30,000 people (24,000 Muslims, 4,500 Eastern Orthodox, and 1,500 Maronites) and the Mina had 5,000. There were four modern hotels (two in the city and two in the Mina), two banks, a telegraph office, and consular representatives of eight foreign countries. Cafés along the waterfront were worthy of mention, as was a café halfway between the Mina and the city on the tramline. There were fourteen mosques, eight native churches, and six churches run directly by foreign missions (Lazarists, Carmelites, Sisters of Charity, Frères des Ecoles Chrétiennes, and American Presbyterians). In 1910, 661 steamers and 1,944 sailing ships had entered and cleared the port. The main imports were cotton goods and other manufactures, while the main exports were, in order of value, raw silk, soap, oranges and lemons, grain, and olive oil. Competition by Beirut was damaging to the port, but people hoped that the new railroad would improve Tripoli's position. Silk weaving and soapmaking (eleven factories) were the city's main industries.[62]

On the eve of World War I, then, Tripoli was a definitely growing city with the facilities and potential for further growth. Travelers were still impressed by its medieval appearance, however, and, more important, its water was still drawn from the polluted river (a probable cause of its being unhealthful, especially at the end of summer), and there was no electric power.

Like Beirut, Tripoli was not part of the Mutaserifiyah of Mount Lebanon, that Christian enclave created in 1861 after the troubles of 1840–60. Correctly dubious of the loyalty of the Christian mountaineers, the Turks blockaded Mount Lebanon during the war, causing starvation and other hardships there. Although Tripoli did not undergo these privations, it did suffer. The new railroad was torn up, and until it was repaired after the war, the hoped-for increase in trade with interior Syria did not occur. Of more lasting damage, the bottom dropped out of the Lebanese silk market, and one of Tripoli's traditional industries began a rapid decline to oblivion.

TRIPOLI SINCE WORLD WAR I

Just before the armistice in 1918, British troops occupied Tripoli, but it soon passed under French mandate. Disregarding the wishes of the inhabitants, the French annexed Beirut, the Biqa' Valley, South Lebanon, and Tripoli to Mount Lebanon, thereby creating the State of Grand Liban.[63]

The Tripolitans were violently opposed to this annexation, and its uneasy consequences are still live issues. Yet Tripoli grew and prospered during, and partly because of, the French mandate.

Population Growth

Concerning patterns of change and growth since 1920, Table 1 recapitulates some details already mentioned and provides some indices of what is to come.

THE GROWTH OF TRIPOLI

TABLE 1. ESTIMATED POPULATION OF TRIPOLI, 1784–1961

Year	Est. population	Comments and questions	Source
1784	4–5,000	Includes Mina?	Volney, 1959 (1787)
1812	15,000	Includes Mina?	Burckhardt, 1822
1881	20,000	Includes Mina?	Yanni, 1881
1886	20,000	14,000 in Tripoli, 6,000 in Mina;	Thomson, 1886
1897	30,000	Apparently included Mina	Verney and Dambmann, 1900, p. 367
1912	35,000	30,000 in Tripoli, 5,000 in Mina	Baedeker, 1912
1914	27,500	25,000 plus 2,500 unregistered residents	President, Tripoli Municipal Council, 1961
1919	32,000	27,000 in Tripoli, 5,000 in Mina	Adib, 1919
1922	36,000	Includes Mina?	UNESCO, 1954
1932	54,876	41,474 in Tripoli, 13,402 in Mina	Official Census
1939	90,000	60,000 plus 30,000 unregistered residents	President, Tripoli Municipal Council, 1961
1943	80,000	Includes Mina?	UNESCO, 1954
1946	78,000	Includes Mina?	Longrigg, 1958
1952	110,000	Includes Mina?	UNESCO, 1954
1961	210,000	100,000 plus 80,000 unregistered residents; plus 30,000 in Mina	President, Tripoli Municipal Council, 1961, and Gulick estimate of Mina

The most obvious ambiguity in the figures shown in Table 1 is that in half of them it is not clear whether the Mina's population was included. Probably the Mina was not included in the 1922, 1943, 1946, and 1952 estimates, but good evidence to the contrary may appear. The distinction between registered and unregistered residents, which the president of the Municipal Council emphasized in his conversation with me, may well not have been taken into account in the other estimates. However, it is a reflection of massive immigration. It also reflects the tendency for many Lebanese to be slow to keep their official place of residence up to date with their actual place of residence, and this in turn seems to be an expression of certain attitudes concerning local or communal identification, to be discussed later. The official census in 1932 probably counted Tripoli's registered residents only.

How reasonable is the estimate of 180,000 people in 1961? The president of the Municipal Council told me that he based his estimate on the fact that there are approximately 30,000 households in Tripoli, a fact deduced, he said, from rental tax figures. The assumption of an average household of six persons is reasonable. A sample survey in Beirut revealed an average household size of 5.76 persons,[64] and another in Amman, Jordan, revealed an average Christian size of 5.6 persons and an average Muslim size of 7 persons.[65]

Population Density

Tripoli's built-up area is about 4 square kilometers, and so on the estimate of a population of 180,000, it would have a density of about 45,000 persons per square kilometer. This compares with 37,000 in Paris, 20,000 in Beirut,[66] and 11,704 in Cairo.[67] However, there are sections of Cairo — parts of Bulaq, for example — which exceed the over-all estimated density of Tripoli by as much as 300 per cent. These are sections of old, multistoried houses reminiscent of Tripoli's. Tripoli has certain features conducive to relatively high over-all density: it lacks definitely nonresidential business districts; it has few extensive open areas and single or semidetached dwellings; and its people live almost entirely in multistoried apartment houses and tenements. Approximately one-third the number of animals are slaughtered for meat daily in Tripoli as in Beirut, whose effective population has been estimated at about 600,000 people.

These scraps of information hardly constitute firm support of the 1961 population estimate, but on the whole they give more confidence than two other estimates of the total population of Tripoli and the Mina I have heard from serious and responsible people: 125,000 and 250,000! A semiofficial source[68] gives Tripoli's 1960 population as 125,000 without reference either to the Mina or to registered or unregistered residents.

Whatever Tripoli's exact rate of population growth may have been, there is no doubt about its tremendous increase in size. From the early 1920's to the end of World War II, its physical growth appeared to consist primarily of continued extensions of the growing areas already mentioned, resulting in the development of Mutran and Bab al-Tibbani into rather closely built-up sections, plus the extension of buildings into al-Qubbah and some scattered structures in Abu Samra. These steady but unspectacular developments are indicated fairly well by a comparison with an aerial photograph taken in 1927[69] and a map based on surveys and photographs published in 1947 which is basically similar to a map published by British Naval Intelligence.[70]

Industrialization

During this interwar French mandate period, modern Tripoli took form. In 1937, while workers in Tripoli's old-style workshops were almost three times the number they had been in 1931, there were also 354 workers in "modern industries," a wholly new development.[71]

In the absence of customs duties between Syria and Lebanon, the produce of northern Syria flowed to Tripoli for export. The jetties, berths, and warehouses of the port were improved, and a seaplane base was established there. In the 1920's electric power was introduced; in 1930 the 'Arida cotton mill was opened at Bahsas, south of the city on the road to Beirut;[72] and in 1934, the terminal of oil pipelines from Iraq went into operation north of the city on the coast.[73] The Iraq Petroleum Company (IPC) and 'Arida Cotton are today the two largest single employers in the city. In 1935, the piped water supply from Rash'ayn north of Zgharta was inaugurated. Two pairs of water storage tanks, one in Abu Samra and the other in al-Qubbah, were built during this period. Economically, the city had more than compensated for the temporary and permanent setbacks of World War I. In 1940, the French improvised an oil refinery near al-Biddawi. After the war, it was acquired by IPC and since then has supplied fuel for local use. In 1942, the occupying British army completed the railroad from Tripoli to Beirut.

The effects of modern education, too, began to be evident. The most important private schools built large new quarters in vacant areas in the city (buildings 40 and 41, Map 3) or on the fringes (buildings 43, 44, 47). By 1932, 3,000 students were enrolled in Tripoli's college preparatory schools.[74] Physicians and hospitals, including Muslim ones, besides those of the American mission, were now active.

The physical expansion of the city necessitated the use of land which had been planted to orchards, and these were owned, primarily, by Muslims. Some sold their land, but others began to build on it themselves for investment. Thus began among the prominent Muslims a slow but steady shift away from agrarian landlordism and toward commercial enterprises of various kinds. 'Arida was, and is, owned by Christians, and the IPC terminal is owned by foreigners, but not all Tripoli Muslims were merely passive observers or employees of these business activities. The small beginnings of a number of now important Muslim businesses took place at this time, as did considerable emigration to places like West Africa, where some large fortunes were made, later to be invested in Tripoli itself.

Politics

In 1929, the administrative structure of Lebanon was reorganized and assumed its present form. Tripoli became the capital of the Muhafazat of the North, an area not dissimilar to the previous provinces of which Tripoli had been the chief town — except, of course, that it did not extend northward beyond the Syrian-Lebanese border in the Akkar. Many outspoken people in the city continued to be dissatisfied with the separation from Syria.

These feelings reached their peak in 1936–37 when Tripoli was torn by repeated riots, demonstrations, and strikes, generally anti-French and for union with Syria. The acknowledged leader of Tripoli was 'Abdul-Hamid Karami, mufti of the city and member of a family with extensive properties. The external political conflict was complicated by an internal one, the traditional opposition to the Karamis of the Muqaddims, another landlord family, and their allies, such as Dr. 'Abdul-Latif Bisar.[75] Wealth and outstanding learning were efficient (though not sufficient) causes of the social prominence of these rivalrous families. It is significant that the examples of outstanding learning involved represented the traditional-theological (mufti) and the nontraditional-technological (physician) types. The Karamis emerged victorious from the struggles of the 1930's, but local opposition to them has not ceased, and Dr. Bisar was the first and not the last of his profession to be a leader in Tripoli politics.

In 1937 there was much talk of annexing Tripoli to Syria in compensation to that country for its loss of Alexandretta to Turkey, and a delegation was even dispatched to Léon Blum, then premier of France, to request this annexation. Yet, on the other hand, Tripoli's leaders were definitely becoming leaders of the Muslims of Lebanon.[76] In fact, 'Abdul-Hamid Karami would soon become premier of Lebanon, exemplifying the principle of always balancing the Maronite presidency with a Sunni Muslim premier. As the people themselves experience it, the issue of whether Tripoli "really belongs" in Syria or in Lebanon has become highly arguable, and this hazy situation first manifested itself in the 1930's.

The refinery and railroad extension developed in reaction to the

34

wartime emergency, and Tripoli benefited from the war in other ways. The British occupation forces stimulated retail business and left in their wake surplus goods and scrap metal, providing a number of entrepreneurs with opportunities for great profit. Advantage was also taken of the greatly inflated prices of such materials as lumber, which Tripoli businessmen were beginning to import and store prior to transshipment.

Some Ironies

There are many ironies in Tripoli's history, and two of the greatest occurred in 1948–1950. The Palestine war, which brought tragedy to so many Arabs, resulted in the removal from Haifa of the entire headquarters of the Iraq Petroleum Company and its reestablishment in Tripoli. This, coupled with an expanded construction program, brought over 2,000 new families, including about 500 foreign ones, to the city. The result was a building boom of unprecedented proportions and great stimulation of all service business — retail shops of all kinds, furnituremakers, electrical and automotive suppliers and repairmen, cinemas, and the like. This chain of events was the greatest single impetus to physical growth since World War II.

All new streets laid out since the war have conformed to a street plan made by the French in the 1930's. Combining grid design with diagonal avenues intersecting at circles surrounded by concentric rings of streets, the plan was conceptually superimposed on the entire triangular plain of Tripoli-Mina. Partial suggestions of it are evident in the newest built-up streets, as shown in Map 3.

By 1950, IPC had a peak payroll of about 4,000 persons. But in the same year Syria, to which so many Tripolitans felt they rightfully belonged, enacted a series of customs regulations, cutting off Tripoli's port from its primary marketing area. During the 1950's, the expansion of the Syrian ports of Latakia and Banyas, the continued mushrooming of Beirut, and IPC's gradual reduction in number of employees, did nothing to improve Tripoli's situation. Yet there were countertrends also, particularly the growth of new, locally owned light industries in Bahsas and the investments in Tripoli business by people who had made their fortunes abroad. Whether such developments would be sufficient to save the city from a serious business recession was the essential economic question troubling its leaders in 1961–62.

In its long history, Tripoli has repeatedly been visited by disaster and then favored with florescence. These vicissitudes have always been caused by external circumstances, forces, and influences. The provincialism and narrowness of mind which some Beirut sophisticates claim is typical of Tripoli people may reflect a sort of emotional isolationism, but Tripoli itself — an agglomeration of human energies and physical structures — is not and never has been isolated. Its characteristics today are the direct products of interests and activities in Asia, Africa, Europe, and even America.

Chapter III

SECTARIAN ACTIVITIES AND

ORGANIZATIONS

ALL OBSERVERS OF Lebanon seem to agree that sect and family are the two groups in the culture with which almost all Lebanese individuals are certain to be identified and to identify themselves. To be identified with a wider range of kinsmen than one's parents and brothers and sisters and children, is expected of and by all Lebanese people. Something is felt to be amiss where this expectation is not met. As far as sectarian identity is concerned, it is impossible for the expectation not to be met, for every Lebanese adult must have an identity card to designate, among other things, his sect. And every Lebanese, regardless of what his personal feelings or private beliefs may be, is considered by others to be a representative of his sect.

LEBANESE IDENTITY GROUPS

What do identities imply with respect to sentiments and behavior? They may, of course, imply nothing other than themselves. However, among the Lebanese, they conventionally entail expectations of mutual and unquestioned trust, financial and other assistance, support in crises, and loyal defense against any person or organization outside the circle of identity. In practice, no Lebanese behaves in all these ways with all his kinsmen and certainly not with all the members of his sect. But with what sample of kinsmen and comembers of sect does he *habitually* behave in these ways, and where do his accompanying feelings lie on the range between willing love and grudging hatred? Furthermore, when called upon to meet his conventional obligations with *other* kinsmen and comembers of sect, what if any reciprocation does he demand if he meets them and how does he justify himself if he does not? And when the choice must be made, does sect or kinship have priority in the meeting of his obligations?

The factors involved in these questions are complex in themselves and even more complex in their permutations. Currently available information on Lebanese culture is not sufficient to answer the questions, but it is sufficient to make possible the raising and consideration of them. To say, as has been said in the past, that sect and family are the primary Lebanese in-groups is to say too little about the truth and to suggest too much of what may be false. For in order really to comprehend these aspects of Lebanese culture it will be necessary to identify, analyze, and delineate all the patterns of mixed and conflicting emotions, of sincere and insincere commissions and omissions of acts, which Robert Frost suggests when he says, "Home is the place where, when you have to go there, they have to take you in."

The formal and institutional characteristics of sectarianism are so conspicuous and important in Lebanese culture that it is probably best to begin consideration of the social structure of a Lebanese community with a discussion of them. As to the family and its interrelations with sectarianism, these, as they are seen in Tripoli, will come later.

SECT AND RELIGION DIFFERENTIATED

In terms of motives and goals, a distinction must be made between sect and sectarianism, on the one hand, and religion and religious behavior on the other. A sect is an organization which has a religious identity but also the attributes and problems common to all social organizations regardless of identity. These attributes and problems include: (1) the daily concerns of administration, and the longer-term one of survival, including the organization's relationships with others; (2) the existence within the organization of hierarchies, cliques, and factions; (3) the constant striving of some individuals and subgroups for power and prestige either within the organization or by means of it; and (4) the various emotional and material mechanisms by and through which the members' sense of belonging is maintained and reinforced.

A religion is a more or less systematized assemblage of beliefs, ritual acts, and symbols. The central belief is that there exists super-human spiritual power conscious of and concerned with human beings. Other beliefs define good and evil in human behavior and assert the ultimate meaningfulness and goodness of life despite the fact that it is burdened with pains, fears, the success of evil, and the defeat of good, and ends in apparently total oblivion, as far as the individual is concerned. The rituals are felt to be communications with the supernatural, acts which promote what is hoped for, forestall what is feared, celebrate joy and assuage grief. Religious symbols are used in the ritual. They represent, and often are actually identified with, items of belief and of ritual itself.

Those Christians who are not intellectually concerned with the matter appear not to see the distinction clearly. To them, sect and religion are blurred together. This is not, however, an indication that the distinction is an artificial one. Jesus saw the distinction between the two and drew particular attention to the ethical conflicts of interest which can arise between them. Christianity as a whole is notorious for the massive atrocities which its sects have committed in direct contradiction to the religious precepts of its founder. And many present-day Americans are certainly at least somewhat aware that the linkage of many of their sects with "ethnic" and social class groups involves behavioral patterns which have little if anything to do with religious motivations and beliefs as defined above.[1] Nevertheless the blurring continues, for the leaders and functionaries of the sects can hardly be expected to encourage any dissociation of their social organization from their religion. And the layman, whose commitment to theology and ritual is often superficial, unthoughtful, and perfunctory, can be expected to justify his sincere ethnic or class sectarian identification on the grounds that it is "religious."

In Lebanon, sectarianism is more ramified and intense than it is in the United States. There is also, at least among intellectuals, the same awareness yet blurring of the distinction between sect and religion. This was well illustrated in an exchange between two Lebanese journalists in the Beirut newspaper, *L'Orient*, in March 1965,[2] which was concerned with how and whether to abolish "confessionalism" in Lebanese politics. Lebanese religious behavior is largely enclosed, psychologically and socially, within the sects. There appears to be very little interest in or knowledge of the religion of other sects than one's own, the sects do not proselytize each other, and inter-sectarian marriages are strongly and quite effectively discouraged. The religion of one of the Lebanese sects (the Druze) is in fact secret, although it is known to be in part a historical derivative of Shi'ite Islam.

And so, as one surveys Lebanese culture, it is sectarianism, rather than religion, which stands out in high relief. Religious behavior, including such pan-sectarian belief systems as that related to the evil eye, will, along with the family, be considered later.

SECULARIZATION, AN AMBIGUOUS NOTION

One of the stereotypes of the character of modern city life is that it is "secular" or "secularized" as opposed to being "sacred." Those who use these labels appear to associate "sacred" with such cultures as that of medieval Europe, of almost any nonliterate society as a whole, and of many peasant villages in the contemporary world. Gideon Sjoberg [3] has shown that this association might as well be extended to include the preindustrial city, too, explicitly focusing the issue on the industrial city, rather than on cities in general. "Secular" is, with some authors, an epithet implying loss of spiritual values that are relevant to contemporary life and of symbols and beliefs that are "meaningful" in terms of it; in short, the loss of religion. With other authors, "secular" is a positive word meaning intellectual freedom of inquiry and release from the bonds of theological dogmatism and the repressions of sectarian membership. Some authors have suggested that both usages are "true," the former representing, as it were, the prices that have to be paid for the latter. "Secular" has many connotations. This disqualifies it for use in the discussion of any urban culture.

Nevertheless, since Tripoli was once a preindustrial city and is now acquiring industry, there are those who will be looking for evidence of "secularization" in the data presented here. If they find and label such evidence, they will do so on their own responsibility. Sects are very important in Tripoli. This could be interpreted as evidence of a "sacred" society, especially if one treats sect and religion as being virtually identical. It could also be interpreted as evidence of a "secular" society on the grounds that many of the sects' activities are nonreligious and that therefore religion per se has lost much of its meaning. For reasons already explained, I would reject both of these interpretations. Yet there are problems in industrial city life we cannot ignore merely because they have been dealt with so clumsily in terms of "sacred" and "secular" types. The term "alienation," too, whose many meanings include some of those of "secularization," is no less clumsy by reason of its being currently fashionable. Surveys of the uses to which it is being put show it to be an omnibus label for all sorts of miseries, by no means limited to the modern industrial urban milieu.[4] Consequently, it is not an accurate enough term to use in generalizing about that milieu. It, like the other catch-all expressions, is a hindrance rather than a help in the effort accurately to identify and analyze the characteristics and problems of modern cities, Tripoli included.

THE SECTS OF LEBANON

Lebanon's only official census was taken in 1932 under the French mandate. In it, the memberships of the various sects were enumerated, and the rank-order and proportions established by it have served ever since as the basis on which candidates for appointive office, and nominees for elective office, are selected. The president of Lebanon is always a Maronite, the premier is always a Sunni Muslim, the president of the parliament is always a Shi'a Muslim, and the various members of the cabinet always represent the major sects. According to the 1932 census, Lebanon had six Christians to every five Muslims, and the composition of the membership of parliament is always fixed according to this proportion. The system is extended down to the lowest levels of the government, and it probably ramifies into the business world also. It is called "confessionalism," and however much some Lebanese object to it because of its promotion of corruption and special favors and its competition with sentiments of national unity, it is thoroughly entrenched not only in politics but in the values of the people.[5]

Some sort of proportional representation of the sects in the government goes back to 1861, and so the 1932 census cannot be regarded as the original principle of the system. However, the balances of power which have been worked out on the basis of it are so delicate and considered so important that there has been no census since then. There have been estimates, however, and according to the latest, the population of Lebanon is now 1,600,000, about 50 per cent more than it was in 1932. But no one has tampered with the rank-order of the sects. In 1951 the populations of the major sects were estimated as shown in Table 2.

TABLE 2. THE SECTS OF LEBANON, 1951

Western Roman Catholics (Latins)	4,000
Roman Catholic Uniates	
Maronites	377,000
Greek Catholics	82,000
Armenian Catholics	14,000
Syrian Catholics	6,000
Chaldeans	1,000
Total Roman Catholics	484,000
Eastern Orthodox	131,000
Syrian Orthodox (Jacobites)	5,000
Armenians (Gregorian)	67,000
Protestants	13,000
Total non-Catholic Christians	216,000
Total Christians	700,000
Muslims	
Sunni	272,000
Mutawilah (Shi'a)	237,000
Druze	82,000
Total Muslims	591,000
Jews	6,000
Others	7,000
Total	13,000
Grand total	1,304,000

Each of these sects is an organized, property-holding group. Though linked to Rome, each of the Uniate sects has its own hierarchy, usually headed by a patriarch, its own special liturgy, its own schools, etc. All of the other sects are likewise discrete, corporate bodies. The Protestant category is composed mostly of Presbyterians who have their own sectarian organization. "Others" is of course a category and not a sect in itself, but it includes such sects as 'Alawites and Isma'ilis. The major sects in order of official size are: the Maronites, Sunnis, Shi'a, Eastern Orthodox, Druze, and Greek Catholics. None is in a majority, and each must constantly seek new balances and rapprochements with the others, for the various Christian groups and the various Muslim ones only rarely coalesce into two unified blocs. Typically, in any location where a sect is particularly small, its members may pledge their votes to officials belonging to other, larger sects in return for favors and advantages. Such reciprocities often cross Muslim-Christian lines despite the much-voiced fears that the larger sects are constantly plotting to better their position at others' expense. The relationships among the sects are a complicated amalgam of competition and accommodation, and of ceremonial deference and day-to-day politeness which are covers for fear, reserve, and memories of grievances.

THE SECTS OF TRIPOLI

According to the 1932 census the sectarian populations of Tripoli and the Mina were as shown in Table 3. These figures are indices of the overwhelming majority of Sunnis in Tripoli, of their formidable numbers in the Mina, and of the definite second place held by the Eastern Orthodox. On the basis of the 1932 census, Tripoli and the Mina always have one Christian and four Muslim deputies in the Lebanese parliament, in sharp contrast to the six-to-five ratio for the country as a whole.

Projections from these figures into the present situation can yield only uncertain results. As mentioned before, the 1932 census probably did not count unregistered residents, but even with this allowance, the actual population has increased at least 100 per cent since 1932. Part of this increase has been due to natural reproduction, whose rate, if Tripoli is representative of Lebanon as a whole in this regard, is higher among urban Muslims than it is among urban Christians.[6] It has also been due to immigration, and there has been, apparently, a large immigration of Syrian 'Alawites (either under the Shi'a or "other" categories in the census) since 1932. Members of the other sects have moved into Tripoli, too, but in what numbers is not known. There is probably a high correlation between recency of immigration and being an unregistered resident, but no statistical

TABLE 3. THE SECTS OF TRIPOLI AND THE MINA ACCORDING TO THE 1932 CENSUS

Tripoli	
Sunni Muslim	32,209
Eastern Orthodox	4,968
Maronite	1,573
Armenian (Gregorian)	668
Protestant	323
Greek Catholic	223
Syrian Catholic	151
Armenian (Catholic)	121
Jews	24
Shi'a Muslims	22
Druze	6
Other	1,186
Total	41,474
Mina	
Sunni Muslim	6,476
Eastern Orthodox	2,364
Armenian (Gregorian)	603
Maronites	250
Syrian Orthodox (Jacobites)	86
Greek Catholics	42
Latins	33
Protestants	30
Other	3,518
Total	13,402

information exists on this, let alone on the present population of the sects.

There are no longer any Jews in Tripoli, and the Druze are few if any. The Armenians, though they have a church in the Mina and a charitable organization in Tripoli, do not play an important role in the city's social and commercial life. The Syrian Catholics (Roman-Uniate descendants of a sixth-century monophysite sect) have a church and primary school near Shari' Kinayis, and have a few hundred members. The Greek Catholics have a church in the Zahriyyah section and two charitable societies, a men's and a women's.

Taking all the evidence, such as it is, into account, the three most important sects in Tripoli are, in order, the Sunnis, the Orthodox, and the Maronites. There is every reason to believe that the Sunnis

44

are still by far the most numerous, followed at a considerable distance by the Orthodox, who in turn are followed (probably more closely than they used to be) by the Maronites. In terms of numbers, the 'Alawites may well surpass the Maronites, but they have no power or institutional significance. The Presbyterians, on the other hand, though numbering only a few hundred, are important because of their hospital, their two big and highly respected secondary schools, and the many ties between them and the prestigious American University of Beirut and Beirut College for Women.

If any credence can be placed in figures which date from about 1897 (Table 4), it looks as if any improvement in the relative position of the Maronites has taken place since 1932, and this is, in fact, the impression that most informants have of the situation.

TABLE 4. SECTARIAN POPULATION OF TRIPOLI CA. 1897

Sunni Muslim	24,841
Eastern Orthodox	3,500
Maronite	1,500
Latin	159
Jews	80
Greek Catholic	30
Total	30,110

SOURCE: Noel Verney and George Dambmann, *Les puissances étrangères dans le Levant, en Syrie, et en Palestine* (Paris and Lyon, 1900), pp. 28–29.

SECTARIAN STRUCTURE OF THE SUNNIS OF TRIPOLI

Mufti, Qadi, Ulama

The organization of the Sunnis of Tripoli is partly a remnant of traditional Islamic procedures and partly a rather loosely structured adaptation (under mostly French influence) to current conditions. The three most prominent officials are the mufti, the qadi, and the chairman of the council of the Department of Awqaf. The mufti, in theory, is the final arbiter in any questions of theology which the qadi, or the chairman of Awqaf, or anyone else, may address to him. The qadi is the judge of the Shari'a court of the city, which adjudicates problems of inheritance, marriage, divorce, guardianship and support of minor children, and like matters, which arise among Sunni Muslims and are covered by Islamic precepts. The court's interpretations are made according to the Hanbali school of jurisprudence. The Department of Awqaf administers Muslim properties in the city.

Before 1920, these operations were carried on fairly autonomously in Tripoli, and the qadi's authority, though the Ottomans had already reduced it by the introduction of a non-Shari'a judicial system, extended over the administration of all Awqaf. Under the French Mandate, the Shari'a courts' jurisdiction was further restricted to matters of personal status among Sunnis, but the courts were also incorporated into the framework of the national Ministry of Justice. The French also set up the Supreme Islamic Council of Lebanon (headed by a grand mufti) and a national directorate of Awqaf with several local departments. Neither of these is directly connected with the Lebanese government, except in the sense that qadis refer to them, but they do participate in the selection of the muftis and chairmen of Awqaf in Beirut, Saida, Baalbak, and Tripoli. The qadi of Tripoli is responsible to the Minister of Justice and can consult with the council of Shari'a judges which is part of the ministry. He can also appeal to the Supreme Islamic Council, and may (but need not) consult with the mufti of Tripoli. The chairman of Awqaf in Tripoli may (but need not) consult with either the mufti or the qadi, and can refer cases to the national directorate, which can appeal them to the Supreme Islamic Council.

The main function of the mufti today seems to be the ceremonial head and spokesman of the sect in the city. The lines of authority are not, however, well defined, and there are unclear and conflicting features in the system. The result, according to informants who themselves have held important positions in it, is much confusion and disagreement. The mufti is elected by the Supreme Islamic Council and by the following personages in the district concerned: Muslim deputies in parliament, delegates from unions and professional organizations, the *imams* (prayer leaders) of the mosques, and the *shaykhs* (doctors of theology); it seems that the consensus of these local people carries more weight than that of the Council in general.

As the authority of the mufti has become diffused and dissipated, so, apparently, has that of the Ulama (Learned Ones), the council of doctors of Islamic theology which is so often referred to in older accounts of Muslim cities as making decisions in company with the mufti. Jessup mentions an incident in Tripoli, apparently in the early nineteenth century, in which the mufti, qadi, chief shaykhs, and Ulama met to decide how to interpret the accidental presence of a

Maronite pig in a mosque as not forever defiling the building. They decided that the pig must have been a lamb in magical disguise.[7]

Although the Islamic world is today in intellectual turmoil over how to adapt the precepts of the religion to present-day conditions, there seems to be little need at every local level for a deliberative body to consider such matters. The Sunni leaders of a city like Tripoli are, in any case, more likely to look to their more prestigeful colleagues in Cairo for answers than to provide them for themselves. The removal of most civil cases, and all criminal cases, from the jurisdiction of the Shari'a courts has perhaps been an even stronger factor in this regard. My informants were completely evasive as to whether there is an Ulama in Tripoli today. Probably there is not; the nearest thing to it would be *ad hoc* meetings of shaykhs at the Muslim boys' *kulliyah*, some of whom were trained at al-Azhar in Cairo.

Department of Awqaf

There are in Tripoli a formally endowed Muslim hospital, a Muslim secondary school for boys and another for girls, five Muslim cemeteries, and about twenty-five mosques. These properties are not owned by the Muslim "church" because there is no such institution in the western sense. They are, however, administered by the Tripoli Department of Awqaf. Administration includes not only staffing and maintenance of the hospital, schools, cemeteries, and mosques, but also the management of the funds which support these operations. These funds derive partly from the direct donations of money for specific purposes (for example, the building of the new mosque on the boulevard) and from endowments (*awqaf*; singular *waqf*). A waqf is almost always real property of some kind, the income from which (rents or sales of produce) is used for the support of sectarian activities. There are two kinds of waqf, *dhurri* and *khayri*. Waqf dhurri is an endowment, 15 per cent going directly to the department but the balance of its income going to the donating family as long as that family exists, after which it accrues to the department. The Shari'a court exercises authority in some issues concerning waqf dhurri.[8] Waqf khayri is a direct endowment with no family entail, completely under the administration of the department. No building or other property originally given as waqf khayri, or apparently any that is supported by waqf khayri funds, can be demolished or other-

47

wise disposed of except with considerable difficulty, and then only if a compensatory endowment of some kind is made. One writer states that 80 per cent of the waqf properties in Lebanon (including those of Christians) are waqf dhurri.[9] This was denied as far as the Muslims are concerned by an informant who had himself been the national director of Awqaf. He said that recently most of the Muslim waqf dhurri has been converted into waqf khayri, and that the latter predominates. The chairman of the Tripoli Awqaf council told me that 60 per cent in Tripoli was waqf khayri.

The real properties for which the department is responsible thus include not only those already mentioned but also the commercial properties from which income is derived. In Tripoli these include storefronts, orchards, a village and its lands in the Akkar, and one of the largest new buildings on the boulevard, containing a cinema, shops, and private apartments. The office of the department consists of several rooms, full of file cases and inhabited by several clerks. The Muslim Awqaf of Tripoli were reported to be the richest in Lebanon and to be worth "millions," but the local officials would not give me any specific or systematic information. One reason for their reticence could well have been the reliably reported fact that they were themselves embroiled in bitter controversy over the proper fulfillment of their responsibilities. Complaints about the administration of Awqaf commercial properties were being voiced in one of the local newspapers.[10]

There is no large-scale, centralized administration of Sunni Islam as a whole. The French tried to establish one for Lebanon, at least, by creating the national directorate of Awqaf, the Supreme Islamic Council, and the office of grand mufti, but in fact these are not a centralized administration. At most they are useful as arbiters of disputes referred to them and as symbols of Sunni Islam in the country. Local autonomy remains strong in regard to the holding and administration of sectarian property, but it has been to some extent weakened by the incorporation of the Shari'a courts into the national judicial system, consisting primarily of nonsectarian civil and criminal courts.

SECTARIAN STRUCTURE OF THE EASTERN ORTHODOX OF TRIPOLI

The Eastern Orthodox of Tripoli are headed by their own archbishop, the ultimate local authority in all religious and sectarian matters. These include the management of Awqaf and the adjudication of problems of personal status which arise among Orthodox people. The archbishop (or priests delegated by him) serves the same function for Orthodox people as does the Shari'a court for the Sunnis, except that he does so outside the framework of the national judicial system. Nevertheless, his decisions are legally binding.

Orthodox Tripoli is part of one of the four original Byzantine patriarchates, that of Antioch, whose patriarch now resides in Damascus, Syria. He is equal in rank to the other three Middle Eastern patriarchs (in Istanbul, Alexandria, and Jerusalem), and there is no higher authority above them. Unlike those of the other three, the hierarchy and priesthood of the patriarchate of Antioch are dominated by Arabs rather than by Greek nationals. In addition to not having an equivalent of the Pope, the lower levels of the Orthodox hierarchy seem to be less authoritarian than they would be in the Roman Catholic sect. In 1961, the office of archbishop of Tripoli had been vacant for about three years; during this time, two factions of laymen and clerics had maneuvered for the appointment of rival candidates. One was said to have Soviet leanings, and the other was supported by, among others, the aristocratic families of Tripoli. The man who was finally appointed in April of 1962 was neither of the rivals. Such a long-delayed appointment would be unlikely among the Roman Catholics.

In addition to the cathedral, which has an elaborate portal and a dome (building 7, Map 5), there are two Orthodox churches near Shari' Kinayis and two each in al-Qubbah and al-Mina. There is a boys' Orthodox secondary school in the Mina and a girls' secondary school on Shari' Zahriyyah, an Orthodox Youth Organization in the Mina, and several benevolent organizations which will be discussed later. Though its structure appears to be more centralized and authoritarian than that of the Sunnis, one has the impression of considerable local autonomy among the Orthodox.

THE STRUCTURES OF OTHER CHRISTIAN SECTS IN TRIPOLI

The residence of the Maronite bishop of Tripoli is, as has already been pointed out, in Hayy Mutran, not far from the new cathedral and the one secondary school (building 48, Map 3) staffed by Maronite nuns. The bishop has duties similar to those of the Orthodox archbishop in regard to Awqaf and to the adjudication of personal status problems arising among Maronites. He is, however, responsible to the Maronite patriarch, who in turn is responsible to the Vatican. The patriarch has great power among the members of his sect and is therefore a force to be reckoned with among all Lebanese people. His rank in the Roman Catholic hierarchy seems to be equivalent to that of an archbishop, but his *de facto* position as the leader of the Maronites as a social group is a special one.

While the Maronite sect is united with Rome, it is not exactly an agency of the Vatican, or, at any rate, it is not the only one in Lebanon. There is a papal legate in Beirut, and the Jesuits and several teaching orders are very active in Lebanon. In Tripoli, the Carmelites, Benedictines, Sisters of Charity, and Frères des Ecoles Chrétiennes are all very important in the educational field. The staffs of their schools include some Middle Easterners, but European monks, nuns, and priests are also present. Such western Roman Catholics (as opposed to Uniate Catholics like the Maronites) are called in Arabic *Latin*, and they have a church in Tripoli (near Shari' Kinayis) and another one in the Mina.

The Presbyterians of Tripoli are people of mostly Lebanese and Syrian origin whose families have been converted (mostly from Eastern Orthodoxy) over the past century or so. The Tripoli congregation, which has churches in Tripoli and the Mina, belongs to the National Evangelical Synod of Lebanon and Syria. The Kennedy Hospital in the Mina and the boys' and girls' schools in Tripoli were founded, and originally largely staffed, by American missionaries. Now, however, the staffs of these institutions are composed mostly of Arabs, and their administration is controlled by the Synod which is no longer an American mission. Nevertheless, the Presbyterians tend to be American-oriented, culturally speaking, in much the same way that the Maronites tend to be French-oriented. Tripolitans in general often refer to the Presbyterians and their institutions as "American." The Presbyterians do not particularly appreciate this, since they consider themselves to be Arabs.

VISIBLE INDICATIONS OF SECTARIANISM

Clothing in General

Carleton Coon has observed that the members of the different Middle Eastern social groups customarily display their identities by means of certain articles of clothing and other symbols. In the Levant (in contrast to some other parts of the area), the widespread adoption of European-style clothing has eliminated many of these practices, and it is not true that all members of each group wear a special uniform. However, Coon's generalization is partially borne out, and these and other visible indications of social groups (namely, the sects) are the subject of this section.

Clerical costumes are the easiest to identify. The mufti, the shaykhs, and imams (all of these being people who are learned in Islamic law or scriptures and have some sort of authority derived from that learning) wear what amounts to a uniform, the same for the mufti and for his juniors alike. It includes a well-tailored coat, usually worn open in front, usually dark brown or gray in color, and extending down to the knees. This is worn over European-style trousers and some combination of vest and shirt, with or without necktie. On the head is worn a fez (properly: *tarbush*), all (except its flat top) wrapped in a white cloth. Evidently made of fine, gauzelike cotton, the wrapping is always spotless, but individuals vary in the care with which they wind it around the tarbush. At its most elegant, it tapers outward toward the top, and the whole has the classic effect of a turban.

Men who wear this costume always also wear a mustache, which does not differentiate them from the average Sunni layman, and quite often a closely trimmed beard, which does. Many laymen wear the tarbush and may also wrap it in some sort of cloth but never in a way that can be confused with the clerical style. However, I did see two men in Tripoli who wore the tarbush with a *green* wrapping in clerical style. One of these men claimed to be a *sharif* (plural, *ashraf*), a lineal descendant of Muhammad. At various times and places in the Middle East, such headgear has indeed been worn by recognized ashraf, or by men who have made the pilgrimage to Mecca. It evidently does not have such significance in Tripoli today, for Sunnis of whom I enquired concerning the two men I had seen derided them as being charlatans.

Christian priests all wear long, black cassocks, over which there may also be a black cloak or overcoat if the weather calls for such an addition. They are differentiated by sect chiefly by their headgear. The Eastern Orthodox priest wears a brimless cylindrical hat whose flat top has a narrow, projecting rim. Higher-ranking Orthodox priests and bishops have a cloth attached to their hats which hangs down the back like a veil. The ordinary Maronite priest wears a black "pillbox" or, *à la mode française*, a beret. His superiors wear what looks like a squat, black turban. The Armenian priest wears a pointed, hoodlike, hat. Christian priests wear beards, and they are usually full rather than trimmed. Their hair also is normally long, sometimes so long that it is tied in a bun behind.

If there are, among males, sectarian differences in the ways in which they have adopted European-style clothes, I have neither heard of them nor perceived them myself. Considering the fact that the Lebanese are acutely aware of the details of European fashions, the rarity of the brimmed man's hat suggests some kind of symbolic rejection, and it may be even more rare among Muslims than among Christians. Nor is there anything specifically sectarian in the non-European clothing worn by men in Tripoli. (The Druze, whose men and women are frequently seen in Beirut in distinctive costume, are not seen in Tripoli.) The tarbush is worn by a considerable number of men, including young ones, often with a costume which is otherwise European, but both Muslims and Christians wear it. *Shirwal*, the pleated trousers with tight legs below the knees and a full crotch which hangs down almost to them, are peasant garb. They are commonly worn by villagers from the Akkar and the adjacent Syrian hills, and these villagers are mostly Muslims, but Christian peasants also may wear shirwal. The same is true of the heavy, black rope-like head circlet (*agal*) and black headcloth (*kuffiyah*) which are often seen in Tripoli. Somewhat less frequent, but not rare, are men dressed in *gumbaz* (ankle-length, narrow gown), white kuffiyah and black agal, and European jacket or *aba* (square cloak with wide sleeves). These men are from the desert fringe areas of Syria, and they are most likely Muslims but not necessarily so. Peasant women from these same areas are usually not veiled, although they always wear some sort of kerchief which can be pulled across part of the face when the need is felt, but Christian peasant women also wear such kerchiefs. Peasant women who wear, under their skirts, flowered pantalettes with ruffles around the ankles seem to be always Muslims and from the interior plains. In general, then, there are cues to sectarian identities among laymen, but they are mostly only approximate.

The Muslim Women's Veil

Of particular interest is the occurrence of veiling among Tripoli women. It is not simply a matter of whether a woman does or does not wear a veil; and in addition to attitudes toward sectarian identity, attitudes toward sex are also involved.

A Tripoli woman who wears a veil is certain to be a Muslim, for gone are the days when Christian women felt it necessary to disguise themselves as Muslims in public. However, not all Muslim women are veiled, and so there is some ambiguity in the matter. The veil must be considered together with the rest of the costume, and three types of ensemble will include most of the cases seen in Tripoli.

1. The neck and head are completely enveloped in a sort of wimple, with an oval opening for the face, spreading out to cover the shoulders. This is black and is worn over a full black gown which reaches to the ankles. Normally, the face opening is covered by the veil, attached above but hanging loose so that it can be raised when necessary. Usually, also, the veil is opaque, but sometimes it is thin enough so that something of the woman's features can be discerned. Women who wear the opaque veil frequently have to raise it when they are out shopping so that they can inspect the goods properly, and some of the older ones may simply throw it back over the top of their heads to get it completely out of the way while they use both hands for other purposes. Occasionally, bright-colored material will show through some gap in the black gown, reminding one that the woman is wearing a regular dress underneath. This outfit serves well its basic purpose, which is to hide the woman's identity and charms from all strangers in public places.

2. The wimple is worn, but more frequently with a thin veil, and without the black gown over the dress.

3. The wimple and attached veil are replaced by a voluminous, sheer black veil which is knotted by the corners behind but can be raised in front. The wearer's features may be quite visible through it. The rest of her costume is westernized, and variable, but may well consist of a short, form-fitting French or Italian suit or dress, sheer stockings, and high-heeled shoes.

Cultural Change and Erotic Stimuli

To American and European men, ensemble no. 3 can have the opposite effect from that intended and achieved by no. 1. The transparent veil may render the woman more interesting than she would be without it, and the rest of her costume may be definitely provocative. But the important question is not what the effects may be on foreigners but what they are on Muslim men. Do they accidentally-on-purpose fail to discourage their women from wearing this apparel because they, too, are pleasantly stimulated by it? Or are they merely allowing their women to follow the current fashions, without having any particular interest in them themselves? A rather peevish-sounding comment in one of the Tripoli newspapers might suggest an affirmative answer to the second question, if it can be taken at face value:

THE DRESS IS ABOVE THE KNEE!

If women are ashamed of showing their legs, and they seem to be because they keep pulling their skirts down, why don't they wear longer skirts? [11]

Erotic stimulation is subject to very different cultural cues, and one must be careful not to jump to cross-cultural conclusions about it. Modern Muslim men seem to be stimulated by the exposure of women's upper arms but not by the exposure of their bosoms. Western men's reactions are approximately the reverse. Many western men seem to feel that women wearing slacks are either uninteresting or definitely unattractive. Many Muslim (and Christian) Lebanese men are so stimulated by such women that they seem to assume that they are whores. To Muslim men (and women), belly dancers are good family entertainment, suitable for wedding parties if one can afford them, and usually to be seen in Arabic cinema comedies. To many westerners, they have the forbidden, indecent aura of nightclub strippers. And so it goes.

Judging from the large number of women in Tripoli who are not veiled at all, there must be many Muslim women and men who do not consider such exposure improper. As to those who are variously veiled and costumed, they may well represent considerable divergence of opinion concerning sectarian and sexual proprieties, complicated by the pressures to be fashionable, for which there is independent evidence. Among other possibilities, it may be that the wearing of the veil which does not really hide the face may at least partly be inspired by the wish to assert sectarian identity. Table 5 suggests some ideas about the frequency of veiling in Tripoli.

The counts of veiled women include all types; my impression is that women wearing type 1 are in the minority, but they are certainly not rare. The scarcity of veiled women in Hayy Mutran is consistent with what we know of its large Christian population and

ACTIVITIES AND ORGANIZATIONS

TABLE 5. OBSERVATIONS ON THE FREQUENCY OF VEILED WOMEN

Place	Time	Veiled	Unveiled
1. Hayy Mutran	4:45 P.M.	2	40
2. Intersection of Boulevard and Shari' al-Mina	9:00 A.M.	7	37
3. Bus Station	8:45 A.M.	5	5
4. Tal	8:30 A.M.	3	17
5. Tal	10:00 A.M.	30	30
6. Tal	12:00 M.	22	50
7. Tal	2:00 P.M.	22	70
8. Tal	4:15 P.M.	10	35
9. Sahit Saraya 'Adimi	9:00 A.M.	11	22
10. Bab al-Raml to Dibbagha	4–4:30 P.M.	73	45
11. Bab al-Raml to Khan al-Sabun	9–9:30 A.M.	90	30
12. Mansuri Mosque, 'Id al-Fitr	6:30–7:00 A.M.	170	110

the heavy proportion of middle class, western-style-educated Muslims and Christians who live there.

Conversely, the strong majority of veiled women in the Old City (observations 10 and 11), is consistent with this section's predominantly non-western-style-educated, lower class Muslim population. Comparison of observations 2 and 4 with observation 11 suggests that at the same time of day when veiled women are out in force on errands in the Old City, there are relatively few of them in the more westernized shopping areas of the city. A greater number of systematic observations might have yielded stronger evidence of patterns in these matters and in diurnal variations such as those suggested by observations 4 to 8 in the Tal, but no amount of such observation by a western man is likely to answer such questions as where the veiled women actually live and what proportion of the unveiled ones are Muslims. For these reasons, and because of observation 12, no further effort was devoted to the matter.

'Id al-Fitr (Break-fast Feast) marks the end of Ramadan, the month of daytime fasting. It is one of the major festivals of the Muslim calendar. Between 6:30 and 7:00 on the morning of 'Id al-Fitr, March

7, 1962, I counted the women who were passing in front of the Mansuri mosque on their return from decorating graves in Bab al-Raml. They were of all ages, and though some Christian women could have been mixed in among the unveiled ones, I think it is unlikely, for the hour was too early for shopping, and most of the stores were closed anyway. Unless a significant number of individuals change their normal veiling practices on festive occasions, I think that my count on 'Id al-Fitr is as representative a natural sample of Muslims as could be obtained. According to it, about 61 per cent of the Muslim women in Tripoli are veiled in public.

Funeral Notices

Of the other types of visible indications of sectarianism in Tripoli, one of the most specific is funeral and mourning period announcements. Lebanese Christians and Muslims alike set aside a period of a month to forty days after a funeral, during which the bereaved receive formal visits of condolence. Deaths and funerals may be announced orally in public places, but they are also posted in printed notices which are pasted on the walls of buildings along with the many commercial advertisements. The Orthodox and Maronite notices are printed on white sheets of typewriter paper size, have heavy black borders at least an inch wide, and meticulously name the individual chief mourners as well as the place and time of the funeral. Muslim notices are the same size but lack the border and generally specify only the names of the mourning families. Protestant notices are smaller and have a narrow black border.

Sectarian Signs

As to sectarian buildings, not all are as obviously Christian and Muslim as are the cathedral in Hayy Mutran and the new mosque on the boulevard. Crosses and belfries are markers of churches, and crescents and minarets are markers of mosques, but these are not always present. All the churches and mosques have names, but these are rarely posted on signs. There are two small mosques in Bab al-Raml which have neither crescents, signs, nor minarets, whose identity becomes clear only if one observes men at prayer inside. The muezzin of one of them simply stands in the doorway and chants his call to prayer to the passersby on the sidewalk. While most churches are identifiable as such, the absence of signs makes it difficult to identify them specifically as to sect. Similarly, only two or three of the secondary schools, which are among the largest institutional buildings in the city, have identifying signs.

As described in Appendix A, there is also a dearth of signs among the industrial buildings in Bahsas. This is a cultural theme, a consistency in style of behavior, which occurs not only in sectarianism but in other aspects of Tripoli's life as well. It may be a reflection of assumptions of long standing, both of them probably unconscious: 1) that signs are useless to the large proportion of illiterates in the population and 2) that only those people who are directly concerned with a particular building care about its identity, and they do not need to have it labeled.

PRIVATE SCHOOLS

Education and charitable activities are two of the most important functions of Tripoli's sects. In fact, the government's contribution to education, though it has increased greatly since 1943, is surpassed qualitatively by that of the sects, while its charitable or social security measures are relatively minor. After all, the concept of government which serves the people is a new one in the Middle East, and even in a country like Lebanon, it is still not very real in the minds of many people.

Chapter IV will discuss the government and private schools in Tripoli in general, but in this section I shall concentrate on those thirteen large schools which have one-third of all the city's school children, including 58 per cent of its secondary pupils. These are the only nongovernment schools providing secondary education. All thirteen, with one marginal exception, are sponsored by sects. Arranged in sectarian alphabetical order, they and some facts concerning them are listed in Table 6.

The information in Table 6 was obtained from the schools individually. Some were cooperative, but others were not, and this accounts for the dearth of information in some cases. In most instances I have not given the actual names of the schools but, rather, descriptive designations. In Arabic, each of these institutions is a *kulliyyah*, a word which in this context means the same as the French "collège," a school whose secondary graduates are qualified to take the nationally standardized examination for *baccalauréat, première partie*. Gradu-

TABLE 6. ENROLLMENT IN NONGOVERNMENT SCHOOLS IN TRIPOLI-MINA OFFERING SECONDARY EDUCATION

Sponsoring sect	School	Kindergarten	Primary	Secondary	Total	Other facts & comments
Eastern Orthodox	Girls (Tripoli)	120	200	330	650	Some boys in kindergarten; 90 boarders, 15% Muslims
Eastern Orthodox	Boys (Mina)		439	283	722	25% girls
Latin	Benedictine Boys		400	90	490	Secondary pupils in vocational classes
Latin	Carmelite				750	Only total enrollment figure provided
Latin	Frères		1250	750	2000	All boys; three separate plants: 2 in Tripoli, 1 in Mina
Latin	Rahbat (Sisters of Charity)		2000	750	2750	All girls; 125 orphan boarders; three separate plants, like Frères
Maronite	'Abrin		650	350	1000	All girls
Muslim	Boys		754	573	1327	300 boarders
Muslim	Girls		310	90	400	36 boarders
Muslim	Kabbara				300	Only total enrollment figure provided
Presbyterian	Girls	118	227	192	537	38 boarders; about 70 boys in kindergarten and primary; 52% Muslim
Presbyterian	Boys		307	194	501	85 boarders; 45% Muslim
Presbyterian	Kulliyyah Trablus		35	315	350	10 girls, 50% boarders; 150 commuters; Presbyterian connections but not sponsored by the church
					11,777	

ating from secondary school and passing the *first baccalauréat* are, in American terms, the equivalent of graduating from high school and passing the College Board Examinations.

Among Lebanese middle class and upper class parents the attainment of this goal is a major criterion of social prestige, gained through their children, and consequently tremendous anxieties and pressures accompany its accomplishment. One informant told me, in terms of great pathos, about the anxious parents who literally camp all day outside the schools in Tripoli when their children take the "Bac" examination.

According to the national Ministry of Education, there were in 1961–62, 14,547 pupils enrolled in the nongovernment schools of Tripoli-Mina, and there were 63 such schools. Therefore, the above thirteen kulliyyahs obviously dominate the city's nongovernment education, for they have about 83 per cent of its total enrollment and all of its secondary enrollment. (There is some secondary enrollment in the government schools, but this is a new development, and high quality secondary education is felt to be offered only in the nongovernment schools.) The remaining fifty nongovernment schools are primary only and have an average enrollment of fifty-six pupils apiece. Some are sectarian, but others are not.

The sectarian kulliyyahs in Tripoli are not uniform in quality or reputation, and not all of them are generally respected. However, at the other end of the scale, it is safe to say that the Frères, Rahbat, and Presbyterian boys' and girls' schools are highly regarded. All four have long been established in Tripoli, the children of important Muslim families traditionally have attended them, and they still do even though the Muslim kulliyyahs are now available. "Frères" and "Rahbat" ("nuns," specifically the Sisters of Charity) are words which have actually become part of local parlance and are used as street names in the vicinities of the two main school buildings. The situation is not static, however. For example, the Eastern Orthodox girls' school has recently been expanding its facilities and has a brand-new modernistic classroom building, adjoining its older building, which contains a biological laboratory which is splendidly outfitted with Russian-made equipment. The Muslim kulliyyahs, too, founded later than many of the Christian ones, have recently been growing and improving. This (coupled with the great increase and expansion of government schools which primarily benefit Muslims

59

in Tripoli) is apparently a counteraction to the long-standing pre-eminence of Christian, and often foreign-oriented, schools in the city.

The educational situation in Tripoli must be viewed in the context of time and Lebanese history. Before the early nineteenth century, the only education was in scriptural schools (*kuttabs*) which were attended by boys only, and by a minority of them. Both Christians and Muslims had them, and the latter also had the more advanced madrasahs. These taught the religious scriptures, and very little else, by rote memorization. Today, in Tripoli and in Lebanon generally, there are no more kuttabs or madrasahs. According to an informant who has a high administrative post in Lebanese Muslim educational circles, the demise of the scriptural schools was gradual but began in the second quarter of the nineteenth century when the Ottomans began to make efforts at establishing a modern school system. In areas like Lebanon, especially, they achieved this by allowing European and American missionaries to set up their own schools. Thus began the present sectarian schools of Tripoli and elsewhere. Though sectarian, they are not direct descendants of the old scriptural schools. Indeed, by law they may not offer scriptural instruction except to members of their own sect, and there are some limitations even on this. A few government schools were established, but it has only been since 1943, when Lebanon became independent, that a full-fledged government school system has come into being. In view of these facts, while it is startling that Muslims for a long time have had to get their best education from Christians, it seems clear that no weakening of the barriers between the sects is involved.

Something should be said about the boarding and commuting pupils, as indicated in Table 6. The Rahbat boarders are all orphans, and I shall shortly discuss this and other charitable activities of the sects. As far as the boarders in the other schools are concerned, I obtained some information about them from the head of one of the schools. Most of them are the children of parents who have emigrated, to West Africa for example. Others are the children of parents who live too far away for the children to commute daily. Still others (girls) have homes in Tripoli but are nevertheless boarders. Personal problems at home, but not a desire on the part of the parents to cloister their girls away from home, are the apparent reasons for this.

Commuting students — those who do not live in Tripoli itself — are not restricted to the one school in the table where their presence is indicated. They come from villages without sufficient educational facilities, especially at the secondary level. There are instances of parents in such cases who will board their children with other relatives in the city, or may even move into the city themselves, so that they can save the cost of boarding fees, but not all are able to make such arrangements. Commuting is the alternative for them.

BENEVOLENT AND CHARITABLE ASSOCIATIONS

According to the 1958 directory, published three years before I began my study, there were forty-five charitable and benevolent societies in Tripoli. I made some spot inquiries about some of these organizations but did not confirm the existence and activities (as listed) of all of them, and therefore I can only assume that the list is largely accurate for 1961–62.

Nine of the organizations are branches of national or international ones:

1. Armenian General Benevolent Society
2. Young Men's Christian Association
3. Young Women's Christian Association
4. Lebanese Red Cross Society
5. Society of St. Vincent de Paul in Lebanon
6. Cercle de la Jeunesse Catholique
7. Young Christian Workers
8. Young Men's Muslim Association
9. Young Women's Muslim Association

The only definitely nonsectarian organization on this list, the Red Cross, is not very strong in Lebanon and is certainly not strong in Tripoli. The YWCA, the YMMA, and the YWMA seem to have only nominal programs. The Armenian society has clearly marked headquarters on 'Azmi Street. Of the YMCA I shall say more later on.

Of more significance in terms of the city itself are the thirty-six local organizations in Tripoli or the Mina. Table 7 lists them in their order of foundation and indicates their functions rather than their formal names, which are often fulsome but not precise.

Study of this list reveals some apparent patterns which can most clearly be discussed in terms of Tables 8 and 9. That the Christians

TABLE 7. SECTARIAN BENEVOLENT SOCIETIES

Society	Sect and year
1. Women's society for needy families, students, orphans	Presbyterian, 1890
2. Society for needy families in the Mina	Orthodox, 1895
3. Society for needy families in the Mina	Christian, 1899
4. Women's orphanage and school for girls in the Mina	Orthodox, 1906
5. Society paying funeral expenses and supplying books to needy students	Christian, 1906
6. Society paying funeral expenses of needy families	Maronite, 1909
7. Women's society for aid to needy families and free medical care	Maronite, 1920
8. Society for aid to needy students	Muslim, 1921
9. Women's society for girls' secondary school scholarships	Orthodox, 1924
10. Women's orphanage and school for girls	Muslim, 1926
11. Society for needy families and free medicine	Orthodox, 1932
12. Women's society for help to needy families, hospital patients, and students, Mina	Orthodox, 1936
13. Women's day care nursery and school expenses for needy children	Muslim, 1937
14. Society for free primary education, adult education for illiterates, medical aid	Muslim, 1940
15. Society for welfare of patients in the Muslim Hospital	Muslim, 1945
16. Women's society for help to needy families and orphans, education	Muslim, 1945
17. Orphanage for boys and girls	Muslim, 1946
18. Women's society for religious and social improvement	Maronite, 1949
19. Women's society for aid to pupils in Maronite schools	Maronite, 1949
20. Women's society providing cash and medical services to needy	Christian, 1949
21. Women's orphanage for girls	Maronite, 1949
22. Society for aid to needy families and free medical care	Muslim, 1950
23. Women's society for needy families and girls' vocational education	Orthodox, 1950
24. Women's society for aid to needy families and free medical care	Greek Catholic, 1950
25. Home for aged and infirm	Muslim, 1951
26. Society for education, employment, aid to needy families, Bab al-Tibbani	Muslim, 1951
27. Women's society for girls' recreation, education, health	Muslim, 1953
28. Women's society for girls' vocational and special education	Christian, 1953
29. Women's society for help to needy families in the Mina	Maronite, 1953
30. Men's society for aid to needy families and free medical care	Greek Catholic, 1954
31. Society for aid to needy families and free medical care	Christian, 1954
32. Union of Muslim welfare societies for coordination and encouragement	Muslim, 1954
33. Society for day care nursery and aid to needy families	Muslim, 1955
34. Men's society for aid to needy families, Mina	Maronite, n.d.
35. Men's society for aid to needy families, Qubbah	Maronite, n.d.
36. Men's society for aid to needy families, Tal	Maronite, n.d.

TABLE 8. FOUNDING DATES OF TRIPOLI CHARITABLE
SOCIETIES BY SECT

Date	Christian	Muslim	Total
1890–1919	6	0	6
1920–1942	4	4	8
1943–1958	10	9	19
None provided	3	0	3
Total	23	13	36

TABLE 9. SEX OF PRESIDENTS OF TRIPOLI CHARITABLE
SOCIETIES BY SECT

Sex	Christian	Muslim	Total
Men	7	7	14
Women	16	6	22
Total	23	13	36

have 64 per cent of these societies when they amount to only about 20 per cent of the population is a striking fact. The Christians' early lead may well have been connected with the early lead they took in establishing modern schools, and both seem to have been related to their earlier receptivity to organizational ideas from Europe and America. Correspondingly striking is the great proliferation of Muslim societies, relatively greater than that of the Christian ones, especially since the attainment of Lebanese independence. There is considerable talk in Tripoli about the Muslims' "catching up" with the Christians, and this is one example of it. Within the Christian category, the great growth of Maronite societies since 1943 is also notable.

Table 9 highlights the apparent fact that women seem to be the predominant participants in these activities. It would seem that the participation of Christian women is predominant, yet the participation of Muslim women, small though it be, is enlightening, especially in view of general notions concerning Muslim women. Some informants commented that a number of these societies, despite their ideal (and reportedly actual) accomplishments, are primarily upper class playthings. There may be some truth in this, but I do not think it is the whole truth. The reported goals of many of the societies seem to be realistic in that they reflect actually felt needs in the culture. It may be that women, whose social roles are now undergoing conscious examination and appraisal in the Middle East, find it satisfying, and possibly easier than men do, to fill the vacuum. Some people have commented that this situation in contemporary Tripoli is reminiscent of what was typical of American cities before World War I.

Partial indications of the scope of these societies' activities are provided in Table 10. For what it is worth, 31 per cent of the Muslim

TABLE 10. CASES ASSISTED BY SOME TRIPOLI BENEVOLENT
SOCIETIES CA. 1957

Type of case	No. cases by sect	
	Christian (57% of societies reporting)	Muslim (55% of societies reporting)
Cash, food, and clothing to needy families	694	93
Free medical care	210	210
Education: aid to needy students, vocational training, etc.	764 (sample excl. YMCA)	1890
Support of aged and infirm		58
Care of orphans	111	125 (excl. figures for orphanage caring for 251 children, 1958–59)
Recreation: sports, summer camps (sample excludes YMCA)	–	180
Funeral expenses	60	

societies reported a combined active membership of 108 people, and 52 per cent of the Christian ones reported a total of 443 active members. I do not know whether a simple percentage projection of these figures would yield a realistic idea of the total efforts of the societies, for, apart from questions of reliability in reporting, the societies are of very unequal size and scope. In any case, the available figures indicate relatively, and in some cases absolutely, less charitable assistance by and for Muslims. Why? The Muslims' greater reticence in providing statistics may be part of the problem. Another reasonable possibility is that among the Muslims the Awqaf organization, private almsgiving, and extended kinship groups provided relatively more assistance than do comparable organizations and activities among the

Christians. It is probable, anyway, that the Muslims would assert this and that the Christians would deny it.

We know from individual cases that all kinds of "charity" is bestowed within Lebanese, and Tripolitan, kinship groups, but even the best of all conceivable surveys would have difficulty in ascertaining what the actual scope of such charity is. In any event, the activities of the charitable societies concentrate on helping people who are not helped, or at least not sufficiently, by or within their own kin groups. Among such people, the easiest to understand, seemingly, are orphans, children who have no parents or other relatives who can care for them *in loco parentis*. Many Lebanese children who have lost both parents through death are cared for within their kin groups; indeed, it is expected that uncles or cousins on the father's side will automatically at least offer to help in this matter. The children in orphanages come from families which obviously cannot or will not care for them, and in the latter case it is very likely that the children are illegitimate. In fact, "orphan," may very often be a euphemism for "illegitimate child."

Illegitimate children among the Arabs are evidence of a major breakdown in the social system. Every effort is made to prevent premarital or extramarital sexual activity among girls and women, and the social segregation of the sexes by which this is in part accomplished makes "affairs" difficult, though it probably encourages homosexuality and men's recourse to prostitutes. Tripoli's illegitimate children are most likely the offspring of prostitutes who have been careless or of other girls and women who have managed to circumvent the sexual security system. Muslims, I was told by Christians, will not adopt children whom they know to be illegitimate.

The great majority of orphanages in Lebanon belong to sects or are sponsored by societies which, in turn, have sectarian identity. However, the Lebanese government makes grants-in-aid to these institutions on the basis of the equivalent of about 35 cents per day per child. It will not provide funds for more than one child in the same family, however. In a sample of twelve Lebanese orphanages, governmental contributions ranged from 8 per cent to 85 per cent of the various institutions' total incomes.[12] Four of these twelve orphanages were in Tripoli and have already been encompassed in the preceding list and tables. Two of them received 25 per cent and two 50 per cent of their incomes from the government.[13] Conditions are crowded, with from 30 to 84 children in one dormitory room, and there is one staff member for every 6 to 12 children.

The sizes of the four orphanages in Tripoli were 251, 77, 42, and 30 children apiece. Qualitatively, Miss Khoury (who was at the time a resident of Tripoli) gives considerable attention to the sectarian emphases in the orphanages, the failure of the government to do anything but supply financial support, and the general lack of emotional warmth which, of course, is not characteristic only of Lebanese institutions of this kind.

In general, and apart from its recent efforts in education, the government's social services in Tripoli (as in all Lebanon) are limited. In addition to partially subsidizing the orphanages, it also maintains a hospital in the Qubbah, and has built a few low-cost housing units in Malulah. This, as far as I know, is all. Sect and family continue to be the preeminent providers of social welfare services in Tripoli and in the culture generally.

SECT AND SOCIAL SOLIDARITY

The fact that interpersonal relationships within each family and sect are by no means always overflowing with loving kindness does not mean that these groups do not display "social solidarity." The charitable activities of the sects are an excellent example of such solidarity, for not only are the societies sponsored by, or identified with, sects, but most of them are explicitly for the benefit of their own sect members. Some groups claim to help others, but few do in any more than a token way. An exception is the Presbyterians' considerable assistance to the Palestinian refugees, most of whom are Muslims, in the Tripoli area.

Sectarian solidarity is less easy to discern in the area of social class, for the Muslims and Christians as a whole are not easily distinguishable on the basis of class. Christian and Muslim families in Tripoli who have high social prestige have a number of interests and tastes in common, and these may actually draw them together even though they would never intermarry. Differences in social prestige within a sect group, on the other hand, may considerably dilute that group's over-all solidarity.

One effect of these cross-cutting factors is that there are only a few residential sectarian clusters in Tripoli, and they are accompanied either by homogeneous class interests or interests related to the same area of origin outside Tripoli. Thus, the 'Alawite cluster in Bab al-Tibbani is reinforced by the facts that the people are lower class and from the same general region in Syria. The most distinct Maronite cluster in al-Qubbah consists of people from the same village (Hadchite) who continue to be laborers and small shopkeepers; the most distinct Maronite cluster in Hayy Mutran consists of shopkeepers and professionals from the town of Zgharta. There are many other instances, but usually involving only ten to twenty families, of people from the same village, and of the same sect and class, but they apparently tend to break up as the economic (and class) positions of their members undergo changes. As a result, there is no single or dominant residental cluster of a long-established sect like the Eastern Orthodox, while the Sunnis are so much in the majority that they are living in every part of the city. About 50 per cent of the people in al-Qubbah, and about 90 per cent in Abu Samra, are Sunnis. As far as residential clustering is concerned, in other words, sectarianism is only one of several contributing factors.

"SENSE OF COMMUNITY"

Lastly, when it comes to that interesting but very elusive subject of "community spirit" or "sense of community," sectarianism is highly relevant, but it is not the only factor involved. The I.R.F.E.D. report on Tripoli, which was frankly evaluative, deplored the lack of "community spirit" in all the sections of Tripoli (see Appendix A). A major reason for this lack is that sentiments of social responsibility are largely confined to sect and family. There are also various attitudes toward the municipal government, none positive, which will be considered in the next chapter.

The Tripoli YMCA is a fitting subject to close this chapter. In terms of Lebanese, and certainly Tripolitan, culture, the "Y" is something of an anomaly. Though identified with Christianity, it is not a sect. It is certainly not a family organization, nor an agency of some foreign country, nor a government organization. It fits few of the conventional assumptions about institutions in Tripoli, and under such conditions, while always in danger of becoming a pariah, it can also be an innovator. Under the leadership of an energetic Palestinian refugee in 1962, it clearly seemed to be the latter. It had 278 adult members (men and women, 46 per cent Muslim), plus 136 student members in various categories. Its programs included sports and various work projects; a hostel; an education division serving about 100 people at a time with courses in drafting, bookkeeping, typing, and languages; a library of about 2,000 volumes which was the only open library in the city, with books in Arabic, English, and French; and a job placement service which cooperated with UNRWA for the benefit of Palestinian refugees.

All of the Y's activities and services except for the hostel are carried out on the principle of sexual desegregation — something which occurs in no other Tripoli institution except the Orthodox youth organization, which is, of course, sectarian. In three years, the annual budget had been nearly quintupled (to the equivalent of about $16,000), and the debt had been reduced to about $1,700.

In connection with these financial matters, the Y in 1961 undertook the first genuinely citywide fund-raising campaign to occur in Tripoli. The Red Cross had, it is true, previously distributed coin boxes for contributions, but the Y's campaign was different. A list of eighty-eight names of individuals and groups, representing various sects and occupations, was drawn up, and teams were assigned to canvass them. Predictably, many people refused to contribute, or contributed very little, because they preferred to give to the charities of their own sect. Individual merchants, on the whole, contributed less than westernized professional people and companies. The goal of the campaign was about $1,350, and it was not met. But about $1,000 was contributed, and this is a tangible sign of the existence of nonsectarian social interests in Tripoli.

Chapter IV

GOVERNMENTAL ADMINISTRATION
AND SERVICES

A STRONG ALLIANCE between the sectarian and civil powers was a long tradition in Islamic cities.[1] However, the nature of this alliance was such that Muslim thinkers never developed any specific or workable concepts of municipal administration and law, as such.[2] In the absence of ethical ideals on the subject, government of, by, and for military and predatory powers became the rule in the Ottoman Empire, if not before; and theocratic roles, such as mufti and qadi, were subordinated to these powers, although they had wider authority than they do today. Some idea of these generalizations as revealed in the specific history of Tripoli has already been conveyed in Chapters II and III.

THE PROBLEM OF OVERCENTRALIZATION

The point of view of the Ottoman administration was highly centralized, in that all provincial administrations were responsible to the Porte and subject to its military discipline. In practice, at many times and places, due to corruption, inefficiency, and poor communications, provincial governors were able to operate relatively autonomously for their own benefit. Yet their point of view, too, remained one of centralization and autocratic control. For example, the provincial governor (wali) of the Tripoli province (generally

69

referred to by his honorific title of pasha) was also the chief authority in the city itself. In other words, the municipal administration was hardly distinguishable from the provincial one, and the functions of both (primarily tax collection and law enforcement) were about the same.

During the latter part of the nineteenth century, the Ottomans made considerable efforts at administrative reform, including the introduction of some government services for the people. Centralization continued to be characteristic, however, meaning that there continued to be a minimum of autonomy at the local level. The fact that the Ottomans chose to model their reforms on the French system only perpetuated the tendency toward centralization, and the French system, in turn, had not become any less decentralized when it was imposed directly on Lebanon after World War I. Tripoli, along with all the other Lebanese cities, was chartered as a municipality in 1922, and the initial details of its administration were very much as they had been under the Ottoman Municipal Law of 1877, based on the Code Napoléon.[3] The French system meant further expansion of services and bureaucracy, but its centralization in the authority of national ministries coincided with preexisting patterns, and so there was little impetus for modifications in this matter. While numerous minor alterations have been made in the intervening years, the general structure has remained essentially the same.

At the time of my study, the Lebanese press was full of complaints about the overcentralization of governmental functions in Beirut which necessitated countless visits to that city on business which was often of purely local import elsewhere. For figures on school enrollments in Tripoli, I was instructed to apply in writing to the Ministry of Education in Beirut. My letter, initialed and stamped all over with endorsements, eventually found its way to the appropriate official in Tripoli, who supplied the figures but would have forwarded them back through channels to Beirut had I not intervened. Evidently some reforms were made in this kind of procedure, for a newspaper article on general progress in Tripoli, subsequent to my study, quotes an official in Tripoli to the effect that decentralization is now in effect 100 per cent and that rarely does anyone need to go to Beirut any more to conduct government business.[4] Ironically, however (from the American point of view), the official in question was the Muhafiz (governor) of the province of the North.

Appointed by the premier of the Republic and the national council of ministers (cabinet), the Muhafiz is not only provincial governor but is also, in law and in fact, the chief municipal authority in Tripoli itself. In some respects, then, there is a genuine continuity between the administrative position of the Muhafiz and that of the Ottoman wali. There are some contingent continuities in public attitudes, too, although signs of change are beginning to appear.

Tripoli is the second largest city of Lebanon, one of the smallest but most "developed" of the "underdeveloped" nations of the world. One of the many current generalizations about such nations is that "government involvement" is more likely to be important in their urban development than it was in the early urban-industrial development of the West.[5] In looking closely at governmental structures and activities in Tripoli, we must not lose sight of this larger context, but we must also be prepared for the possibility that the generalization may need to be qualified if it is to represent the realities of this particular city. This caution is especially important in view of all the implications that can be attached to the expression "government involvement."

THE ZA'IM

Technically separate from, but actually interwoven with, the formal structure of the Lebanese government are several regional political bosses (Arabic *zu'ama*; singlar *za'im*) and their coteries.[6] Some of the zu'ama operate with the trappings of western-style political party leaders, but this is only nominal, for western-style political parties are incompletely developed in Lebanon. The strength of each za'im is anchored in his sectarian and kinship identity and support and in the wider regional following which he can muster. A few of the zu'ama are also widely thought of as being latter-day feudal suzerains, but this can easily be exaggerated. By no means do the zu'ama collectively constitute a unitary power structure, for there are continual rivalries among them, and their alliances are always temporary. Individually, however, they may have very great power within their own districts, but their identities are well known. The za'im is not an anonymous, behind-the-scenes figure, and, in fact, most zu'ama hold formal governmental offices as well as exercising their power informally.

During the period of my study, the za'im in Tripoli, acknowledged as such by everyone including his enemies, was Rashid Karami. He had grown into this role since the end of World War II, initially assisted by the reputation built by his father and paternal uncles. Like several of the other Lebanese zu'ama, Karami was one of the elected deputies in the Lebanese parliament. The fact that he was also, at the time, the premier of Lebanon greatly enhanced his prestige in Tripoli as well as Tripoli's prestige in the eyes of its inhabitants. His rise to the premiership was due in part to his leadership of the Sunnis of Tripoli, but there were other factors as well, related to national affairs. In other words, it was partly coincidental that Karami was premier of Lebanon at the same time that he was za'im in Tripoli. This coincidence, however, made it very difficult to differentiate the effects of the two roles in contributing to his prestige and influence. Also, his being premier removed him physically from Tripoli much of the time, and therefore he may have been less accessible to his own local clients than zu'ama often are.

PUBLIC ATTITUDES

Once again, we must consider Tripoli in a wider, even international, context, for the interaction of sects and za'im with its governmental structure reflect certain characteristics widespread in the politically "transitional" nations of the world: the primary involvement of political behavior with tightly knit social groups, the primacy of a leader's personal status over his specific views, the preemption of political party interests by those of subsocieties or influential individuals, the prevalence of cliques, and the assumption that the leader's first concern is for the interests of the group to which he belongs.[7]

Concerning these political acts and structures, the Lebanese and Tripolitan layman has a set of attitudes, and these are essentially as follows.

A person's first social responsibility is to his family and his sect, for it is primarily by members of these groups that social responsibility is reciprocated. The government is aloof, not subject to ordinary citizens' influence, and is corrupted by the bribes, nepotism, and pressures of other groups or individuals who are trying to better themselves in or by means of it. It is wise to avoid involvement with the government, but if the individual cannot avoid it, he at least needs intermediaries who have "pull." Kinsmen in the government can be very useful in this connection. If and when these fail, he needs the patronage of a za'im, who, in return for votes and other demonstrations of loyalty, will apply pressures in his behalf. Government is now doing more for the people than it used to, and it ought to do more, but it continues to be aloof and corruptible, and therefore the layman continues to need "pull" and the zu'ama.

Thoughtful people recognize the circularity in this set of attitudes but ask what can the "little man" do except go along with the system. This political orientation is similar to that found among the "ethnic minorities" of the United States; but in Lebanon everyone belongs to a minority, and the actuality of despotic rule is so close in historical time that it is still felt to be imminent.

THE MUHAFIZ: IMAGE OF "GOOD GOVERNMENT"

During the greater part of my study, the regularly appointed Muhafiz was on leave of absence in the United States, but the acting Muhafiz seemed to maintain the same kind of administration. Personally, both men were as unlike the stereotypic pasha as can be imagined. Both were Druze, and were appointed partly on that account since they had no relatives and few cosectarians in the city and province. Both were lean, intelligent, energetic, and apparently outspoken about the city's problems. One of them even undertook physically to direct traffic one afternoon as a way of emphasizing the need for better traffic control in the city. Both projected an image of integrity which seemed to be accepted at face value and appreciated by the normally wary and cynical populace, if one can judge from casual remarks and comments in the newspapers.

Some months after my study had been completed, the Muhafiz said in a newspaper interview that after years of aloofness, the governor and people of Tripoli were now working in harmony, that there was great cooperation between the government and the various organized groups in the city, and that respect for law and order was in general increasing. The reporter added that everyone in Tripoli seemed to feel that the Muhafiz was ready at all times to listen to the complaints and problems of all people regardless of who they were.[8] Perhaps all this is an indication of incipient changes in public attitude and performance, but one could also interpret it as being only an instance of the "good ruler" who is a traditional (but rare and fortuitous) figure in Middle Eastern history. Among the traditional good ruler's attributes are impartiality and effectiveness in law enforcement and accessibility to the ordinary citizen.

The strong association (in the people's minds) of "good" government with strong enforcement is reflected in the complaints which are voiced in editorials and letters to the editor in Lebanese newspapers and magazines. Most of these are published in Beirut, but they are widely read in Tripoli. Frequent complaints are concerned with such matters as garbage dumped in the streets, inconvenient or dangerous holes in the pavements, chaos in automobile traffic, predatory taxi drivers, and so on, all being complaints with some justification. In every case, the plea is that the government should enforce the laws better or pass new laws in order to eliminate these problems. People, it would seem, according to their own prevailing attitudes, are incapable of making self-generated changes in their public behavior.

FORMAL STRUCTURES

As I have already indicated, the formal government of Tripoli is dominated by that of the Muhafazat al-Shamal (Governorate, or Province, of the North). There is also a municipal government responsible to the Muhafiz. Administratively separate from both are the law courts of the city (and province), agencies of the national Ministry of Justice. The various offices of the Muhafazat and the courts are housed in the new Saraya on the boulevard. While they have direct jurisdiction over Tripoli itself, they also have jurisdiction over the whole province, and so the new Saraya is both a municipal office building for Tripoli and the capitol building of the province.

The Muhafazat and Ministries

The Muhafiz is a functionary of the Ministry of the Interior, but he is responsible for the direction of the local activities of all the other ministries except justice and defense.[9] A major defect in the system, apparently, is that while the department heads are responsible to the Muhafiz locally, they are also responsible to superiors in their respective ministries in Beirut. This is the source of considerable difficulties.[10] The Muhafazat is responsible for public health measures, tax collection, registration of all property transfers, highways and roads, public works (including renewal and street-widening in Tripoli and other towns), public education, collection of commercial statistics, veterinary and agricultural inspection services, and inspection of local administrations. These functions are carried out through each *qada'* (subdistrict) of the province. Tripoli, the Mina, and the outlying areas to the east and northeast of Tripoli constitute a single qada'.

Not included in the functions of the Muhafazat are the collection of customs duties in the Mina, supervision of the army barracks and hospital in al-Qubbah, or anything to do with the judicial system. On the other hand, the Muhafiz may, with the approval of the national Minister of the Interior, dismiss the members of the Tripoli municipal council. He appoints some of the members of the council and he may abrogate the election of the others. The council must submit to the Muhafiz, for his approval, the municipal budget, all decisions concerning taxes and fees, contracts for more than three years, and all decisions relating to municipal services (such as police, sewage, fire brigades, water supply, electricity, health, hospitals, public transportation, and inspection of markets, graveyards, slaughterhouses and cinemas).[11] In the fall of 1961, Tripoli was one of the few places in Lebanon where *arabiyyahs* (horse-drawn, four-wheeled carriages) were still available for public transportation. There were about eighty of them, and despite the competition of taxis, they were still popular for leisurely rides. In November, they suddenly disappeared from the streets, having been outlawed on the grounds that they aggravated traffic congestion. The owners were subsequently compensated in the amount of about $670 per carriage.[12] This affair was executed by the Muhafiz, not by the municipal council.

Considering the high degree of local control exercised by the Muhafiz, it is not surprising that it seems to be of little interest or concern to people in general that Tripoli and the Mina are separate municipalities, that several of the newer sections of Tripoli are not within the municipal borders, or that there was little complaint (or even comment) when the municipal council elections were abrogated in April 1962.

THE MUNICIPALITY

Officers. From 1922 until 1952, the Muhafiz was actually also the chairman of the Tripoli municipal council. Between 1952 and 1957, the offices were separated, but there was a sort of deputy Muhafiz who was in charge of Tripoli and the Mina. The council, partly elected and partly appointed in 1952, remained in office until 1960 (its four-year term having been extended by decree) when it was replaced (by appointment) with a council of nine men, most of whom had been members of the previous council.[13] Mostly Muslims, the members are primarily businessmen and landowners from important families. The majority are partisans, also, of the za'im. The council annually elects a chairman (*ra'is al-baladiyyah*, usually translated as "president of the municipality") and a vice-chairman. In 1961–62 they were, respectively, a Sunni and an Eastern Orthodox.

Those functions of the municipal council in which it has some measure of autonomy seem to be limited to routine matters concerning the administration of municipal property, granting of licenses, maintenance of law and order, and basic health and sanitation services. The police department had a force of 178 in 1960.[14] The fire brigade of seventeen is part of the administrative department, which also takes care of municipal personnel matters. The engineering department is concerned with planning, street maintenance, and the public parks. The health department keeps records of diseases, supervises public sanitation and veterinary and meat inspection. These offices and one police station are housed in the municipal building in the Tal. There are also police stations in Bab al-Raml, Bab al-Tibbani, and al-Qubbah. In addition to the municipal police, there are units of the national gendarmerie (Ministry of the Interior) who also have stations in the city. The total number of municipal employees, not counting street cleaners, apparently amounted to about 220 persons in 1960.[15]

Budget. Between 1945 and 1959, the annual municipal budget increased over 300 per cent to 3,180,000 Lebanese pounds, about $1,060,000. Of this, the national government had provided about two-thirds, having collected most of the taxes involved.[16] In 1960, about three-quarters of the central government's revenue for Tripoli was derived from customs duties paid in the Mina. Most of the municipality's own revenue was derived from taxes and license fees, the most important being the rental tax, slaughterhouse and meat tax, sewage tax, and cinema tax.[17] About 32 per cent of the expenditures consist of payments on the municipal debt. Any large projects, such as the widening and straightening of the Abu 'Ali River's bed and the building of new avenues and streets, must be planned, adminis-

tered, and financed at the national level, although the financing sometimes (as in 1956 for the initial work on the river) may be in the
form of a loan. This point, as well as the need for greater efficiency
in the municipal government, was brought out in a meeting in Tripoli
in March 1962, attended by the premier of Lebanon, the Muhafiz
of the North, and the president of the municipal council.[18]

Administrative Districts. Tripoli is divided into ten administrative
districts, and their locations are indicated on Map 4. Each of these
districts has one or more *mukhtars*:

Bab Hadid	2
Al-Mihaytrah	1
Al-Rimani	1
Bab Hadadin	4
Swayqah	2
Al-Nuri	1
Bab-al-Tibbani	4
Al-Qubbah	2
Al-Zahriyyah	1
Al-Tal	1

Since 1947, the mukhtars have been appointed by the municipality
(rather than elected). Previously, according to an informant who
lived and had his business in the Tal administrative district, there
was a mukhtar representing each major sect in the district, but this
is no longer the case. The mukhtar's duties (which are part-time)
are to record births and deaths, report any crimes or serious health
crises, cooperate with the police, tax collectors or any other officials
who may need his aid, and keep records on the registered residents
in his district. These are essentially the same duties as those of the
mukhtars of Lebanese villages. Supposedly, the mukhtar knows everyone in his district, but this is no longer true in many instances, and
many residents do not know who their mukhtar is or, offhand, where
he can be found.

It is obvious from Map 4 that the formal districting of the city has
not kept pace with its growth, for there are a number of newer
sections which are not included at all. Residents of these sections
apparently are more or less under the jurisdiction of adjacent districts. The records for people in Abu Samra, for example, are kept
by the mukhtars of Bab Hadadin, whence many people originally
moved to Abu Samra in the first place. Otherwise, these formal dis-

MAP 4

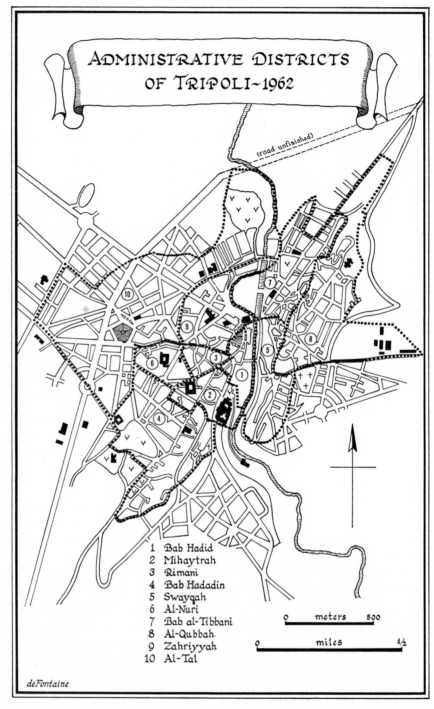

ADMINISTRATIVE DISTRICTS
OF TRIPOLI~1962

(road unfinished)

1 Bab Hadid
2 Mihaytrah
3 Rimani
4 Bab Hadadin
5 Swayqah
6 Al-Nuri
7 Bab al-Tibbani
8 Al-Qubbah
9 Zahriyyah
10 Al-Tal

meters   500

miles   ½

deFontaine

tricts appear to have little significance among laymen. They are not even systematically represented by the Municipal Council, for its members, when they are elected, are elected at large.

The fact that the names of most of the administrative districts are also the names of informal quarters calls for comment. A comparison of Maps 3 and 4 shows that the Tal administrative district comprises the following informal quarters: Tal, Hayy Mutran, Shari' Madaris, Shari' Yazbik, Hayy Ghuraba, and parts of Shari' 'Azmi, Shari' Latifi and Zahriyyah. The Zahriyyah administrative district includes only part of the Zahriyyah quarter (as popularly conceived) and also includes Shari' Kinayis, Dibbagha, and Tirbi'a. The Swayqah and Qubbah administrative districts do, on the other hand, coincide fairly closely with the informal quarters of the same names. It is the informal quarters which are real in people's minds and important in daily usage. The administrative districts, whose names derive from those of true quarters, are largely abstractions in the popular mind. For this reason, and also because of the poorness of fit between the administrative districts and the newly developing sections of the city, the unavailability of population figures for each administrative district is not as tragic as it might be. If such figures were available, I would of course present them, but such presentation would immediately call for a discussion of what social significance they might have, and that would be rather inconclusive. Previous references in this book to "quarters" or "sections" have been to the socially significant informal locations, and I shall continue to use these words (interchangeably) in this sense. I use the word "district" only in the sense of formal administrative unit.

The Law Courts

The Lebanese judicial system is modeled on that of the French. All decisions are made by judges, singly or in panels; there are no juries. Public prosecutors are attached to each court. Of necessity, the lawyers are trained in French law, and a significant proportion of them are Christians. In fact, a strike by the Beirut Bar Association, which ended in January 1962 without resolution of the issue, was a protest against the government's approval of non-French legal training.[19] The Tripoli Bar Association, however, did not take the same stand, and was less opposed to the accreditation of Egyptian-sponsored legal training in Lebanon, which was the central issue of the strike.[20]

There are essentially three levels in the court system: (1) Courts of First Instance; (2) Courts of Appeal; (3) Supreme Court of Appeal, of which there is only one, in Beiruit. The first two levels are present in Tripoli, and they handle all cases which arise in the Muhafazat, including the city itself. All cases are first taken before a *juge d'instruction* who decides in what court each should be tried.

The civil division of the Courts of First Instance has chambers with only one judge who tries cases involving less than $5,000, and it has chambers with three judges which try cases involving more than this amount. The criminal division tries cases in which conviction carries a penalty of up to three years in prison.

The Courts of Appeal hear cases which have been appealed from the Courts of First Instance. They also directly and originally try criminal cases in which conviction carries a penalty of more than three years in prison.[21] Also present in Tripoli, as discussed earlier, is the Shari'a court which tries cases of personal status arising among Muslims.

I do not know the number of cases which are tried in the Tripoli courts. The nine-month lawyers' strike in Beirut created a backlog of 100,000 cases,[22] and since the population of the Muhafazat of the North is less than that of the Muhafazat of Beirut, the volume of cases is presumably less. There is some reporting of court convictions in the Tripoli papers, and during 1961–62 the Beirut papers printed several items on murders committed in Tripoli. The Tripoli papers regularly print notices from the Shari'a court having to do with pending decisions on the disposition of inherited property, judgments of the type, for example, that Mr. X, whereabouts unknown, is ordered to pay a stated amount of money for the support of his wife and children; and so forth.

Attitudes Toward the Law

Noninvolvement. There is a general feeling among the Lebanese people, as there is elsewhere, that they would prefer to settle their problems out of court if possible. There may be a greater readiness than in the West, however, to keep what would be criminal cases from coming to the attention of the police and the courts (although at least one murderer gave himself up to the police in Bab al-Tibbani during the period of my study). The feeling that judges and prosecutors are routinely corruptible is a factor in these attitudes.

Aside from periodically voting for a slate of five deputies in the national parliament, the registered men and women residents of Tripoli have very little opportunity formally to participate in their government. It is understandable why many nonnative residents of the city have little incentive to become registered, for they can continue to vote for parliamentary deputies in the localities where they are registered.

Disregard (Street Traffic). There is yet another matter of some importance connected with attitudes toward the government. Beirut in particular, and Lebanon in general, are notorious for the ineffectiveness of law enforcement in the control of automobile traffic. Traffic jams are not the least of the symptoms of this problem, for careless and often exceedingly disagreeable driving behavior is very widespread. There are, of course, limits to what even the most efficient police force can do in this matter. The police cannot directly affect such attitudes and emotions as the defiance of authority and hostile aggressiveness which seem to be involved. The Lebanese government, however, is concerned and apparently aware that the issue has many facets. In 1961–62 there was considerable discussion in the press about the advisability of a moratorium on the importation of cars into the country, for the number of registered vehicles had increased from 16,471 in 1951 to 66,305 in 1961.[23] During the last week of 1961, there was a concerted traffic safety campaign in Beirut. This included the display of posters and wrecked vehicles, a large corps of auxiliary traffic policemen (students), and even a dramatic tableau: people in numbers equal to the year's fatalities sprawled as if dead in the center of a traffic circle. In defense of themselves, some Lebanese will say that although they may be wild drivers, they are very well coordinated and therefore "safe." Besides the fact that this avoids the question of courtesy and consideration, it is not entirely convincing in view of the figures shown in Table 11, in which Lebanon is contrasted with Connecticut, the American state which most closely resembles it in both area and population.

Lebanon had a little more than one-twentieth the number of cars, but it had one fatality for every 4,322 vehicles. In the same year, California, which has a high accident rate, had one fatality for every 2,157 vehicles.

It should be noted that, in Connecticut, the number of pedestrian fatalities was reduced from 263 in 1934 (more than half of that year's

TABLE 11. TRAFFIC CASUALTIES IN 1961

	Lebanon	Connecticut
Registered vehicles	66,305	1,223,635
Fatalities	298	278
Injuries	3,000	25,086
Population	1,600,000	2,535,234

SOURCES: Klat, *Middle East Express* (1962), p. 3; *La Revue du Liban,* December 30, 1961, p. 10; Connecticut Department of Motor Vehicles.

total) to 66 in 1961. It is interesting to speculate (1) how much of this improvement has been due to increased general understanding of the problems of driving — of what is involved in stopping a moving automobile, for example, and (2) how many of Lebanon's fatalities are due to the lack of such understanding among pedestrians. This is a specific instance of the problems of adaptation to technological change. It is possible that more injuries become fatalities in Lebanon than in Connecticut because of less effective emergency medical care. However, it is also probable that injuries are more thoroughly reported in Connecticut.

Klat was unable to obtain figures for each Muhafazat, but outsiders to Tripoli have the impression that the traffic situation there is better than it is in Beirut.[24] Tripoli has relatively, as well as absolutely, fewer automobiles (about 5,000), for one thing. Also, its areas of streets which are passable yet inadequate for vehicular traffic are much less extensive. The route through the Tal and Zahriyyah to Bab al-Tibbani is the most seriously congested, a condition which should improve when the Boulevard is extended across the river (as indicated on the maps) permitting through traffic to bypass most of the city. While Tripoli's traffic is less congested than Beirut's, there is, however, no evidence that the attitudes toward driving among Tripoli people are any different from those of the Lebanese in general.

PUBLIC UTILITIES AND SERVICES

Communications, Water, Sewerage

Among those government agencies and services in Tripoli which have not yet been mentioned are the post office, telephone and telegraph, and water and sewerage.

There is only one post office, and it is located on the Boulevard. It has several hundred delivery boxes, but the rest of the mail in Tripoli is home-delivered. The mail carriers must be familiar with the inhabitants, and/or with the names of buildings' owners, in their areas, for no buildings are numbered, and street names are used very loosely. Members of the post office department were therefore a helpful source for the names of quarters used primarily by their own inhabitants. There is some thought that the single post office, supplemented only by mailboxes and by seventeen shops which have stamp-selling concessions, is not sufficient and that there ought to be branch post offices.[25] Telegrams are sent from the post office.

There are approximately 4,057 telephones in Tripoli-Mina, about 90 per cent in Tripoli itself. (Beirut, with an estimated one-third of the country's population, has about three-quarters of all its telephones.) There is in Tripoli-Mina one telephone for approximately every fifty-three persons. By contrast, there is in highly urbanized states like California, Connecticut, New Jersey, and New York about one telephone for approximately every two persons, and in a rural state like North Carolina one for approximately every four persons. The central exchange, in the Tal section, has given its name to the street where it is located ("Sintral"). Calls within the Tripoli-Mina area can be dialed, but long-distance ones must be placed orally. There are thirteen public telephones, three in the central exchange itself. The other ten are on private premises in the Mina, Bab al-Tibbani, the Tal, Abu Samra, Bahsas, al-Biddawi, Bab al-Raml, and al-Qubbah.

Tripoli now has complete systems of piped water, piped sewage disposal, and electrical supply. This does not mean, of course, that all individual households are sufficiently served. There is little to say about these services except to note the recency of their installation (none existed before 1920); this recency may be part of the reason why they seem to be better in Tripoli than in Beirut, where such public utilities were initiated in the 1870's.

The Government Schools

Another government service which has been, and is being, expanded very greatly is education. I have traced the general background of this subject in the preceding chapter. In 1961–62, there were sixty government schools in Tripoli and the Mina; the enrollments are shown in Table 12. Eight of these government schools are in the Mina; their enrollments are shown in Table 13. For comparison, the enrollments in the nongovernment schools of Tripoli and the Mina are shown in Table 14.

TABLE 12. ENROLLMENT IN THE GOVERNMENT SCHOOLS OF TRIPOLI

School	Boys	Girls	Total
Primary	7,400 (45.6%)	6,048 (37.4%)	13,448 (83.0%)
Secondary	1,622 (10.1%)	1,124 (6.9%)	2,746 (17.0%)
Total	9,022 (55.7)%	7,172 (44.3%)	16,194

TABLE 13. ENROLLMENT IN GOVERNMENT SCHOOLS OF THE MINA

School	Boys	Girls	Total
Primary	1,080	1,010	2,090
Secondary	169	152	361
Total	1,249	1,162	2,451

SOURCE: Lebanese Ministry of Education.

TABLE 14. ENROLLMENT IN NONGOVERNMENT SCHOOLS OF TRIPOLI AND THE MINA

School	Boys	Girls	Total
Primary	5,924 (40.0%)	4,796 (33.7%)	10,720 (73.7%)
Secondary	2,050 (14.8%)	1,777 (11.5%)	3,827[a] (26.3%)
Total	7,974 (54.8%)	6,573 (45.2%)	14,547

[a] The sum of the figures from the individual secondary schools is 3,844 (see Ch. III).
SOURCE: Lebanese Ministry of Education.

The grand total of schoolchildren in Tripoli-Mina is 30,741. Of these, 52.7 per cent are in government schools and 47.3 per cent are in nongovernment schools. Boys comprise 55.3 per cent of the grand total and girls 45.2 per cent, and there is a difference of only about 1 per cent between the government and nongovernment schools in this regard. However, the number of secondary pupils and the proportion of girls among them are significantly larger in the non-government schools. Since the Christians prefer to send their children to non-

government schools, even at great financial sacrifice, the proportion
of Muslim schoolchildren in the government schools is probably
even higher than the proportion of Muslims in the population as a
whole. Government secondary schools have less prestige than the
nongovernment ones, most of the schools are in rented quarters in
older buildings which were not designed to be schools, there is very
little communication between teachers and parents (nothing equivalent to the American Parent–Teacher Associations, and there is
the problem of the sociopsychological gulf between middle class
teachers and lower class pupils. However, most of the Tripoli government school system in 1962 had been created in only twenty years,
for in 1943 there were only three government schools in the city.
From this perspective, the problems and limitations of the system
seem entirely understandable.

In regard to the proportionate number of schoolgirls, too, it is
less appropriate to criticize the fact that they are fewer than the
boys, than it is to appreciate their magnitude in a culture which, not
very long ago, provided no formal education for girls at all.

CONCLUSION

Felt Needs for Reform

The potential for new directions in future cultural change, through
greatly increased literacy among the Muslims of the city, must be
noted. At the moment, it appears that changes in education philoso-
phy, teaching methods, and curriculum will probably come from
the top of the administration without much pressure or inspiration
from the parents or the adult public at large, for the latter seem to
accept the schools very much as they are and to regard them almost
entirely as a means to the end of advantageous status for their children. Yet there are signs of ferment and restiveness among the youngsters themselves. In March 1962, the Tripoli Student Union published a list of requests of the Ministry of Education which is worth
reproducing: [26]

1. Increase the number of primary schools in the north from 255 to 410.
2. Increase the number of secondary schools in Tripoli.
3. Establish more secondary schools for boys and girls in the Mina.
4. Establish playgrounds and kindergartens for small children.

5. Construct new school buildings to replace the old, rented quarters which are unsuitable for schools.
6. Modernize the school curricula, discarding the outmoded French system of examinations.
7. Make textbooks available at cost.
8. Train more teachers.
9. Abolish the various fees which are a hardship for students from poor families.
10. Develop vocational schools.
11. Establish a public library in Tripoli.
12. Expand the technical departments of the Lebanese National University.
13. Establish a scholarship loan program.
14. "Deal with and solve" the problem of people who cannot find occupations commensurate with their educations.

The government would have to go far in meeting these practical as well as visionary needs felt among the young, if the generalized cynicism of the populace were to be lessened. This cynicism is apparently equally frequent among Lebanese Christians and Muslims (at least among villagers), and has recently been succinctly stated as follows: "If you give us a camel by way of our government, we will get only its ears." [27]

Street Demonstrations

One association that western laymen have with modern Middle Eastern cities is the political demonstration, which, with "students" as prominent participants, turns into a violently rioting mob. It is usually only when this ugly turn of events takes place that the western layman is likely to be aware of the demonstrations at all. As a matter of fact, by reason of one of its very rare appearances in the American press, Tripoli itself may be known to many Americans only in this context. Personal injuries and property damage in Tripoli and Baghdad, from riots protesting against West Germany's diplomatic recognition of Israel, were the subject of a page-one story in *The New York Times* on March 17, 1965.

However, another aspect of the truth is that nonviolent political demonstrations by students are also characteristic of Middle Eastern cities; in fact, they may be more characteristic, numerically speaking, than the violent ones. Such a demonstration took place in Tripoli on

November 16, 1961. The same student union (*Al-Ittihad al-Tullab*) mentioned above had called for a one-day "strike" which was to be a manifestation of support for several FLN leaders being held as hostages by the French in Algeria. The following is a description of this event taken from my field notes:

Most of the children went to school this morning but were dismissed by about 9 A.M. At the Boys' School, at least, the Tripoli student union leader had in advance asked the principal to excuse the boys for the occasion. At the Rahbat School, however, the decision to dismiss the girls for the day was made only after some delay. The school, with its French identification, has an armed guard outside. On such occasions in the past, the nuns have disregarded these demonstrations, but this time they finally decided otherwise.

Before leaving the house, I watched some small boys roil by in the street, chanting for Nasser, their leader beating time with a stick.

I encountered the main demonstration near the Frères School. About half a dozen leaders, each carried on shoulders in the midst of about a dozen supporters, were chanting away and getting applause. About twenty others carried one-man or two-man slogan banners, Algerian flags, etc. Frequently, someone would toss into the air blue, green, and red slips of paper with slogans printed on them. They were immediately picked up by small boys who darted in and among the larger demonstrators (all male).

The demonstration had clearly been well arranged in advance, and it may have been part of a larger plan, for the university students in Beirut were demonstrating at the same time, I later learned.

As the ragged procession formed and began to move through the streets, about a dozen gendarmes armed with rifles took up the rear and sauntered along behind it to its destination. It went across Shari' Zahriyyah into Shari' Madaris, past the municipal building and into the Tal, past the bus station and left into the boulevard, down which it proceeded, coming to a halt at the main entrance of the new Saraya. Few onlookers followed it all the way as I did. Rather, some joined it for part of the journey, walking along passively or chatting casually with each other. Women came out on balconies as it passed, and then went back indoors. In general, people seemed to continue about their business except to watch briefly as the procession passed them.

The new Saraya is not yet quite finished, but the office of the Muhafiz has already been set up there. The Muhafiz himself met the group on the steps of the building. He talked with them for about five minutes, getting several rounds of applause. Then they began furling up their banners and started back toward the Tal, most of them dispersing. But one leader rallied a small group around him which returned to the new Saraya. The Muhafiz reappeared, this time on the balcony above the entrance. There was a brief shouted exchange, terminated by the Muhafiz with a gesture which seemed to be saying, "Well, you fellows just run along now, like good boys." And they did.

The authorities were ready for trouble, but it did not develop. By how narrow a margin it was averted I do not know, but I think it probably was not very narrow, for the whole affair seemed more pro-Algerian than anti-French and, though loud, it was generally good-natured.

Chapter V

WORK AND COMMERCE

TRIPOLI IS THE distribution center of the agricultural products of northern Lebanon (north of Batrun) and of products imported to north Lebanon. Both of these activities are concentrated in Bab al-Tibbani. It is also a transshipment point in international commerce, and the activities associated with this are concentrated in the Mina, in Bahsas, to some extent also in Bab al-Tibbani, and, of course, at the Iraq Petroleum Company's terminal. Regional distribution and international trade coincide in the export of local and regional products, of which olives, apples, citrus fruits, olive oil, sweets, soap, concrete building materials, plywood, and cotton cloth are the most important. For the sake of these local products, Tripoli depends on and directly imports from abroad: raw cotton, lumber, and sugar. The concrete is made of mostly locally extracted materials. Probably the bulk of the goods sold in Tripoli but manufactured in Europe, America, or Japan are imported indirectly — that is to say, through Beirut.

TRIPOLI AS A REGIONAL TRADING CENTER

Transportation Facilities

I do not have any quantitative information on Tripoli as a regional agricultural distribution center, but I do have some figures that will give some idea of the city's role as a transshipment point. Some of these figures give an impression of the economic damage to Tripoli which everyone says was done by Syria's erection of customs barriers in 1950. Tripoli still imports Syrian cotton overland, but apparently the major damage was the city's virtual elimination as a seaport for Syria. Decline of the port, despite the enlargement of its docks and the extension of its breakwaters in the 1950's, is attributed by everyone to Syria's action in 1950. It should also be recognized, however, that the continued growth of Beirut as a seaport and airport has given Tripoli severe competition. Furthermore, the steady improvement of overland transportation between Tripoli and Beirut (better highways and more vehicles) has made it increasingly easy for Tripolitans to have shopping sprees in Beirut rather than to patronize their own city's retail outlets. The latter, in turn, are often discouraged from stocking the latest goods; these have to be imported from Beirut anyway. This was brought out in a series of interviews with local businessmen which appeared in one of the Tripoli newspapers.[1]

Before 1909, vehicular travel all the way from Beirut to Tripoli (about forty-three miles) was impossible, for it was only in that year that a passable carriage road was completed. By 1961, the two cities were connected by a good paved highway; about one-fifth already had four lanes. The Beirut-Tripoli railroad was not completed until 1942. No figures are available, unfortunately, on the amount of highway traffic in and out of Tripoli, but all informants were of the impression that the railroad was less important for both passenger and freight transportation than automobiles, buses, and trucks. In 1959 the railroad carried 276,000 tons of freight and 32,700 passengers between Beirut and Tripoli. It carried only 98,000 tons from Tripoli north into Syria, but its passenger traffic in that direction (41,400 persons) was higher.[2] These contrasts may reflect (1) the effects of Syria's import barriers and (2) the probability that most of the passengers were through travelers between Beirut and various points in Syria. Certainly, I never heard of any Lebanese even considering the railroad for traveling between Beirut and Tripoli. The train, a diesel locomotive car, leaves Beirut only once or twice a day. In contrast, express buses for Tripoli leave every quarter of an hour, the trip takes 90 minutes and costs only one Lebanese pound ($0.33), and there are many other buses, as well as taxis. The railroad can, however, be a preferable mode of travel north of Tripoli, where the highways are generally not in good condition.

Bab al-Tibbani is the main terminal area of buses to and from Syria, and it may not be at all coincidental that it is also the main residential area of Syrians. At any rate, it has been noted that village emigrants living in Cairo tend to settle near the bus terminals serving their own rural areas.[3] Bab al-Tibbani is also the main terminal of trucks carrying wholesale vegetable foodstuffs. At an earlier time, the bulk of these may have come from the north, hence the location of the market area on the northern edge of the town, but the trucks now come also from the south (necessarily going through the Tal and Zahriyyah) and from the plains and mountains to the east (going through al-Qubbah). Trucks carrying other types of freight use the Mina, the Tal, and Bahsas as chief focal points.

The express buses for Beirut, which are owned by one company, have their terminal in the Tal. There are three or four other companies operating "country buses" to various parts of Lebanon, making stops wherever requested. Typically, their roofs, while in transit, are loaded with all sorts of baggage, including small livestock in crates. These buses have termini in al-Qubbah and Sahit Saraya 'Adimi (for the Cedars area), and in Sahit Kura and Bab al-Raml for points south.

In 1961 there were 3,200 licensed taxicabs in Lebanon; this figure by law had been held virtually constant for the previous ten years. If their distribution throughout Lebanon followed the same pattern as that of other new technological devices, the great majority of them were probably concentrated in Beirut, but there might well have been two or three hundred in Tripoli. For those able to pay, there is taxi service along the same routes followed by the buses out of Tripoli, the group fare per person to Beirut being about one dollar. Probably most of the taxis, however, are used within the city, for they are the only means of local, "public" transportation. The taxis congregate in the Tal area, and many of them operate on the *service* principle. A *service* taxi travels a regular route, picking up and discharging passengers as it goes along. Each passenger pays the same standard fare (25 piasters, or about 8 cents). The maximum payload is five passengers, and the drivers prefer not to start a trip until they have at least four. Consequently the cries of the *service* drivers announcing their destinations (e.g., Bab al-Tibbani, Abu Samra, al-Qubbah, and the Mina) are among the many voices heard in the Tal. *Services* waiting in the Tal cluster in particular places according to their destination.

The main nodes of transportation are Bab al-Tibbani and the Tal area (including Sahit Saraya 'Adimi and Sahit Kura). Two other nodes, but secondary ones, are in Bab al-Raml and al-Qubbah. Service stations and automotive repair shops tend to be clustered at these same nodes, and so do cafés and coffeehouses. Many of the latter, in turn, cater to specialized clienteles. Thus there are Maronite-owned cafés which specialize in serving Maronites traveling to and from the Cedars area; Orthodox-owned cafés which serve Orthodox travelers to and from the Kura area; Muslim-owned cafés serving Muslim travelers to and from the Akkar and Syria; and others. In these establishments, various ties — local, sectarian, and familial — are continually reinforced. The cafés are used not only for rest and refreshment, but also as meeting places, message centers, and temporary baggage rooms. Each café consequently has a core of regular customers; among them are groups of cronies who use the premises as a sort of headquarters in much the same way that the British pub is used. Cards, backgammon, and checkers are among the favorite games played in these informal but tightly knit clubs. In addition to coffee and various snacks, the house also provides tobacco and charcoal for narghile smoking, and it also provides the narghiles, although many habitués prefer to bring and use their own mouthpieces.

The Port

Tripoli's condition as a port is indicated in Table 15. Aside from certain trends, the most striking thing about these figures is the extreme variations from year to year; this surely must result in diffi-

TABLE 15. MOVEMENTS IN THE PORT OF TRIPOLI

Year	No. vessels	Goods imported (tons)	Wood imported (cu.m.)	Goods exported	Wood exported (cu.m.)	Petroleum transferred from pipe-lines to tankers (tons)
1950	802	86,869	3,520	62,605	6	5,434,469
1951	948	181,238	34,337	33,847	1,964	7,333,296
1952	898	63,181	27,314	27,255	13,987	7,035,808
1953	927	90,733	59,091	43,871	15,539	7,070,257
1954	816	86,711	22,139	51,685	9,880	7,151,635
1955	886	126,961	57,151	65,242	11,038	7,147,148
1956	784	122,896	50,624	37,149	5,857	. . . . . .
1957	641	100,223	71,281	51,118	17,534	3,055,720
1958	556	60,770	40,810	24,618	7,124	7,290,624
1959	598	84,140	39,091	12,529	1,659	7,290,600
1960	677	108,895	92,814	28,094	. . . .	8,990,853

SOURCE: *Le Commerce du Levant* (Beirut), 15:29 (1961).

culties and uncertainties for the businessmen of Tripoli. Such fluctuations have occurred in Beirut, too, but the trends there have all
been unmistakably towards increase, and the scale of operations is
many times larger, as indicated in Table 16.

TABLE 16. MOVEMENTS IN THE PORT OF BEIRUT

| Year | No. vessels | | Total | Goods imported (tons) | Goods exported (tons) |
	Ships	Schooners			
1950	1,317	792	2,109	832,475	218,974
1960	2,129	886	3,015	1,442,575	280,484

SOURCE: *Le Commerce du Levant*, 15:26 (1961).

Beirut is not a petroleum terminal at all. The advantages accruing
to Tripoli in being one inhere largely in the number of Tripolitans
employed by the Iraq Petroleum Company, rather than in the amount
of flow through the terminal. The great increase in the import of
wood in Tripoli reflects one advantage the city does have. The Arab
countries in general are very poor in wood and must import it; since
land is cheaper in Tripoli than in Beirut, it costs less to store lumber
there. The wood is imported mostly from the Balkan countries and
from West Africa, and comes in the form of very large, unmilled
logs. Several new industries in Tripoli have been given impetus by
this development.

The efforts to make Tripoli an airport have so far been an expensive failure. The French-built seaplane base in the Mina did not survive World War II. Subsequently, an airport was built at Klayat,
northeast of Tripoli, and from 1952 through 1957, it handled an
annual average of about 1,100 aircraft carrying about 5,500 passengers. However, the runways were so severely damaged during the
troubles of 1958 that they could thereafter only be used for occasional, unscheduled landings. In 1962 they had not been repaired,
nor was there, amid all the publicity about development projects in
Tripoli, any reference to putting Klayat back into service. Beirut,
meanwhile, had developed into a major international airport.

Tourism

Tripoli's problems in maintaining itself as something more than
a provincial trading center are reflected in the number and quality

of its facilities for visitors. Their number is disproportionately small considering the city's size, as the figures in Table 17 show. Not only are Tripoli's facilities few; they are also almost entirely antiquated. Informants attributed this situation to the decrease since 1950 of overnight visitors from Syria, coupled with the ease of transportation to and from Beirut, which permits many people to conduct their business in Tripoli without having to spend the night there. In the

TABLE 17. NUMBER OF HOTELS AND RESTAURANTS IN TRIPOLI AND OTHER PARTS OF LEBANON

Place	No. hotels	No. hotel rooms	No. hotel beds	No. cafés, restaurants, etc.
Beirut	303	4,202	7,933	1,362
Mount Lebanon	335	6,431	12,682	804
Tripoli	27	236	441	250
Saida	6	64	136	99

SOURCE: Le Commerce du Levant, 4:32 (1960).

spring of 1962, there were reports in the Beirut newspapers of plans for building a new modern hotel in Tripoli in conjunction with a projected International Trade Fair there. But the challenge facing all such plans is that Beirut and Mount Lebanon province (which includes Beirut's suburbs) already have a disproportionate share of the nation's industry and commerce (including the fledgling tourist business), and they are not likely to relinquish it. Tripoli might attract many more Middle Eastern and western tourists who now visit the Cedars area in summer and in winter, but it would have to offer them exceptionally attractive accommodations in order to deflect and delay their return to Beirut.

To western tourists, particularly, Tripoli has the inherent interest of possessing the only authentic "old Arab city" in Lebanon; but in order to capitalize on this, the Tripolitans would have to preserve and enhance the Old City rather than neglect or demolish it, which is their present inclination. The conversion of the upper levels of the citadel into a luxurious modern restaurant, with a magnificent view of ocean, river, city and mountains, and adjacent to a restored Old City, could be an attraction which Beirut might not be able to match. It would not destroy what little historical and architectural interest the citadel itself now has, nor would it spoil its impressive appearance from the river. But whether such necessarily major projects could be achieved, given the values, attitudes, and resources of Tripoli's people, is another question entirely. These comments, though they are in the nature of an aside, are nevertheless relevant to the contemporary culture of Tripoli, for in 1961–62 there was much talk in Tripoli and Beirut about the need for expanding the tourist business, but there was only routine consideration of how specifically to improve the quality and interest of its offerings.

THE AGRARIAN-COMMERCIAL BASE

Orchards

Oranges, lemons, and olives have been the major crops of Tripoli for a very long time, the citrus fruits for at least a thousand years. Not only is Tripoli a producer and an exporter of these fruits, but for a long time it has also processed them in various ways. In Tripoli itself (meaning the qada' of Tripoli) the citrus plantations are far more important than the olives. The latter occupy only 5.4 per cent of the area and are actually merely an extension of the groves of the contiguous Zgharta and Kura plains which comprise the major olive-growing region of Lebanon.

In addition to occupying most of the un-built-upon area of the Tripoli-Mina plain, the citrus orchards also fill the coastal plain of al-Miniyah, which is about the same in size and lies northeast of Tripoli, directly north of Mount Turbul. Ownership of these orchards has for a long time been a major source of the wealth of Tripoli's aristocratic Muslim families, who also, however, own more distant agricultural properties. The Zgharta and Kura areas are primarily Maronite and Eastern Orthodox strongholds, but their olives contribute to Tripoli's economy by being marketed and processed there.

The lemon harvest begins at the end of September, oranges are harvested from the end of November to April, and the olive harvest begins in November also.[4] Unfortunately, no information is available on the demography of the laborers involved in these activities. How many of them are villagers, how many are residents of the city? No one could tell me. The closeness of so many villages to the city, and the customary ease with which people move back and forth between city and village make this a subject of no interest to

Tripolitans. One item, however, is noteworthy: the villagers of Hadchite apparently originally established themselves in Tripoli to work in its orchards, and many of them still do this. Others serve their fellows as shopkeepers. The village, like its neighbors, is very cold and often snowbound in winter, and there have always been winter migrations to the lowlands. This, instead of remaining a seasonal migratory pattern, became a colonization. A parallel and better known case is Zgharta, the lowland colony of Bsharri, a large village which, like Hadchite, is very high in Mount Lebanon in the vicinity of the Cedars.

In 1961–62, the orchards of Tripoli contributed much to the beauty of the city — glossy green foliage all year around and the perfume of their blossoms in the Spring — as well as to its economy. They were faced, however, with three serious threats: (1) continued outright destruction to make room for more new buildings, (2) parasitic disease, and (3) the competition of more productive stock and techniques in the coastal regions of southern Lebanon. In view of the second two threats, it is understandable how some Tripolitans have themselves become agents of the first, for building sites are commanding increasingly tempting prices. One authoritative report comments as follows on this situation: "Since the city of Tripoli will, during the next twenty years, absorb only part of the land occupied by the orchards, it would be useful from now on to set limits to the zone of its extension in order to facilitate [the renovation of the orchards]." [5] As far as disease is concerned, this Beirut newspaper report is significant:

A delegation representing the orchard owners of Tripoli was received yesterday by Mr. Joseph Skaf, the Minister of Agriculture. . . . They explained the damage which has been suffered as a result of the spread of the "red parasite" disease in the orange orchards. A large number of trees have been cut down in order to prevent the contamination of neighboring orchards. At the same time, the growers asked for compensation, so that they could replace the felled trees, and they asked for the Ministry of Agriculture's assistance in the total eradition of this disease.

Mr. Skaf promised to order an inquiry to evaluate the damage and eventually fix the amount of indemnification.[6]

The orange trees are planted very close together, and the groves of different owners are separated by screens of very tall reeds, some growing, others cut and woven in. Some time before the above account appeared in *L'Orient*, a Tripoli informant, who was in a critical mood at the time, told me about the parasite problem. He said that sprays were being used on the trees but that the screens, which harbor the parasite, were often not sprayed because the adjoining owners could not agree on an equitable division of labor and costs.

In Tripoli, about two-thirds of the trees are oranges, one-third lemons. There are, on the average, about 1,000 trees per hectare (2.47 acres) in contrast to the 300 or less per hectare which is one of the newer methods of cultivation being used in the south. So far, it costs about the same in Tripoli and in the south to cultivate and irrigate the land and harvest the crop (about 2,000 Lebanese pounds, or $670 per hectare). However, while the average income in Tripoli is 5,850 Lebanese pounds per year per hectare, the average income of the newer orchards in the south, when they mature, is expected to be about 10,000 Lebanese pounds. The quality of the Tripoli fruit, also, is not as high.[7] Radical changes in production techniques will obviously be necessary if the Tripoli citrus business is to remain of major importance.

Whole oranges and whole lemons are consumed in Tripoli itself, and are also exported. The export business has recently been facilitated by the local manufacture of wooden crates, which, in turn, is an adaptation to the greatly increased importation of wood.

Confections

Citrus fruits and flowers also contribute ingredients to the confectionery business, one of Tripoli's specialties. The city no longer produces and exports its own sugar, as it did long ago, but rather imports it for the manufacture of sweets. These include liquid orange and lemon extracts sold in bottles, sugared fruits and nuts, and variously flavored sugar-and-nut candies of the nougat sort. There are seven or eight major manufacturers, employing about two hundred people, and many smaller ones. The shops of three of the major manufacturers are in the Tal and are considered to be fashionable. In the spring of 1962, furthermore, one of them opened a branch in Ras Beirut. The affair was marked by a gala reception, attended by important Beirut personages including the premier himself.[8]

Soap

Another such traditional business is the manufacture of soap. Tripoli has for a long time been famous for its soap and recently has been the center of the traditional Lebanese soapmaking industry.[9] The laundry soap is made from olive oil (in abundant supply in Tripoli), while the toilet soap is made from coco or palm oil which must be imported. The shops are mostly small. The oil base is boiled with lye in vats for 30 to 40 hours. It is then spread out on a prepared floor, and cut and stamped when it is cool but still soft. For two months, it is stored in conical stacks to dry — notably in the Khan al-Sabun. Then it is trimmed and packed in bags and aged for four months. The square cakes are sold by weight, not individually wrapped, and there is little advertising.[10]

In 1956, the traditional soap industry was in serious straits owing to the exclusion of the Syrian market area, the high cost of olive oil, and the competition of packaged detergents and powdered soaps. The main hope for the continuation of the industry at all seemed to depend on the development of good quality, moderately priced toilet soaps.[11] In 1961–62, there were only about eight soap factories in Tripoli — employing about 150 people — all small except for a relatively new one in Bahsas. They no longer used very much olive oil, but relied on vegetable oils and sheep fat. One factor here was that they could no longer offer the olive oil producers high enough prices. They were still surviving, despite the competition of detergents, but business was down to about 20 per cent of what it had been 10 or 15 years earlier. Unless the soap industry could somehow modernize, it was, according to the informant who provided me with these details, doomed to eventual extinction.

There are olive presses in Tripoli, but it is not so much a center of olive oil making itself as it is a distribution center for the oil which is made in northern Lebanon generally. For some time, an entrepreneur in Bahsas had a plant which prepared the olive oil residue (crushed seeds, skin and flesh) for use as fuel for water heaters and the like. The increasing competition of electricity and kerosene, however, was too much, and in 1961–62, the works had recently been converted by another entrepreneur into a cottonseed oil and fertilizer plant employing about 150 people.

These, then, are the traditional agrarian-commercial businesses of

Tripoli. All of them are facing, with varying degrees of success, the challenge of "adapt or die."

Fishing

The fishing business of Tripoli (strictly speaking, of al-Mina) is equally traditional, though not agrarian, and it is faced with a similar challenge.

In 1961 Tripoli was, by a slight margin, the largest port of the Lebanese fishing industry, as indicated in Table 18. However, Leba-

TABLE 18. NUMBER OF FISHERMEN AND FISHING BOATS
IN TRIPOLI AND OTHER PORTS

Port	No. fishermen	No. boats
Tripoli	650	267
Saida	645	128
Beirut	525	216
Sur	514	127
Juniah	391	94
Shikka	376	84
Jubayl	152	52

SOURCE: "La pêche au Liban," *Le Commerce du Levant*, 11:26 (1961).

nese fishermen were receiving an average annual income of only 750 Lebanese pounds (about $250) as contrasted with the average national income of nonagricultural workers in general, which was 2,581 Lebanese pounds, or about $860.[12] Unable to invest in better equipment and not assisted by the government, the fishermen could not compete with Turkish, Greek, and Italian boats in the same waters, and many resorted in desperation to the illegal practice of using dynamite. Yet consumer prices for fresh fish were very high, and the market was relatively limited. Government support (and utilization of the country's many new refrigerated warehouses, including Tripoli's) in increasing the output and the fishermen's incomes, while lowering consumer prices, was being discussed in the press at the time.[13] Though a problem of national scope, it was relatively more important to Tripoli as a city than to Beirut.

Crafts and Commerce

Of the traditional occupations not directly connected with the production of foodstuffs, silk weaving was the only one for which Tripoli was ever renowned. It was dependent upon the silk production of Mount Lebanon. This, having been a major activity for centuries, became nearly though not entirely defunct during World War I, and the subsequent decline of the world silk market forced a change in land use. Most of the mulberry trees in the highlands were replaced by fruit trees, especially apples, which were new to Lebanon. Lebanon's production of 90,000 kilograms of cocoons in 1961 was but a tiny fraction of world production and of its own former production, although it represented an increase over immediately preceding years.[14] If there is any silk weaving in Tripoli today, it must be on a very small scale. I heard of some looms in Mawlawiyyi, but the city (in contrast, for example, to Damascus with its brocades) no longer has any reputation for products of this sort. It is possible that the inauguration of the 'Arida cotton mill in 1930 was facilitated by the availability of unemployed silk spinners and weavers.

The Suqs. Appendix A describes the way many shops in the Old City are concentrated by specialty on certain of the narrow, old streets. Such concentration in itself is a traditional pattern. So is the very small size of the shops, and so, too, are the specialties themselves: cloth, tailoring, woodwork, leatherwork and shoes, metal utensils, and gold jewelry. It is very important to understand, however, that though these are "traditional" in some important ways, they are not "living fossils" from the past. They exhibit some direct continuities with the past, but they are continually adapting to new conditions. The merchants in Bazarkan sell cloth from bolts mostly imported from Europe. They also sell imported, ready-made clothing and plastic materials which are not only imported but are the creations exclusively of twentieth-century technology. Even the tailors in Suq Khayyatin, who make traditionally styled garments, use factory-made cloth and sewing machines. The leather workers in Birkat al-Millaha and Suq al-Haraj use some of the hides still tanned in Dibbagha, but they also use imported leather and factory-made threads, metal accessories, and tools. Some of the shoes, and especially the sandals, sold in Kindarjiyyi, are locally made, but most are ready-made imports from Europe. The tools and styles of product of the woodworkers and furniture makers are, as I remarked much earlier, entirely European. The tinsmiths and coppersmiths of Nahhasiyyin do make old style trays and cooking pots for conservative householders, but they also sell factory-made imports from Europe. Those who make brass and copper trays, bowls, and coffeepots for the tourist market copy old styles, but they use sheetmetal from Europe and they stamp on the designs with a hammer and a set of variously designed punches. They do not do the etching, incising, and inlaying characteristic of the old metalwork and of some of the higher-priced work still done in Damascus. The goldsmiths' product is not only traditional, but much of the demand for it is traditionally motivated (i.e., investment in gold jewelry rather than in a bank account). Yet the gold itself is subject to international price fluctuations, and the smiths are liable at any time to be subjected to direct inspection by the national government and to arrest if they are using debased gold.[15]

It has been observed in old Arab cities that shops selling imperishable, low-turnover, and relatively high-priced goods will be located near the grand mosque.[16] One can find examples of this in Tripoli. The best one is the short street of goldsmiths, one end of which adjoins the Mansuri mosque. Then, too, around the corner, in the long street called Sagha, there are a few spice shops and stationery stores which also sell books, but these are intermingled mostly with groceries and butcher shops, and the occurrence here of the latter does not fit the generalization.

My oldest informants could not remember a time when the "traditional" shops were not concentrated in their present locations, but this does not necessarily mean that there have not been any shifts for centuries. To be sure, Dibbagha, because of its name and its location downstream from the rest of the Old City, has probably been a section of tanneries for a very long time, and so leather workers may have adjoined it for a very long time, too. But during the past fifty or sixty years, many Christians have moved out of the Tirbi'a section, and it may be that there are more furniture and metal working shops there now than there used to be. And then, what about Bab Hadadin? It means "Blacksmiths' Gate," but there are no blacksmiths there, and in fact only a few miscellaneous shops. Was it once a blacksmiths' section (nonautomotive iron workers are now concentrated in Zahriyyah and Tirbi'a), or does the name refer to families named Hadad who may once have been dominant there? It is true that names become attached to locations because of the craftsmen (or other features) in them, and that either the names or the craftsmen, but not necessarily both, may subsequently shift location. "Sagha" refers to goldsmiths, but it is applied not only to the short street where the

MAP 5

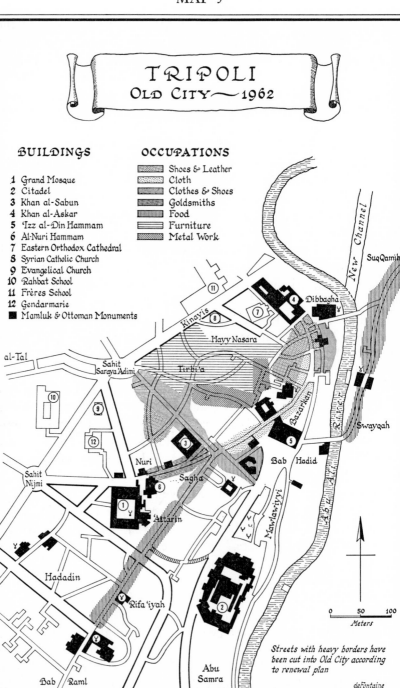

TRIPOLI
OLD CITY — 1962

BUILDINGS

1 Grand Mosque
2 Citadel
3 Khan al-Sabun
4 Khan al-Askar
5 'Izz al-Din Hammam
6 Al-Nuri Hammam
7 Eastern Orthodox Cathedral
8 Syrian Catholic Church
9 Evangelical Church
10 Rahbat School
11 Frères School
12 Gendarmerie
■ Mamluk & Ottoman Monuments

OCCUPATIONS

Shoes & Leather
Cloth
Clothes & Shoes
Goldsmiths
Food
Furniture
Metal Work

al-Tal

Sahit
Saraya'Adimi

Kinayis

11

8

7

Dibbagha

Hayy Nasara

SuqQamih

New Channel

Tirbi'a

Ras el Nahr

Bazarkan

10

9

12

Nuri

3

5

Swayqah

Bab Hadid

Sagha

6

1

'Attarin

Nawlawiyyi

Abu Ali

Sahit
Nijmi

Hadadin

Rifa'iyah

2

0   50   100
Meters

Abu
Samra

Bab Raml

Streets with heavy borders have
been cut into Old City according
to renewal plan

deFontaine

jewelers actually are, but also to an adjacent but long segment of the main street running north-south through the Old City. One of the new streets extended out from Sahit Saraya 'Adimi, sixty to seventy years ago, became the location of Tripoli's printing presses. There is still one there, while the other presses are now widely scattered, but the street is still called Shari' Mitab'ah.

I was not aware of any guild organizations among the Old City's craftsmen-merchants. In view of the character of their "traditional" appearance, this should not be surprising. What is not traditional about them is their source of materials and their techniques of production. Yet these were the very kinds of issues with which the guilds were concerned, and as they changed, the guilds lost their function. There is an incipient labor union movement in Tripoli, but as in the West, it is something entirely new and is not a modernized continuation of the ancient guilds. Nevertheless, there is still a possibility that those shops clustered by specialty do have some kind of remnant of guild organizaiton. Weulersse, in his detailed analysis of the suqs of Antioch (about a hundred miles north of Tripoli) says that each cluster belonged to a "corporation," but he does not say what the corporations were.[17] He also points out that the clustered shops represented ethnic or sectarian groups, and correspondingly Tripoli's goldsmiths are nearly all Christians. At that time (about 1933), Antioch was smaller than Tripoli, was predominantly Turkish (rather than Arab) in language and architecture, and the sharp delineation of its quarters and suqs was beginning to break down owing to new means of transportation and production.

Merchants. The merchant (singular *tajir*; plural *tujjar*) is a man who buys and sells for a living. He may be a shopkeeper who actually handles the goods he buys and sells. Or he may be a commission agent or broker who does not. This is a well recognized role among the Lebanese and one for which they are famous the world over. It is clearly to be distinguished, in their eyes, from peasant, laborer, craftsman, and (in modern times) a specialist in one of the learned professions.

So far, one might conclude that when a Lebanese talks about a tajir, he means exactly the same thing that an American does when he talks about a businessman. However, I have a notion — and it is admittedly only that — that a Lebanese would be more content to limit himself to the general designation, whereas the American would more likely want to know (or to designate) the particular kind of businessman. Connected with this notion are two others: (1) Lebanese references to an individual tajir need less often to specify the kind of business, since the individual's identity and specific business are more likely than in America already to be known by those talking about him; (2) while the Lebanese tajir must have expert knowledge, he is likely to need less specialized knowledge than the American businessman, who is more likely to be an expert in a particular field within a larger business organization and more likely to be a member of a professional organization composed of fellow specialists.

These notions developed as a result of my consideration of the listing of occupations in the Tripoli telephone directory [18] and of my analyses of this material. The number of listings in the directory are:

Tripoli	3,367
Mina	281
Unlocated	74
	3,722

All of these are the telephones of individual persons. In addition, there are 335 institutional telephones, but at this point I will consider only the 3,367 individual ("personal") telephones in Tripoli. Of these, 581 are double listings (separate telephones for home and business), and consequently the actual number of persons involved is 2,786. Of these persons, 1,693 gave their occupations as well as their addresses. The telephone directory is a biased sample in that those listed are presumably in better-than-average financial circumstances. The occupational subsample is further biased, but for reasons on whose nature we can only guess. The 1,693 people who provided their occupations or specialties wanted to do so, although they did not have to pay an extra fee, but I do not know why they did. Since the directory has no "classified" section, advertising (of a rudimentary sort) comes to mind, of course, as one possible motive.

Those occupations or specialties by which ten or more persons identified themselves are listed in Table 19. The "merchants" constitute 46.4 per cent of the total. The total includes certain occupations which I think neither the Lebanese would classify as "tajir" nor Americans as "businessmen." Accordingly, let us subtract the 219 dentists, engineers, lawyers, pharmacists, and physicians. Let us also subtract the 178

TABLE 19. NUMBER OF PERSONS IN SELECTED
OCCUPATIONS

Merchant	785
Physician	127
Restaurateur	56
Grocer	45
Lawyer	42
Electrical appliance seller	31
Engineer	29
Garage and service station operator	27
Nouveautés seller	24
Furniture maker and seller	21
Transport agent	19
Tailor	19
Clothier	18
Bookseller	16
Pastry seller	16
Butcher	16
Dressmaker	15
Hairdresser	15
Maritime agent	14
Sweets seller	11
Shoe seller	11
Pharmacist	11
Dentist	10
Mechanic	10
Moneychanger	10
Baker	10
Other (89 specialists)	283
Total	1,693

dressmakers, bakers, mechanics and automobile servicemen, butchers, hairdressers, tailors, grocers, and furniture makers. Lastly, let us subtract 37 other specialists who are in the "other" category in the list by reason of their small numbers. They include drycleaners, dyers, printers, cabinet makers, newspaper proprietors, midwives, and heads of schools. These subtractions leave us with 1,365 individuals, each of whose self-identification is one of 83 commercial specialties; but of these, 785 persons (57.3 per cent) classify themselves simply as "merchant." There seem to be some patterns in the frequency of "merchants" depending on their location within the city, as suggested by Table 20.

TABLE 20. *DISTRIBUTION OF MERCHANTS AND OTHERS IN VARIOUS SECTIONS OF TRIPOLI*

Section	Merchants		Others		
	No.	%	No.	%	No. specialties
Bazarkan	35	77.7	10	22.3	(7)
Bab al-Tibbani	157	71.4	63	28.6	(36)
Sagha	26	61.9	16	38.1	(12)
Zahriyyah	34	38.2	57	61.8	(36)
Boulevard	26	33.8	53	66.2	(29)
Tal	32	26.2	130	73.8	(43)

Of all the Tripolitans who have telephones, those who identify themselves as "merchants" are significantly more frequent in the old (Sagha) and/or commercially specialized (Bab al-Tibbani and Bazarkan) sections. Conversely, the majority of (presumably) prosperous businessmen in the newer or more westernized sections prefer to identify themselves more specifically in terms of their commodities or services.

It does not follow that the "merchants" all deal in the same commodity or service. In fact, one of the points of this discussion is that the reverse is true. It is a good bet that a "merchant" in Bab al-Tibbani is a dealer in foodstuffs, but that a "merchant" in Bazarkan deals in cloth. Everyone accepts this, and for the people concerned, "merchant" is a sufficient identification of role. Sagha is not so specialized, but, like Bazarkan, it is a section of very small shops which tend to have a stable, customary clientele. Those who are content to call themselves "merchant" are reiterating a traditional role label, supported by the probability that their specialty and personal identity are already known by those who wish to do business with them.

In Tripoli, then, the "merchant" role is, in part and in a particular sense, a traditional one. That there is a distinctively conservative motivation in this matter is suggested in a classified telephone directory, supported by advertising fees, which a private publisher in Beirut has produced.[19] It reprints most of the occupationally identified names in the official Tripoli directory and puts them under 113 headings based on occupation or specialization in commodities or services. The largest single category is "merchant." By contrast, the Beirut section of this book is fourteen times longer and includes

1,576 specialties. Not only is "merchant" not the largest category in the Beirut section; it is not even included as a category!

Traditional though it may be in the conception of Tripolitans, the merchant role, like the others which I have considered, is also being adapted to changing conditions.

NEW FORMS OF BUSINESS

Types

Because of the actual continuities between "old" and "new" occupations, I have already of necessity given some consideration to the latter, but there are also occupations and businesses which are new and clearly nontraditional; there are no obvious continuities between them and the past.

The most important single concern is the Iraq Petroleum Company, which in 1961–62 employed about 1,100 people. Not only is it the largest single employer in Tripoli, but its role in stimulating growth and change in the city has been very great. Also, the municipality receives considerable revenue from the national government which is a share of the royalties paid by IPC. Physically, IPC has three main locations: the terminal and adjoining refinery northeast of al-Biddawi, the office compound in al-Qubbah, and the residential compound above Bahsas where forty-three families live. In May 1962 it was announced that IPC, in agreement with the government, would expand the Tripoli refinery so that it would produce not only kerosene but high-grade benzine and aviation fuels. Previously, the Tripoli refinery had compared very unfavorably in both output and quality with the one at Saida which is not owned by IPC.[20] A major contribution to the Lebanese economy in general, this development would presumably not compensate for the many IPC lay-offs which posed problems for many Tripoli people in the late 1950's.

The 'Arida cotton mill is the second largest employer in Tripoli, with a payroll of about 900 people. Many of these are not residents of Tripoli itself, but of the villages of al-Kura. Still further removed from Tripoli are the cement factories at Shikka, but some Tripolitans are employed by them.

Both IPC and 'Arida began operations in the early 1930's, shortly after the introduction of electrical power in Tripoli. In fact, we can legitimately think of the industrialization of Tripoli as beginning about 1930. In 1937, there were in Tripoli 12,523 workers in "old industries" and 354 in "new industries," the latter presumably being 'Arida and IPC.[21]

In addition to 'Arida, there are five other large businesses in Bahsas, which, with their approximate number of employees are:

Sugar refinery	400
Plywood factory	200
Cottonseed oil plant	150
Bottling plant	20
Construction company	50

The first three, together with a shipping company and an orange crate factory in the Mina and a refrigerated warehouse in Tripoli, are owned by five Muslim brothers whose father began the whole enterprise on a small scale in the 1930's. The shipping company owns and operates three small freighters, the largest of which is 5,000 tons. There are six other vessels and about ten other refrigerated warehouses owned by Tripoli businessmen, but the most conspicuously successful modern family enterprise in the city is the one first mentioned.

The refrigerated warehouses are a response primarily to the great increase in the production of apples in Mount Lebanon and in the production of hen's eggs. The latter was particularly stimulated by the United States Point IV program. Tripoli's merchant fleet primarily imports wood and exports concrete products.

Of smaller scale, individually, are the many shops in Tripoli which have come into being during the past twenty to thirty years as a result of new domestic architectural styles and the prevalence of the automobile. Plumbers, electricians, western-style furniture makers, automobile servicemen, electrical appliance salesmen and repairmen, taxi and bus drivers — all of these are cases in point. Changing tastes, as well as technology, have resulted in various new types of dry goods stores, thirty-two movie theaters, and twelve banks in addition to the semigovernmental Banque de Syrie et du Liban. All branches of larger concerns, the Tripoli banks are:

Banque Libanaise pour Le Commerce
Union National Bank
Commercial Business Bank

Intra Bank
British Bank of the Middle East
Arab Bank
Development Bank
Bank of Beirut and the Arab Countries
Crédit Foncier d'Algérie et de Tunisie
Compagnie Algérienne de Crédit et de Banque
Banco di Roma
Bank Misr-Liban

Besides the newness of all these enterprises in Tripoli, there are in their operations some elements of "industrialization." There is some mass production, there is some white collar bureaucratization, there is some national and international financing, and at IPC there is even some automation. Unfortunately, I cannot quantify these phenomena. Nor are figures available which would enable a precise comparison of "traditional" and "new" enterprises in terms of numbers of workers, their salaries, and the market value of their products. Yet even if such figures were available, and if such ambiguous categories as "merchant" could be clarified in these terms, I wonder if we would really be significantly closer to the answers to what appear to be the really bothersome questions about industrialization, and, specifically, about the degree to which Tripoli is now an industrial city. These bothersome questions — about "rootlessness," "fragmentation," "anonymity," and the like — seem to have arisen in the first place more from qualitative and moralistic observations, and it has not been demonstrated that strictly economic statistics can elucidate them.

Number of Businesses and Employees

More can be said, however, about the important and more straightforward problem of how the people of Tripoli earn their living. In the fall of 1961, the president of the municipal council told me that there were in Tripoli about 10,000 shops of all kinds and sizes. Early in 1962, the Ministry of Social Affairs announced that in 1961 in the province of North Lebanon there were: 2,511 productive establishments, employing 10,850 people (9,716 men; 1,124 women), whose total earnings were 28,480,000 Lebanese pounds and whose average annual per capita income was 2,626 Lebanese pounds.[22]

The 1960 population of North Lebanon was estimated at 338,000,[23] and the 1961 population of Tripoli-Mina was an estimated 210,000; it is reasonable to assume that at least two-thirds (or 1,674) of the productive establishments in the northern province were in Tripoli-Mina. These 1,674 establishments would, presumably, be a subsample of the 10,000 "shops" to which the council president referred.

Another approximation to the wage-earning situation in Tripoli can be gleaned from an industrial census of Lebanon taken in 1955 (see Table 21). In 1955, Tripoli-Mina had 89.6 per cent of the pro-

TABLE 21. TYPE OF BUSINESS ESTABLISHMENT BY NUMBER OF EMPLOYEES

Type	5 or more employees, North Lebanon		5 or more employees, Qada' of Tripoli	
	No. Estab.	No. Emp.	No. Estab.	No. Emp.
Mining and quarrying	12	37	10	. . . .
Food manufacturing	100	1,138	90	. . . .
Beverages	4	42	3	. . . .
Textiles	10	1,041	9	. . . .
Footwear, clothes	19	141	17	. . . .
Wood and cork	17	128	15	. . . .
Furniture and fixtures	26	234	22	. . . .
Printing and publishing	4	26	3	. . . .
Chemicals, oil	8	682	7	. . . .
Nonmetallic minerals	22	1,495	20	. . . .
Metal products	9	110	8	. . . .
Other	10	99	9	. . . .
Total	241	5,173	216	3,645

SOURCE: Republic of Lebanon, *Industrial Census of Lebanon, 1955* (Beirut, 1957–58), I, table 10.

ductive establishments in North Lebanon, employing five or more persons. Further details on this are shown in Table 22. Two of the largest establishments in Batrun Qada' would have been the cement factories at Shikka, while the two largest establishments in Tripoli Qada' would have been IPC and 'Arida. However, Tripoli's large sugar refinery and plywood factory have been established since 1955,

TABLE 22. NUMBER OF EMPLOYEES PER BUSINESS ESTAB-
LISHMENT BY LOCATION IN NORTH LEBANON

Qada'	5–9	10–24	25–49	50–99	100 or more	Total
Tripoli	137 (90.1%)	67 (93.1%)	5 (100.0%)	3 (60.0%)	4 (57.1%)	216 (89.6%)
Kura	9	2	..	..	..	..
Batrun	5	1	..	..	3	..
Zgharta	1	2	..	..	..	..
Akkar	..	..	..	2	..	..
Total	152	72	5	5	7	241

SOURCE: Republic of Lebanon, *Industrial Census*, II, table 3.

but no general figure on the number of establishments with five or
more employees is available for 1961. Whatever that figure is, it is
presumably not very different from 216, and it is certainly a subsample of the total number of productive establishments, of which,
in 1961, there were possibly about 2,000 in Tripoli-Mina.

The industrial census provides some further information about
Tripoli-Mina in 1955, of interest and perhaps importance. The total
inventories held on December 31, 1955, by the establishments with
five or more employees were valued at 7,294,000 Lebanese pounds,
and the total receipts during 1955 had been 62,995,000 Lebanese
pounds. Tripoli's inventories were one-quarter of the value of the
inventories of comparable establishments in Beirut, where there were
more than four times as many (995). Beirut's establishments also had
more than four times the number of employees and a larger proportion of female employees (23 per cent versus Tripoli's 12 per
cent). Of the 294 working owners of the Tripoli establishments,
four (1.3 per cent) were women, as compared with 47 (3.5 per cent)
women working owners in Beirut. Capital formation in Tripoli-Mina
in 1955 was 1,708,000 Lebanese pounds (somewhat more than a quarter of Beirut's).

The relatively greater availability of physical space in Tripoli is
indicated in the figures in Table 23, which have reference, again, to
the productive establishments with five or more employees in 1955.
It will be recalled that availability of land is an important factor in
Tripoli's lumber business.

The most serious limitation of the 1955 industrial census is not
that it is slightly dated but that it excludes all the establishments
which employ less than five persons. In the aggregate, these are prob-

TABLE 23. *SPACE USED FOR BUSINESS PURPOSES IN TRIPOLI AND BEIRUT*

Location	Space used Floor	(sq. meters) Land
Beirut	319,000	378,000
Tripoli	112,000	303,000
Lebanon	1,024,000	3,934,000

SOURCE: Republic of Lebanon, *Industrial Census*, I, 57.

ably far more numerous than the larger businesses covered by the census. Most of the establishments in Tripoli, both in the Old City and in the newer sections, are small enterprises which were probably not surveyed in the census. The latter gives, then, only a partial insight into the economic life of the city. This is also true, unfortunately, of the 1961 figures, which, though more inclusive, are less detailed than those of 1955.

However, there is a way of estimating the total number of productive establishments in Tripoli, and this is by projecting from comparable findings in the nearby Arab nation of Iraq. According to that country's 1954 industrial census, about 90 per cent of its productive establishments employed less than five persons, about 45 per cent being one-man shops.[24] If a similar proportion obtained in the qada' of Tripoli, the qada' would have had approximately 2,160 productive establishments in 1955. This is not an inconceivable figure, considering the fact that North Lebanon had 2,511 establishments in 1961–62. Thirty-eight per cent of the productive employees in Iraq were hired by the smallest establishments, and projecting on this basis, the total number of industrial employees in the qada' of Tripoli would have been about 5,879, which is also a conceivable figure. However, it is not consistent at all with the figure of almost 13,000 workers in 1937, noted earlier. One problem here may be the ambiguity of the terms "industrial" and "worker."

The New Professions

As noted earlier in this chapter, there are 219 individuals in the telephone directory who are dentists (10), engineers (29), lawyers (42), pharmacists (11), and physicians (127). One physician told me that there were 125 of his kind in Tripoli, and I am inclined to think that the telephone directory sample represents the universe of this profession in the city. I think it is probable that this may also be very nearly the case with the lawyers and engineers, but I have no evidence on this. It is difficult to believe that there are only 10 dentists in Tripoli when there are 127 physicians, but I have no further information about the dentists. Twenty pharmacies are listed in the directory, and I know that there are at least two more (in the Mina) which are not listed. Therefore, there are probably more than 11 professional pharmacists in the city.

Except for the lawyers, all of these professions are, in their present form, outgrowths of modern science and technology. The fact that there have always been healers in Middle Eastern culture does not make today's medical, dental, and pharmacological professions in any sense "traditional." Engineer seems to be a rather eclectic socioeconomic status which includes people who are practicing chemists, physicists, architects, and builders. As for the lawyers, most of their training and practice derives from models that date from no earlier than the nineteenth century. All these specialists had to receive their training elsewhere than in Tripoli — in many cases, in Europe or America.

In terms of prestige and numbers, the physicians are the most important of these professional groups. They have their own medical association, and some of them are the proprietors of twenty-six private hospitals and large clinics in Tripoli and the Mina. Several of the physicians own pharmacies, also. Each of the private hospitals is known simply by the name of its proprietor: "Dr. So-and-So's Hospital." Several of the hospitals are housed in their own buildings, and the largest and newest in 1961 had about fifty beds, with room for expansion. It had air-conditioned operating rooms and various types of equipment from Europe and America.

There are only four hospitals in Tripoli-Mina not privately owned: the Muslim and Presbyterian hospitals, the government hospital, and a hospital which is operated by a benevolent society. Thus there are thirty hospitals and large clinics in the city. At the beginning of World War I there were only three.

The large clinics have some beds, and they specialize in surgical cases. On the whole, the medical institutions in Tripoli are, however, general in service, and many patients who need special treatment must go to Beirut for it. A psychiatrist from the mental hospital in

Beirut spends one day a week at the Presbyterian hospital in the Mina — the only service of this kind in Tripoli.

Half of Tripoli's physicians are Muslims. Compared to the total population, this is a disproportionately small number, but it is a reflection of the general educational situation, as discussed earlier. Two or three of the physicians are women, and one of them is a Muslim who has her own hospital. Forty-three per cent of the physicians have offices separate from their homes, and these are concentrated in the Tal and the small area immediately south of it, and to some extent along the Boulevard and adjacent avenues. Their residences (some are used as offices) are similarly concentrated, although more of them live in Abu Samra and al-Qubbah than have offices in these sections. Very few physicians live or have offices in the Old City, Bab al-Tibbani or Maluli, or in the Mina.

Twenty-five of Tripoli's lawyers (a little more than half) are Christians, and the head of the Tripoli Bar Association in 1961 was a Christian. There are two partnerships (one Christian pair and one Muslim pair), but otherwise the lawyers seem to work singly. Their physical concentration, on which I have remarked before, is very striking, for almost all of their offices are on Shari' Yazbik, the Boulevard, and Shari' Sintral, a short street connecting the other two. Their residences, also, are more concentrated in the general area of the Tal section than are those of the physicians.

The pharmacies, rather than being scattered throughout the various residential areas, are also concentrated, but differently from the physicians' and lawyers' offices, and they are found chiefly along two axes: Tal to Sahit Saraya 'Adimi and Sahit Nijmi to Tirbi'a via Shari' Kinayis. There are also two in Sagha and two in Bab al-Tibbani, but none in either Abu Samra or al-Qubbah, and only one in Hayy Mutran. It looks as if the pharmacies were systematically kept in lower rent areas than the physicians' and lawyers' offices. The poorer people who live in these same areas are not, however, necessarily the pharmacists' best customers, for the very high price of pharmaceuticals was a much-debated subject in the Lebanese press in 1961–62.

The proprietor of a pharmacy in the Mina told me that by law there is supposed to be no more than one pharmacy for every 7,000 persons (minimum). Since there were, at the time, three pharmacies in the Mina, I said that I supposed that Mina's population was at least 21,000. He answered that it was definitely more than that — that, in fact, there could legally be a fourth pharmacy in the Mina. If we can trust the *ad hoc* population estimates that are obviously made in this matter, the twenty-two known pharmacies in Tripoli-Mina imply a total population of, at the very least, 154,000.

PROFESSIONAL ORGANIZATIONS AND CLUBS

An aspect of the development of "new" businesses and professions in Tripoli has been the establishment of several ancillary business organizations and of some labor unions. I have already mentioned the local medical and bar associations. Tripoli's pharmacists, too, are organized — at least they are members of a national association of pharmacists whose president was public spokesman for the members in regard to the price problem in 1962 and its possible solutions. There is also an engineers' association in Tripoli.

Clubs

Rotary International and the Lions have chapters in Tripoli. The former was founded in 1949 by an Orthodox physician and a British IPC executive. The Lions chapter was founded in 1953 and reorganized in 1960 after a temporary dissolution caused in part by the discovery that there were Lions organizations in Israel. In 1961–62 these two organizations had memberships as indicated in Table 24. By mutual agreement, no individual is a member of both clubs.

TABLE 24. MEMBERSHIP IN TRIPOLI SERVICE CLUBS, 1962

Members	Rotary		Lions		Total
	Christians	Muslims	Christians	Muslims	
Businessmen	13	5	7	3	28
Physicians	3	1	7	1	12
Lawyers		1	5	1	7
Engineers	2			1	3
Landowners		1		1	2
Pharmacists				1	1
Dentists	1				1
Foreigners	4				4
Totals	23	8	19	8	58

Total Rotary	31 (incl. 4 foreigners)
Total Lions	27
Total Muslims	16
Total Christians	34 (excl. 4 foreigners)

The four foreign members of Rotary include two Britishers, both of whom are IPC executives, and one of whom was a cofounder of the club. The other foreigners are the representative of the French cultural mission in Tripoli and a Swiss engineer who works at one of the cement factories in Shikka.

Disregarding the foreign members, the two clubs are identical in size, in their 2-to-1 ratio of Christians to Muslims, and in the fact that 31 per cent of their membership represent seven of the ten most prominent Muslim families and seven of the ten most prominent Christian families in the city. Six other individuals (two Muslim and four Christian) represent five additional families which are among the second ten most prominent families in each sect category. (These ratings of families, which I discuss further in Chapter VI, were made, without any reference to Rotary or the Lions, by a set of informants who were not members of either club.)

There are, however, some subtle differences in upper class sectarian representation between the two clubs (see Table 25). One

TABLE 25. UPPER CLASS MEMBERS OF ROTARY
AND LIONS CLUBS

Rank	Rotary		Lions		
	Christian	Muslim	Christian	Muslim	Totals
First 10 families	5	4	2	7	18
Second 10 families	2	2	2	0	6
Total	7	6	4	7	24

Tripolitan (who had not seen my lists of members) commented that he thought the Rotary had more well established upper class people than the Lions, in which, he felt, there were more social climbers. Table 25 might be seen as supporting this evaluation as far as the Christians are concerned, and the informant was himself a Christian. The sectarian representation among the Christian members of the clubs was 19 Orthodox, 9 Maronites, 2 Presbyterians, and 8 whom I could not identify.

Neither club had, in 1961–62, a very active service program, but the Lions were awaiting a shipment of white canes for blind people, and Rotary members were involved in the distribution of some scholarships and medical assistance. Both clubs were concerned with the economic status of the city and were actively discussing such matters as the projected trade fair and other hoped-for economic stimulants. Both the president and the vice president of the Municipal Council were members of Rotary. Comprising representatives of the major sects and a good cross-section of the political and economic elite of Tripoli, these clubs could, in the future, become spearheads of new developments of all kinds. Or they could, of course, merely become upper class and upper middle class self-interest groups. Members of both clubs commented on the difficulty of recruiting additional members because of the unwillingness of many eligible people regularly to attend meetings. There is a Chamber of Commerce in Tripoli but, according to a Rotary member, it had in 1962 no program and few activities.

Labor Unions

At a different point in the socioeconomic spectrum of Tripoli, that of workers and employees, there are other organizations — unions — but I had no contacts with them. The labor unions of Lebanon in general are currently under study, and only partial information is available. It is clear that the unions, though modeled on those of the industrial West, are neither so powerful nor so well organized. Among the factors in this weakness are (1) the tacit or open opposition of owners and managers, many of whom tend to be paternalistic and sectarian in their recruiting and personnel policies; and (2) the assumption among both management and workers that the family is the main bulwark of an individual's security.[25] Then, too, the Lebanese government forbids collective bargaining and discourages union political activities, yet, in sharp conflict with the generally laissez-faire attitudes of the culture, provides that no employee may be dismissed without an indemnity. For these reasons alone, it has apparently been impossible, so far, for the unions to find any clear focus of purpose. The government does mediate management-labor disputes,[26] but these do not necessarily involve the unions.

As of 1962, there were 87 labor unions in Lebanon. Sixty-four of them were organized into four legally recognized federations, one of which, Federation of Unions of Workers and Employees of North Lebanon (FUNL), was centered in Tripoli. Some of the remaining twenty-three unions were independent, while others were organized into two federations which were not legally recognized.[27] The North

Lebanon Federation was established in 1954, became affiliated with the Confederation of Arab Trade Unions in 1956, and (along with two of the other legally recognized federations) with the Confederation of Lebanese Labor (CLL) in 1962. In 1962, it had fifteen member unions, and there were four other unions in Tripoli which were not affiliated with it. Details concerning the nineteen labor unions in Tripoli are given in Table 26.

TABLE 26. LABOR UNIONS IN TRIPOLI, 1962

Name of union	Affilia-tion	Date estab-lished	Member-ship
Bakery workers	FUNL	1948[a]	225
Barbershop workers	FUNL	1953	75
Carpentry workers	FUNL	1952	315
Commercial employees	FUNL	1953	400
Construction workers	FUNL	1954	300
Qadisha electric workers	FUNL	1956	350
Hotel, restaurant, café workers	FUNL	1946[b]	125
Machinists	FUNL	?	550
Printers and bookbinders	FUNL	1956	100
Cinema projectionists and workers	FUNL	1955	150
Radio and electrical workers	FUNL	1948	130
Sawmill workers	FUNL	1956	150
Shoeworkers	FUNL	1952	380
Tailorshop workers	FUNL	1946	170
Tricot workers	FUNL	1956	125
Actors and actresses	Indep.	1953	75
Taxi owners and drivers	Indep.	1949	245
IPC employees	Other CLL	1948	400
IPC refinery workers	Other CLL	1960	325
Total membership [c]			4590

[a] Originally branch of Beirut union; Tripoli union after 1953.
[b] Originally branch of Beirut union; Tripoli union after 1958.
[c] Subtotal for FUNL: 3,545.
SOURCE: Samir G. Khalaf, "Managerial Ideology and Industrial Conflict in Lebanon," unpubl. diss. (Princeton University, 1963), p. 340.

In 1962, the Federation had an office in Sahit Kura and a health center on the top of the Tal, close to the office of the Department of Awqaf. The Taxi Owners' and Drivers' union also had an office, on Sintral Street. Except for noting a few elections of union officers and an official protest by some of those officers against the general high cost of living, the Tripoli press paid little attention to union activities in the city. The officers of Tripoli's unions were almost all Muslims.

LACK OF ANONYMITY

To each resident of Tripoli the vast majority of Tripolitans are strangers. Furthermore, there are tendencies on the part of various individuals to insulate themselves from people of other sects and other social strata. In these senses, there is anonymity in Tripoli, and there is social distance which discourages familiarity, although it requires knowledge of identities.

Yet the predominant style of life in Tripoli — as in Lebanon generally — is for most people a set of interactions with known persons. The emphasis on intrafamilial and intrasectarian activities is an important contributor to this, and a reflection of it is the constant search for, and use of, personally known mediators when one is dealing with the governmental bureaucracy or any other organization of which one is not a member. Conversely, anyone who has a position in a bureaucratic organization is expected to express his personal obligations through nepotism and the granting of special favors to those he knows.

These are the ethical foundations on which a generally personal style of behavior rests. As far as the organization of work and commerce is concerned, this style is reflected in the highly individualized (hence "personal") identity of business concerns. Sometimes this is expressed by what seems superficially to be lack of concern for announcing identity in public. Earlier, I mentioned the almost complete lack of signs on the industrial buildings in Bahsas. It is assumed that those who have business in them already know their identity through personal contacts, and there is little interest in advertising their identity to any hypothetical "others" who may happen to pass by.

Several of these large businesses are legally incorporated and have corporate names, some of which are listed in the telephone directory, but among Tripolitans these plants are not referred to by their corporate names but by the personal names of their proprietors. Similarly, only two of the private hospitals even have impersonal formal names, and all of them are known by the names of their owners. The pharmacies, on the other hand, do have impersonal names, but in the telephone directory the name of each proprietor is included in parentheses. In fact, all but about 335 (8 per cent) of the listings in the directory are individualized. The vast majority of them are simply personal listings, and yet half of them are included explicitly for business purposes. Of the 335 impersonal or institutional listings, 150 are for the various government offices, and 75 are for the various offices of the Iraq Petroleum Company, both of which are indeed, in many ways, psychologically exterior to Tripoli. Of the remaining 110 institutional telephones, 27 belong to schools (with whose personnel most adults have little reason for contact), 18 belong to movie theaters (with which there is little occasion for negotiations which require a personal touch), 16 belong to banks and insurance companies, all of which are branches of larger concerns in Beirut, 15 belong to private clubs or associations of the sort which have been considered earlier in this chapter, and about 15 belong to commercial enterprises which are the agents for foreign companies (automobiles, for example). In other words, strictly local impersonal listings are very few in number, and the most ready explanation for this is that it is assumed generally that contacts will be made with individual persons as such, rather than with institutions through the medium of anonymous individuals.

Chapter VI

PRIVATE LIFE AND
PUBLIC FACE

ONE OF THE most persistent misunderstandings about Middle Eastern culture is that the typical Arab household consists of a patrilocal extended family — that is to say: a man, his wife (or wives), their unmarried children, their married sons, and the sons' wives and children. This group is usually pictured as being dominated by the senior male and living in a compound of adjoining rooms.

KINSHIP GROUPS

The factual evidence on kinship groups is rather considerable, and all of it indicates that the supposed typicality of the extended family household is a false notion — false whether one considers Christians, Muslims, villagers, or city dwellers.

The misunderstanding may have originated with western travelers who, untrained in the behavioral sciences, accepted as literal fact an idealized pattern about which some Arabs told them. One factor in the persistence of the misunderstanding is probably the tendency of Arabs, Muslims particularly, to shield their family life from scrutiny, thus discouraging research. Another is that there is indeed much evidence of concern and mutual aid among the members of Arab extended families, even though only a minority of them actually live together in the same menage. But there are also indications of severe hostilities and suspicions among the very same extended family members — feelings which would (some Arabs themselves have said) become unbearable if (and when) these relatives actually have to live together.

Quantitative studies which have been done since World War II show that Arab households (village and urban) are definitely larger than North American ones. This fact is illustrated by Table 27.

TABLE 27. *AVERAGE HOUSEHOLD SIZE IN VARIOUS ARAB COMMUNITIES*

Location of household	Persons per household	
City of Beirut	5.76	Churchill, 1954, p. 30
City of Amman, Christian	5.60	Hacker, 1960, p. 75
City of Amman, Muslim	7.00	Hacker, 1960, p. 75
Southern Lebanon 8 Shi'a villages	6.60	Gorton et al., 1953, p. 8
Biqa' Valley, Lebanon 13 mostly Shi'a villages	5.50	Churchill, 1959, p. 3
Central coastal Lebanon 1 Orthodox village	6.00	Gulick, 1955, pp. 48–49
United States, March 1962	3.31	U.S. Statistical Abstract

To what extent the existence of extended family households contributes to the largeness of Arab households in general is a moot question, as shown in Table 28 where "extended family" includes the so-called "stem family" in which one married son only, with his wife and children, lives with his parents. These two villages, predominantly Orthodox and Sunni, respectively, are almost identical in

TABLE 28. *HOUSEHOLD SIZE AND COMPOSITION IN TWO ARAB VILLAGES*

Household	Al-Munsif, Lebanon	Tell Toqan, Syria
No.	87	56
No. extended family	2	14
Per cent extended family	2.3	23.4
Population	523	326
Average size	6.0	5.8

SOURCES: John Gulick, *Social Structure and Culture Change* (New York, 1955), pp. 48–49; Louise E. Sweet, *Tell Toqaan: A Syrian Village* (Ann Arbor, 1960), p. 165.

average household size, yet they represent opposite extremes in the relative frequency of extended family households among the half-dozen villages in the area recently studied on this subject. Generalizing from Munsif, one would guess that extended family households have a negligible effect on average household size. Generalizing from Tell Toqan, one would have to admit the probability of some effect, at least. On the whole, it seems that more important in this matter than the extended family are: (1) the larger number of children produced per couple than in the United States, and (2) the tendency for single adults (unmarried, separated, or widowed) not to live alone but to live, as the case may be, with their parents, or married siblings, or married children, or more distant relatives sometimes. This second factor is very clearly illustrated in my earlier study of village social structure, where the personnel of every household in the village is precisely specified.[1] By contrast, single-person households, which comprise about one-fifth of all households in the United States, are regarded as strange and unnatural by Arabs, even highly westernized ones who admit that their own kinship ties can be very irksome.

As to the attitudes toward those extended family households which do exist, there is some specific information. In two Lebanese Christian villages (one of them Munsif), it was found that the extended or stem family households were regarded as temporary and undesirable arrangements. In a third case (a predominantly Muslim Arab village in Israel), where extended or stem family households amounted to 16 per cent of the total, they were held together either by dire economic straits which forced the pooling of resources (often much against the personal desires of individuals) or by the force of will of older men who wanted to be surrounded by a large menage.[2] The latter fitted the stereotype but, rather than being typical, they comprised only a very small minority of household heads.

Recent studies show, then, that in several Arab villages, extended or stem family households do occur, but that they are in a small minority and that feelings about them are decidedly mixed. As to average household size, the figures so far shown are inconclusive as to differences between cities and villages (contrary to some of the favorite assumptions of rural sociologists and urban theorists), and it is not a reliable index of the frequency of extended or stem family households.

Household and Family in Tripoli

All of this is a necessary preamble to a discussion of household and family in Tripoli. The data presented provide direct clues to the situation in Tripoli, for they are from the same culture area, and there are many Tripolitans who came originally from Syria, Palestine, and other parts of Lebanon. My information from Tripoli itself is derived from the statements of informants, from a few observations, and from responses to a questionnaire completed by Tripolitans who were students of the American University of Beirut in 1961–62. The composition of this sample, referred to hereafter as "the AUB Sample," is shown in Table 29. Actually, there were about sixty Tripoli-

TABLE 29. SEX AND SECTARIAN COMPOSITION OF
AUB SAMPLE

Sex	Muslim	Christian	Total
Male	14	6	20
Female	5	10	15
Total	19	16	35

tan students at the university, but these were the ones who were willing (some not without persuasion) to fill out the questionnaire. All were unmarried, their average age was about twenty years, and most of them were from middle or upper class families. Rather than being representative of Tripoli, this small, biased sample is a probe into it. A larger, stratified sample would obviously be better, but it was quite unfeasible at the time to conduct the necessary survey in Tripoli.

In my first chapter I mentioned that the president of the municipality apparently assumed that the average household size in Tripoli was six persons. His assumption may have been based on some independent evidence, and not an interpolation from other sources,[3] but this is uncertain. It is very unlikely that he had read these works, but it is not inconceivable that he had heard about them. Perhaps, on the other hand, he and the vice-president, who was participating in the conversation, were generalizing from the situation in their own social circles (Christian and Muslim upper middle class) in Tripoli. At any rate, the average household size of the members of the AUB Sample (Table 30) was very close to the official assumption.

TABLE 30. HOUSEHOLD SIZE OF TRIPOLI (AUB SAMPLE)

Sect	No. households	Av. house-hold size (persons)	Av. no. children in household	Av. no. children per couple
Muslim	18	6.7	4.1	5.6
Christian	15	5.7	3.5	4.0

The AUB Sample members' families appear to have more children than those in the much larger sample of village and Beirut families whose mothers were interviewed in Prothro's study of child rearing in Lebanon (see Table 31).

TABLE 31. NUMBER OF CHILDREN PER FAMILY BY SECT AND CLASS

Sect	Class	Beirut	Biqa' Valley
Sunni	Lower class	4.8	4.3
	Middle class	3.1	5.0
Orthodox	Lower class	2.5	4.4
	Middle class	2.8	3.3

SOURCE: E. T. Prothro, *Child Rearing in the Lebanon* (Cambridge, Mass., 1961), p. 45.

It is possible that the Tripoli AUB Sample parents were generally older than those of the Prothro samples (which were purposely selected for the presence of small children), and hence tended to have produced more offspring. At any rate, the total number of children per couple in the Tripoli sample is less than the average number of live births by city-dwelling Christian and Muslim Lebanese women generally,[4] and this adds a little more fuel to the hope that the AUB Sample has some generally representative value.

The Tripoli AUB Sample is also consistent with Prothro's and Yaukey's studies in that it indicates that Muslim urban sibling-sets (children per couple) are larger than Christian urban ones when one holds social class constant. There is relatively little difference in size, too, between Muslim village and Muslim urban sibling-sets, whereas Christian urban sibling-sets are often smaller than Christian village ones. Some urban theorists might interpret this by saying that urban Muslim families remain "ruralized," whereas Christian ones have become "urbanized." In actual fact, however, the Muslim families in the AUB Sample have very few village connections, whereas the

Christian ones not only do have many, but several of them originally were village families. The lower fertility of urban Christians is not due to any mysterious "urban influence." Rather, it is probably closely related (as Yaukey points out) to increased age of women at marriage and to increased use of contraceptives. Both of these factors are probably connected in several ways with the Christians' greater acceptance of high education and nondomestic occupations for women and of the western technological orientation toward the meeting of life's problems.

This discussion of Muslim-Christian differences must not be misconstrued to mean that the Christian Tripolitans' attitudes toward children and the family are indistinguishable from typical western urban ones. The differences between the Muslims and the Christians are matters of degree only, and the Christians are far more appreciative of large numbers of children and of woman's place in the home than would be considered normal in urban America and probably in most of rural America, too. As to contraception, it is not easy for women to obtain the equipment in Lebanon, and the Muslim and Christian sectarian authorities are either opposed to it or are unenthusiastic about it.[5]

The household composition of the AUB Sample is indicated in Table 32. Further details can most conveniently and clearly be pre-

TABLE 32. HOUSEHOLD COMPOSITION OF AUB SAMPLE, I

Type of family	Christian	Muslim	Total
Nuclear	12	10	22
Nuclear and dependents	2	2	4
Other	1	4	5
Sometimes stem or extended	0	1	1
Definitely extended	0	1	1
Total	15	18	33

sented in tabular form also (see Table 33). The suggestion is that in Tripoli, as elsewhere in Lebanon, the nuclear family is the typical household group among both Christians and Muslims, and that the extended family household, when it does occur, is most likely to do so among Muslims.

Five men provided further impressions of household composition in Tripoli. All were Christian, but all were longtime residents of the

TABLE 33. HOUSEHOLD COMPOSITION OF AUB SAMPLE, II

Type of family	Christian	Muslim
Nuclear (parents and unmarried children)	All complete except: 1. absent father	All complete except: 1. absent father 2. absent father
Nuclear and dependents	Dependents: 1. mother of 1 parent 2. mother of mother	Dependents: 1. mother of 1 parent 2. mother's brother
Other	1. Two sisters with 2 children each	1. Three cousins (Palestinian refugeees) 2. Four siblings 3. Parents, 4 children, and sometimes a married daughter and her son 4. Parents, 3 daughters, son of 1 daughter
Sometimes stem or extended		1. Parents, 7 children, 2 grandchildren
Definitely extended		1. Parents, 3 daughters, 3 sons, 2 son's wives, 1 grandson

city who had Muslim friends and acquaintances. Two were physicians with experience among people of all social classes, two were teachers, and one was a businessman. One of the physicians made inquiries among Muslim friends. The gist of the impressions of these men is that extended or stem family households are exceedingly rare among Christians, that extended family households among Muslims occur, though they are unusual, but that Muslim stem family households are relatively frequent. Some of the older people approve of such households because to them they symbolize family unity and solidarity. Extended and stem family households have been becoming less frequent among middle and upper class people. Two factors in this appear to be (1) various influences from western-style education and (2) moving from the Old City (where the house was likely to be owned by the family and was perhaps more adaptable to the accommodation of several nuclear families) to an apartment in one of the new sections, which is smaller and less adaptable, though not impossible, for such accommodation. It follows that extended and stem family households are found primarily among poorer people, including immigrants from rural areas. (The one definitely extended household in the AUB Sample was an 'Alawite family from Syria.) Though the pooling of resources is an important reason for such households, each of the component nuclear families usually has its own food budget although they share the same kitchen.

The typology of families I am using is, of course, a conventional device designed to make some order out of a situation which is a mass of sometimes conflicting attitudes, values, and expectations. I had some glimpses into those actualities in Tripoli. One was afforded by a well-to-do Muslim family which was apparently going to become a stem family household. The house resembled a modern apartment building and had three floors, a semibasement, and a roof. The first floor was devoted to reception and dining rooms. The family (parents and six children) lived on the second floor, while the third was rented as an apartment to tenants. The eldest son had recently earned his medical degree in Damascus, and his father had set up for him in the semibasement an office with some laboratory equipment. One of his sisters was serving as laboratory assistant. Negotiations were under way for the son to marry a Syrian girl, and after they were married they were to move into the third-floor apartment.

By contrast, a not unusual arrangement among well-to-do people is for a married daughter to remain living with her parents. This is contrary to the conventional expectation. Usually this arrangement involves the economic dependence of the son-in-law, or his junior partnership in business with his father-in-law, especially when the latter has no sons of his own. However, a mere count of household personnel may not reveal what is really going on among them. Not infrequently, a well-to-do man will have his wife's parents as dependents in his household. The personnel in the two types of household are identical, but the quality of their relationships is obviously very different indeed.

Some Delicate Problems. The question of dependent relatives is a very touchy one in Lebanese culture, and, as noted in Chapter III, the various conflicts among jealous resentment, ideals of loyalty, and fear of the neighbors' gossip are very troublesome. Eldest sons are expected to be responsible for the parents in their old age, even though they will by law inherit in equal shares with their younger siblings.

Some eldest sons never marry, so that they can devote their resources to their younger siblings. Siblings are expected to share and share alike in all things, but enough of them take advantage of this expectation to make acute jealousies endemic. Yet above all, neighbors and friends should not know of such rifts; in one case the father did not make a will because to have done so would have implied to outsiders that the sons were already in hopeless conflict. The fact that a will might have prevented conflict was not the major consideration at all. This was not a Tripoli case, but it was described as being typical. Adults with children may support dependent adult brothers or sisters in their households, but they must be careful about appearances, lest the neighbors begin to say that the dependent siblings are really being used as servants, which, in fact, may be the truth! One of my informants, whose shop and house were in Hayy Mutran, told of a case of mistaken servitude on his own street. An elderly Muslim man was living with his son, a grocer. Every morning the father opened the shop and set out the vegetables. He did so because he enjoyed it, but the gossip began going around that he was being obliged by his son to do this work. When he heard of the gossip, he was so chagrined that he moved out and went to live elsewhere with another son.

Another touchy matter is polygamy among the Muslims. Islam does indeed permit a man to have as many as four wives, but very few do, and in fact most Muslims are monogamous. Some years ago, a survey of Palestinian villages indicated that only about 10 per cent of the men had ever in their lives been polygamous, and that nearly all of them had had only two wives. In Baghdad, a predominantly Shi'a and Sunni city four times larger than Tripoli, about 5 per cent of the married Muslim men (according to the official 1957 census) were polygamous and nine out of ten of them had two wives only. Churchill's sample survey of Beirut households yielded only two cases of polygamy (a tiny fraction of one per cent), but since the proportion of Muslim households in the sample is unknown, this finding means very little.

Muslims know that westerners disapprove of polygamy and consider it to be evidence of Middle Eastern backwardness. Consequently they are defensive about it, and this complicates their reactions to inquiries. Westerners' attitudes, in turn, seem to be befuddled by daydreams or nightmares (as the case may be) of irresponsible sensuality, and their objectivity is also suspect. Actually, polygamy is under attack in the Middle East itself, and in 1959 the Grand Mufti of Lebanon stated that although polygamy is permitted by Islam, it is only a stage of evolution toward monogamy.[6]

As far as Tripoli is concerned, none of the Muslims in the AUB Sample participated in a polygamous household, but about half of the respondents (Christian and Muslim) indicated that they knew, or knew of, specific cases of polygamy. One of them (a Muslim) guessed that 5 per cent of the Muslims in Tripoli were polygamous. In Tripoli itself, one of my informants cited a Muslim friend as saying that 2 per cent of the Muslims in the city were polygamous. There seemed to be general agreement that middle and upper class Tripolitan men had generally ceased to practice polygamy and that it was most frequent among poorer, less western-educated people. Additional wives, when they occur, normally have different rooms for themselves and their children, or may even live in entirely separate households. The additional expense to the husband may be offset by the fact that often each of the wives works.

Among middle and upper class people, the modern apartment is not in itself a cause of the decline of polygamy or of the practice of *harim*, the sequestering of the women from male visitors to the home. The apartments available to such classes in modern Lebanese cities are very large and relatively very inexpensive by the standards of similarly placed people in urban America. And a rich Lebanese may simply rent two adjoining apartments on the same floor or adjacent floors. In such establishments, it is easy to set aside a parlor where strangers can be entertained quite separately from the life of the household, and this is all that is really necessary for harim. Harim is practiced in some modern apartments in Tripoli, and it is not any influence of modern domestic architecture dictating the apparently steady abandonment of it. Illustrating the latter point, one informant told me of a Muslim family of his acquaintance which, with the same personnel and living in the same place, has within just a few years completely given up harim and everything associated with it, such as veiling of the wife.

Middle and upper class householders, Christian and Muslim alike, insist on domestic help. Over half of the AUB Sample reported at least one maid living in their homes, not to mention the servants who come in during the daytime. Many of the living-in maids are barely into adolescence, and many of them (by arrangement with their parents) are working under terms not unlike indentured servitude. To have the "help" of resident indigent relatives has certain obvious advantages.

Some Deeper Dimensions of Kinship

Expectations and Conflicts. The nuclear families which constitute most of Tripoli's households are normally linked to other nuclear families, through the brothers and sisters, and to a lesser extent the parents, of the parental pair in each nuclear family. The conventional expectations of Lebanese culture (and of Arab culture generally) are that adult brothers will remain in contact with each other, and be mutually loyal and helpful, throughout life. Each man is normally the head of his own nuclear family, but he also has obligations to his brothers and to his parents as long as they live. In a minority of cases, as we have seen, these considerations result in the extended family household, but normally the extended family is separated into different households. The conventional expectations of the brother-sister relationship are a little more complex. As long as she is un-married, a girl or young woman is thought of as being under the direct care of her parents, brothers, and other sisters. When she is married, the sentiments involved in that care are not erased, but the woman also comes under the care of her husband and his brothers. However, if the marriage ends in separation, or if the woman is widowed and has no children to care for her, her brothers are still responsible for her. Many of the dependent relatives living in Leba-nese nuclear family households are such women — sisters of the male head of the household.

To meet these obligations (however unwillingly) is a matter of family honor (*sharaf*). To fail to meet them (however willingly) is a matter of family shame (*'ayb*) if it is discovered by outsiders.

If the system of familial obligations really relied primarily on the motivations of altruism, unselfish affection, and solicitude, 'ayb would presumably not be a major phenomenon in Lebanese culture. How-ever, recent and sensitive observations (some of them by Leba-nese people) make it plain that the concern about 'ayb is quite acute. Consequently, it seems as if many Lebansese actually were behaving or feeling in ways which they know warrant 'ayb. One is further led to look for evidence of severe emotional conflicts in Lebanese familial relationships, and one finds it. True, it is usually hidden beneath the mask of "moral make-believe" which constitutes much of Lebanese verbal behavior. According to Khatchadourian,[7] there is a prevalence of the forced showing of respect, loyalty, and devotion to relatives, elders, and people in authority, a forced showing which covers actual feelings of great resentment and lack of respect. The latter feelings are exacerbated by the fact that the culture does not allow for their at least partial relief through frank expression. This lack of frank expression of feeling is related, Khatchadourian believes, to the coincidence of (1) religious precepts which make destructive thoughts as sinful as destructive acts and (2) the making of all sorts of intense demands on individuals' inward selves, characteristic of Lebanese behavior among relatives and friends.[8] The former leads to suppression, repression, and all the consequences of these processes exposed by the psychoanalytic approach to human behavior. The latter, an aspect of the personal character of Middle Eastern social life, consists of constant demands for the show of affection ("Do you love me more than you do that person?" "Why haven't you come to visit us for such a long time?" "We have been waiting for you every day," etc.). One defense against such onslaughts is to learn to keep one's true feelings to oneself and to put up a barrage of elaborate verbal reassurances and compliments. These *mujamalat* are a fine art in Lebanese and in Arab culture generally, and an even finer art is the second-guessing game as to whether the speaker really means all, some, or nothing of what he is saying.

So far, I have said only that hostile and negative feelings within the family are worsened by the various complex pretenses that they do not exist. They are occasionally expressed, as one might expect, by outbursts of passionate violence which further worsen them. The feud among kinsmen is a classic, but nevertheless actual, example of this, and it is of interest that Arab feuds are often described as having begun with trivial incidents. We may surmise that these incidents were only triggers or catalytic agents.

But closer to the root of the emotional conflicts within the family is the fact that, while the culture demands absolute solidarity among siblings, it also characteristically creates and perpetuates jealousies and hostilities among them. How? In the first place, there is some evidence that parents typically take advantage of sibling rivalry as a disciplinary device ("Why aren't you as smart as your brother?"

said not only privately but in the presence of outsiders). In the second place, while the legal system specifies equal inheritance among brothers, social realities make unequal demands upon them; frank discussion and adjustment is made difficult if not impossible.

The "Vulnerable Ego" Hypothesis. The ability of people to cope with these problems is impaired by the operation in both men and women of what I call the "vulnerable ego." The vulnerable ego most usually expresses itself in great sensitivity to real or imagined slights, in demands for the constant demonstration by others of their affection, and in the practice of emotional blackmail ("If you do not accept my hospitality, it means you do not love me, and I will therefore act accordingly."). Its genesis is in part that there is considerable Middle Eastern folklore the gist of which is that women are inherently inferior to men. Women as well as men internalize this notion and pass it along to their children. Girls acquire it from their parents, and their subsequent experiences may well reinforce it. The various legal advantages of males in Arab culture certainly would seem to reinforce it in the eyes of a growing girl. Yet there is considerable evidence that it is not true. Arab women tend to dominate the internal workings of households and thus appear as dominant personalities to both boys and girls. This is accentuated in the cases of women who actually are of greater than average intelligence and general competence. The girl is taught that she is by nature inferior or at least passive (often equated or confused with being inferior). She may, later on, try to compensate for her impaired ego by achieving success as a seductress, but the culture allows her only limited scope for such a talent. She is more likely to succeed as a fertile mother, but in this, almost by the definition of the situation, she as a fertile *woman* is still an inferior person.

Resuming the hypothesis, the female ego is made vulnerable by initial damage and later frustration. So, too, is the male ego, but it happens in a different way. Hamed Ammar's discussion [9] is one of the clearest descriptions of certain crucial aspects of the process. The baby boy, through the toddling stage anyway, is smothered by his mother's attention, affection, and oral gratification. Then, typically, when a younger sibling arrives, he is thrust rather abruptly into an all-male pecking order consisting of older brothers and/or cousins. Dominated and gratified by a female ego with which he cannot identify, he is now dominated by male egos with which he can identify, but only after having been passive to, and often humiliated by, them. Not infrequently, one encounters in the same adult man bullying and verbal bravado combined with self-pitying protestations of incompetence. This combination could well be a consequence of these earlier experiences.

This picture of the vulnerable ego and the several phenomena which I have connected with it is not particularly edifying. Many Arabs will not enjoy reading this discussion. I, too, have not enjoyed reading analyses by foreigners of certain self-defeating elements in American character structure. But such elements may well be present in every culture, and when descriptions and analyses of them may help to account for certain aspects of an important segment of life like the family, they are necessary.

I did not do any original research on these matters in Tripoli, but I did encounter there further examples of behavior which seem to be relevant. In Tripoli, I saw no overt patterns of kinship behavior not encountered elsewhere in Lebanon, and more widely in Arab culture. To the extent that the more covert aspects of kinship behavior discussed in this section are applicable to Arab and Lebanese culture, I assume them to be applicable to Tripoli. The reader is of course free to question these assumptions, but if he exercises this freedom he may be called upon to provide better explanations of the phenomena with which we are concerned. It must be understood that postulation of the vulnerable ego as a factor in certain aspects of Lebanese behavior does not imply that all Lebanese persons have it, or that its effects always obtrude into all relationships.

The fact remains that Lebanese, and Tripolitan, families continue to function as groups. One reason is that genuine affection and solicitude are interwoven with the various divisive factors just discussed. Another is that, regardless of how they may feel about each other, people know that their relatives are the source of ultimate support in times of crisis. One can without excuse ask a relative for help, and if he does not give it, he must at least justify himself. Apparently there is enough reciprocation of favors among kinsmen to maintain the system, though the emotional cost often seems to be considerable.

Wider Dimensions of Kinship

Kindreds. Beyond the individual's own extended family (his or her brothers and their children, or the father's brothers and their children, depending on the individual's age), there are two kindreds of some importance. The patrilateral kindred includes the extended family plus the married aunts, married sisters, and married female cousins. I have already mentioned the mutual expectations between a man and his married sister. The matrilateral kindred consists primarily of the mother's brothers and, to a lesser extent, of the mother's sisters.

There are no legal ties with these people (no inheritance is expected, for example), but there is some evidence that for this very reason youngsters can find some release and relief from emotional pressures among their matrilateral kinsmen. The subject has not been systematically studied in Arab culture, but it deserves to be. Of course, when the mother is a relative of the father, one's matrilateral relatives are not distinct from one's patrilateral ones. Despite its idealization among Muslims, the marriage of first cousins is unusual, although the marriage of more distant relatives is quite common. Table 34 provides a small glimpse into these practices in Tripoli. This sug-

TABLE 34. MARRIAGE PATTERNS IN TRIPOLI (AUB SAMPLE)

	I Relatives recently engaged or married to relatives			II Friends recently engaged or married to relatives		
Cases	Christian	Muslim	Total	Christian	Muslim	Total
None	7	9	16	5	3	8
Some	1	7	8	8	10	18
Total	8	16	24	13	13	26

gests that engagements and marriages between relatives are more common among the Muslims than among the Christians, but the table indicates nothing, of course, about the actual frequency of such marriages.

Lineages and Clans. The extended family is a patrilineal group, that is to say, membership is inherited (by cultural definition) only from males. In theory, this inheritance extends as far back in time as one is able (or cares) to trace one's ancestry. A group with a common patrilineal grandfather is an extended family. A group with a common patrilineal great-grandfather is a four-generation patrilineage. Many Lebanese can trace their ancestry back five or six generations to such an ancestor, and they often use his name as a "family" name. All people with this name and particular ancestry are members of the same five or six-generation patrilineage; the youngest members will include third or fourth cousins. Even more remote common ancestors (and consequently a larger number of more distant living relatives descended from them) may sometimes be recognized, but in such cases all the genealogical connections usually cannot be traced. Such groupings can be called "clans" to distinguish them from "lineages" in which all connections can be traced.

The literature is full of loose references to the importance of "clans" in Lebanese and Arab culture, and it is usually only a short step from them to loose references about "tribalism." The Lebanese themselves contribute to the imprecision by using three words interchangeably for nuclear family, extended family, lineage, and clan. These words are *'a'ila* (family), *bayt* (house), and *al* (people). The last is sometimes used in a wider sense than the others, but this wider sense is itself vague.

While no systematic studies have been made of this matter except within the confines of single Lebanese villages, there are certain impressions of the wider scene which seem to fit consistently together. First, the majority of Lebanese appear to be bound by enforced loyalties and obligations within their extended families — this including their first cousins on their father's side. But beyond the extended family, practices vary greatly. On the one hand, the divisive factors lead people to disregard kinship obligations beyond the extended family. Unless there is something to be gained, in other words, these obligations will be honored more and more in the breach as the relationships become more distant. On the other hand, if there is something to be gained, as there may be in the political sphere, reinforced ties at the lineage and clan levels may occur. And for those Lebanese who are not at any given moment participating in anything more than extended family relationships, there is always the potentiality of wider participation, for the ties of patrilineal kinship can in theory be extended and invoked ad infinitum.

Among the Druze, there is maximum recognition of remote patrilineal ties, and one often encounters references to the "tribalism" of the Druze. For those who tend to equate "tribalism" with the desert-dwelling Bedouin, it should be pointed out that the Druze are not Bedouin, nor were they, even in the remote past, sedentarized Bedouin.

Obligations and Evasions. In Tripoli, mutual obligations at the lineage or clan levels apparently occur among some people, but not all, in these categories:

(1) Poor, recent immigrants from rural areas, who need to pool their economic resources and to strengthen their weak political position by the strength of organized numbers.

(2) "Old families" of Tripoli (mostly Sunni, but some Orthodox) whose poorer, less influential members want to maintain close ties with their richer, more influential clansmen. When the latter have political ambitions, they can make good use of the loyalty of their poorer, remote relatives, as well, of course, as of the loyalty of those nonrelatives for whom they can do favors. The political bosses (*zu'ama*) build their power partly in this way, and those who seek to wrest their power from them try to do likewise. I will have more to say about this in the section on social class.

As for the rest of the Tripolitans (the great majority, probably), the issue of wider or narrower kinship organization beyond the extended family seems to be in constant flux. The less-favored people continually importune their more prosperous kinsmen for jobs, loans, and spouses, while the more prosperous kinsmen must decide either to grant the favor (perhaps in return for some immediate or potential price) or somehow to evade the importunity without incurring 'ayb. This problem of decisions is also seen in the solidarity (or lack of it) among Tripoli residents who originally came from the same village. Those recent immigrants who need help seek it from their better-established fellow villagers (if not from their relatives), and the latter must continually decide whether or not to help. Sometimes they must decide in effect to ostracize themselves, for the pressures can become unbearable, but because of 'ayb this tactic cannot be admitted openly. It is not really surprising that many Lebanese emigrants to foreign countries remain away for many years at a time — if not forever — often sending remittances home, but, if they do, controlling the gift-giving rather than being badgered by requests for it.

Residential Clusters. One Muslim informant said that it is not uncommon for brothers to wish to live near each other. This is, of course, the conventionally proper thing to say. If in fact the brothers in successive generations of a clan did live close to each other, the result would be a residential cluster of clansmen.

Other informants felt that in the days when Tripoli consisted only of the present Old City, there were definite residential clusters of clansmen in it, but when asked for specific examples, they did not provide them. In Chapter II, I mentioned a reference to a Bani Baraka quarter (no longer known by this name) and the possibility that the Rifa'iyyi quarter may be named for the Rifa'i clan once concentrated there. The telephone directory indicates that members of the large Barudi and Shami clans continue to be concentrated in the Old City, and there may well be others.

However, the significance of these clan residential clusters is not easy to determine. Formerly, when there was nothing but the Old City, many clan clusters may have occurred more by chance than deliberate will, for the area of the Old City was only about eighty-five to ninety acres. Nowadays, the fact that some appear to remain concentrated in the Old City may be indicative of some group-minded conservatism. The members of the most prominent lineages and clans appear now to be widely scattered in residence, at most exhibiting partial clustering. A Muslim informant said that the "thousand" members of Bayt 'Awayda lived in Zahriyyah. Probably many of them do; eight of the eighteen 'Awayda telephone subscribers live in Zahriyyah, but the rest are scattered. Several of the Karamis live in Karm Qullah, the quarter where 'Abdul-Hamid Karami's mansion is located (most of them do not live in the mansion itself), but other Karamis are scattered elsewhere. The 'Abdul-Wahhab clan is concentrated in the Buwwabi quarter of the Mina, but the numerous 'Adras are scattered all over Tripoli.

Whatever people's personal desires may be in regard to residential kinship clusters (and we can safely predict a number of contradictory ones), there is an economic factor very important in any decisions about place of residence. Persons occupying the same house or apartment since before World War II have the advantage of a rent ceiling enacted at that time. Such persons may continue to occupy such premises out of economic necessity only. More prosperous relatives may, on the other hand, prefer to pay the price of newer, more fashionable accommodations. These realities, some informants themselves suggested, tend to separate brothers and close cousins, not to mention more distant relatives. Only three persons in the AUB Sample had relatives other than their own nuclear family living in the same building as themselves. Twenty-three had relatives living in the same street or quarter, while fifteen had relatives living in other parts of Tripoli. Kinship clusters may well be less frequent and less sharply defined in the newer quarters of apartment buildings than they were (and occasionally may still be) in the houses of the Old City. But this in itself does not necessarily imply any breakdown in kinship structure; in fact, it may even provide some relief from the tensions physical concentration can magnify.

There is bound to be some kinship clustering in the regional-sectarian residential clusters: the 'Alawites in Bab al-Tibbani, the Hadchite Maronites in the Qubbah, and the Zgharta Maronites in Hayy Mutran, but in these cases the kinship clustering at most reinforces the other criteria of unity which seem to be the paramount ones.

Familial Awqaf. What holds the members of Tripolitan lineages and clans together is largely an informal network of reciprocal, advantageous expectations. Beyond the extended family, there are few legally binding ties, but there are two phenomena which deserve mention. One of these is property held as waqf dhurri (see Chapter III). This will be inherited in the same lineage until that lineage either "dies out" or ceases to have any male members who can perpetuate it. Common interest in waqf dhurri property, if nothing else, can serve to perpetuate awareness of lineage. However, according to the Islamic-Ottoman inheritance laws applying to everyone (including Christians), this property is inherited on the basis of equal shares to all heirs. Hence, waqf dhurri properties are subdivided and resubdivided in each successive generation to the point where each person's own share may be infinitesimal.

As a result of this, there are in Tripoli not only single parcels of land with many owners, but even single floors of buildings with many owners. This is common enough to have been remarked upon by S. G. Shiber, the Arab city planner, and by one of my informants in Tripoli. The possibility of bitter quarrels, rather than greater solidarity, resulting from this system is very great. Its troublesome effects can be, and are often in fact, mitigated by consolidation through purchase and exchange, but these procedures tend to eliminate the lineage emphasis in the whole matter. When the government takes property by eminent domain in Tripoli, it fixes the amount of compensation, but it leaves the division of this sum to the discretion of the various owners. Their problems will be very much easier if their rights are certified by specific deed than if they are traditional shares of lineal inheritance.

One implication of all this should now be clear: Tripolitan lineages and clans are linkages of interpersonal sentiments, but they are not corporate groups.

Family Associations. The other phenomenon deserving mention consists of the efforts of a number of Lebanese in recent decades to incorporate the lineages or clans to which they belong. This is done by certain members of a kin group forming a "family association" (*jama'iyat al-'a'ila* or *jama'iyat al-al*), which has a charter, officers, and membership criteria, and is formally registered with the Ministry of the Interior.

Between 1928 and 1961, 210 such associations were registered. The earliest ones were apparently mostly Christian, and mostly in the Beirut area or the mountains adjacent to it. In 1961, 102 were Christian, 95 were Muslim, and 13 were Druze. The proportion of Muslim ones was apparently increasing, especially among the Shi'ites of southern Lebanon. "Family solidarity" and mutual charitable or educational benefits were the most commonly stated purposes of the associations, and active membership (as opposed to membership automatically ascribed by inheritance of the name) usually entailed the payment of dues. In several instances, women apparently lost their membership when they were married.

These associations are currently under study by social scientists in Beirut, and as yet many important questions about them are unanswered. In particular, the most obvious explanation of them (that they are efforts to preserve the traditional structure and advantages of lineages which are otherwise felt to be doomed to extinction) remains to be tested. In any case, in 1961, the associations seemed to be least common in northern Lebanon, and only six were registered in Tripoli:

Al Kabbara (Muslim). Founded 1946. Purpose: family solidarity and mutual benevolence. (There were 49 Kabbaras in the telephone book, and it was one of the recognized distinguished lineages in the city.

Al Tabbikha (Muslim). Founded 1951. Purpose: family solidarity and mutual benevolence. Membership: over age 18 and inheritance of the name. (There were two in the telephone book.)

Al Dabbusi (Muslim). Founded 1953. Purpose: family solidarity and mutual benevolence. Membership: name, application, fees, and oath. (There were 14 in the telephone book.)

Al 'Alush (Muslim). Founded 1955. Purpose: family solidarity and mutual benevolence. Membership: by application and oath. (There were three in the telephone book, all in Bab al-Tibbani.)

Al Hajr (Muslim). Founded 1959. Purpose: family solidarity and mutual benevolence. Membership: by application of people over 18 with the name. (There were eleven in the telephone book, over half in the Old City.)

Al al-Khoury (Christian). Founded 1960. Purpose: family solidarity and mutual benevolence. Membership: name and paying dues. (Khoury means "priest" and is a very frequent Christian family name. Common possession of it alone does not imply kinship. Therefore, this must be a particular Al al-Khoury.)

In 1961–62, none of Tripoli's most distinguished lineages, except Al Kabbara, was incorporated. Furthermore, Christian informants were puzzled about the whole phenomenon. Some of them seem never to have heard of it. As to the AUB Sample, only two persons indicated that their families belonged to associations, and neither of these had headquarters in Tripoli.

HOME-CENTERED PERSPECTIVES

One author has discussed at some length "the usual Moslem town which is simply a scene for the unfolding of family life." [10] Corollary to the elements in this depiction were the traditional Muslim urbanite's tendency to limit his public behavior to trade, worship in the mosque, and gossip in the coffee house and bath. Otherwise, he had no sense of municipal or civic responsibility and simply hid himself at home with his already hidden family.[11] Much of the preceding material has borne on these points, showing that, despite many innovations, there still appear to be in Tripoli some very subtle continuations of attitudes and reactions which fit Planhol's generalizations. More needs to be said on this subject, however, and in this section I shall focus on certain aspects of life in Tripoli which seem to be fundamentally home-centered.

The Roles of Women

Conflicting Values. The traditional role of women in Tripoli (and in all Muslim cities) was strictly domestic. Without doubt, the great majority of Tripoli women are still primarily concerned with the care of their children and households. This is also true in the most industrialized cultures where, however, a many-sided debate is in full career as to how women most satisfactorily can find fulfillment in various alternative occupations. The debate and the experimentations which accompany it appear to be quite far from resolution, and the feelings and attitudes of all people concerned are as confused as they are intense.

Lebanese culture has already embarked upon this stressful reappraisal and readjustment. In fact, it has probably moved more quickly into it than did, at first, the industrializing West. In Tripoli, education for girls at least through secondary school appears to be widely accepted, even by some of the more conservative Muslims. Of course, one reason for the acceptance by some parents is that such education has become fashionable, but there is also recognition (and probably some apprehension) that it is potentially a widener of horizons and an opener of opportunities. Most of the secondary school girls in Tripoli will not go on to university studies (necessarily elsewhere), but some of them will, and many already have. In the past, most of them have eventually become mothers and primarily housewives, but there are women physicians, too, in Tripoli, and the girls know it. They are also exposed in the newspapers and magazines to open discussions of the debate itself and to examples of actual women who have nondomestic occupations.

Nurses have for some time been in this category, but now the variety is widening. And for those who probably say to themselves and to each other, "Yes, but I'll still get married and when I do, I'll give all that up," there are the novels of Layla Ba'lbaki (member of a Shi'a family from southern Lebanon), which uncompromisingly stand for complete freedom of choice of occupations for both men and women as well as for a single standard of sexual behavior for both. While they know that they are unlikely to experience all that Ba'lbaki advocates, at the very least they can think about approximating it. In Beirut, there are some waitresses, women ticket sellers at cinemas, and even some women attendants at automobile service stations. In conservative eyes, this verges on the unrespectable if not scandalous. Yet in one of the Beirut weekly magazines there was an illustrated article whose gist was that these women and girls are entirely respectable and should be treated accordingly.[12] In some cases, of course, apparent signs of "emancipation" may by their very frivolity conceal a fundamentally unchanged attitude toward the roles of women. The beauty-queen complex is a conspicuous and frequently encountered example in Lebanon, and a Tripoli girl (a member of one of the incorporated Muslim lineages mentioned in the last section) was elected and displayed as "Spring Queen" at Beirut College for Women in 1962.[13]

According to a column in one of the Tripoli newspapers, "Tripoli women cannot quickly get on an equal footing with men. They should work for the betterment of Lebanon and their children rather than worrying about status." The author was a woman, and she proceeded to describe a series of interviews with nurses in Tripoli hospitals and to discuss the fact that the city needs more social workers and more education in health and civic responsibility.[14] In Chapter III, I noted that some Tripoli women are already at work (at least on a part-time basis) on such problems, but clearly a need is felt for more concentrated efforts, and perhaps for less conventionally acceptable ones.

The problem of expanding what is now conventionally acceptable (home and family-centered activities) apparently remains more profound than might be supposed from what has been said so far. This was very neatly shown in a series of articles published in the Beirut newspaper *L'Orient* in 1961–62. In one of these, the author (a Frenchwoman) reported on conversations and visits she had had with several young Lebanese women. All were middle class, well educated, unmarried, and some even had professional jobs. All were also modern in terms of their chic clothing and coiffures, and they represented the Maronite, Sunni, and Druze sects. Despite all the modernity, all knew that they were expected to become housewives and mothers, in preparation for which some had for years been working on their trousseaus. Yet each was strictly limited in the opportunities she had to meet men. "Dating" was virtually impossible; one mentioned that she could go to parties only in the company of her brother (a lawyer who was usually too busy to oblige), and another said that she had never been to a beach in a bathing suit. For them, regardless of some of their individual ambitions, the future was likely to be that of married housewife, and it was likely to be a marriage closely circumscribed by sexual segregation and family supervision. One of them expressed confidence that, in time, Lebanese women would achieve a greater degree of essential (as opposed to superficial) independence, but she pointed out that such changes necessarily take place imperceptibly.[15]

Work and Social Class. It is important to keep in mind that two of the ways in which the roles of Lebanese women seem to be restricted to home-centered matters are simply examples of limitations experienced by Lebanese men also. Lebanese women have the right to vote, but they do not vote very often. Nor do men vote often, for reasons explained in Chapter IV. Second, for middle and upper class women (and my references have primarily been to them), manual tasks are considered menial and degrading and are therefore avoided. For this reason alone (there are others), a Lebanese middle class college girl would not even consider taking a job as, for example, a waitress in a summer hotel, though there are many such hotels in Mount Lebanon. The same kind of restriction applies, however, to middle class Lebanese males.

As to the lower class, semiliterate, or illiterate women of Tripoli, their activities are also home-centered, but by reason of their minimal educations they are probably less aware of the debate about the roles of women, and less able to experiment with new alternatives. Out of financial necessity, however, many of them have to work outside of their own homes, often as domestic servants. The women of the Hadchite community in al-Qubbah, whose menfolk are mostly laborers and small shopkeepers, have made a group speciality of daytime domestic service (they will not "live in" with their employers).

In Chapter V it was pointed out that there were 1,124 women working in 2,511 productive establishments in North Lebanon in 1962. They amounted to about 10 per cent of the labor force in these establishments. It is safe to assume that virtually all of them were lower class women, and that some of them were working in textile mills. I do not know anything about their conditions of work in North Lebanon or Tripoli, but Mme. Delprat published an interview with a Beirut textile manufacturer revealing conditions which, if representative of Beirut, are very likely representative of Tripoli also. This textile plant employed 600 people (about two-thirds the size of 'Arida's mill in Tripoli), half of whom were women. This sex ratio was the same as that of the Lebanese textile industry as a whole. On the average, the women were employed for five to ten years, often beginning about the age of fifteen and remaining until they got married. Most were recruited either through relatives or neighbors who already worked in the plant. They worked 48 hours a week at an average of about $0.20 an hour which was about 40 per cent less than the men's wages. All were unmarried, and the employer implied that husbands would not permit their wives to do such work.[16]

The existence of day-care nurseries in Tripoli implies, of course, that there are some working married women there who cannot afford maids and are therefore probably lower class women.

The prestige of having a maid, preferably a resident one, is something to which all middle class Tripolitans (and Lebanese) aspire, and the labor market is such that even minor clerical workers can actually have them. This is, again, a reflection of the disdain of manual labor, an established theme in the culture. Another expression of it is the middle class man's avoidance of household maintenance chores. One of them told me in all seriousness that he would never answer the door dressed in old clothes for fear that if strangers were calling, they would think he was a repairman or servant. Lounging about in pajamas, however, is a display of leisure and therefore prestige, and in Abu Samra close friends walked across the street to each other's houses, late in the afternoon, in pajamas and brocaded dressing gowns.

Maids are apparently not hired primarily to take care of the children so that the mother will be free to go out in the evenings. They sometimes serve this function, of course, but "going out in the evening" consists primarily of visiting relatives and friends *en famille*. Babies and young children are often taken along or left at home with older siblings. The only other night life in Tripoli is going to the movies, and this, too, is likely to be either a family affair or an affair of groups of young men and groups of young women who "mix" only at a distance.

Upper class women in Tripoli have regular days on which they receive guests. Probably few if any of these women resemble odalisques in harems, but among middle class people in Tripoli they have the reputation of being idly luxurious and of indulging too much in gambling. No foreign man could possibly get any direct information on what happens at these gatherings, and the following description may or may not be fairly applicable to Tripoli. However, it was written by a Palestinian Arab novelist who put the words into the mouth of a 20-year-old upper class Muslim girl living in present-day Baghdad:

Mother receives a flood of women visitors every Tuesday. From morning till midnight they play cards and drink tea, and talk, talk, talk like a thousand parrots about husbands, children, boy lovers, girl lovers. You would think the whole of the Arabian Nights were coming back to life in the shape of these fat-breasted women. Finally they go away leaving behind their gossip, their stories of sex and money and scandal, hanging over the dirty plates and glasses and remnants of food and shells of pistachio nuts.[17]

Rites of Passage

Some General Points. Rites of passage are ceremonies which mark the transition of an individual from one socially important phase of life to another. Among Christian and Muslim Arabs, the most important rites of passage are weddings and funerals. In addition, boys' circumcision ceremonies are important among the Muslims. All of these ceremonies have been described in some detail in the Middle Eastern literature, but those descriptions often fail to specify whether they are of idealized patterns in the past or of procedures actually performed at the time of writing.

In all my wanderings in Tripoli, I saw only part of one rite of passage, the Maronite funeral procession described below. I was not invited to any circumcisions or weddings and had no occasion to attend any funerals.

Thus there remain some unanswered questions about these aspects of life in Tripoli. Do wedding and circumcision processions still move through the streets, as they did in Cairo long ago when Lane saw them? I certainly did not see any. Informants said that they "sometimes" did. To what extent are bride-wealth payment negotiations, sexually suggestive dancing, and display of a stained cloth as proof of the bride's virginity still components of Muslim weddings? Again, informants said that they "sometimes" were, but they also admitted that these things were more frequent in the past. Newspaper accounts make it clear that some of the trappings of western weddings have in part been adopted by middle class Muslims. However, brides may privately show a bloodied towel or cloth to their closest relatives in order to forestall a favorite gambit of some erring husbands: claiming grounds for divorce on the charge that the wife was not a virgin in the first place.

One reason for the relative inconspicuousness of all these ceremonials is that they are home-centered, even if the mosque or church may also be involved. Weddings must, by Lebanese law, be performed by a sectarian official, but the actual ceremonies consist primarily of observances at the bride's and the groom's homes.

Similarly, when a person dies, the body is kept in the home until the time of burial, and traditionally it is cared for by friends and relatives. Among middle class people living in apartments in the new sections of Tripoli, it is customary for the close friends of a newly bereaved family temporarily to take charge of the latter's household, supplying food, preparing meals, and helping to receive callers. This is similar to village behavioral patterns, and if it happens among this class of people, one can safely assume that it also does among poor people in the older parts of the city.

Muslim funeral processions are definitely standard, but they are usually less conspicuous than the Christian ones. If a Muslim dies before the last call to prayer in the afternoon, he or she is buried on the same day. If the death occurs later, a vigil is kept around the body overnight, but it is buried as soon as possible the next morning. The death is announced by a crier in the markets, followed later, in some cases, by a printed notice. Under these circumstances, a Muslim funeral and funeral procession can hardly be very elaborate. The body is not put in a coffin, but is wrapped up, marked with a fez if the deceased was a man, and carried to the cemetery on a litter. In contrast, Christian funerals may take place any time up to three days after death, and so the ceremonies can be more elaborate. If there are any morticians in Tripoli, I did not hear or see anything of them. None, in any case, had a telephone. (In Beirut, there were fourteen morticians with telephones. Judging from their names, eleven were definitely Christian, the other three not unmistakably Muslim.)

A Funeral Procession. During an afternoon in December 1961, I watched a Maronite funeral procession. The bracketed comments in the following description were received when I later discussed the event with informants.

I was walking toward the Tal on Shari' al-Mina, and just west of the Boulevard I saw about fifteen people standing around on the sidewalk and among the automobiles parked in the center of this broad street. Then I noticed that adjoining balconies were fairly crowded with people looking down at about two dozen preadolescent or early adolescent girls wearing brown or blue uniforms and berets, each in charge of a floral wreath or cross. [These were orphans recruited from one of the institutions.] There were a couple of nuns with them. They were standing in the street along the curb, more or less in formation, adjacent to an alleyway which gives access to the off-street entry of an apartment building.

A priest and a crucifer emerged from the alleyway and went to the head of the column of girls. In leisurely fashion, some men donned broad black velvet bandoleers on each of which was worded in big silver Arabic letters, "Maronite Burial Society." When the procession formed, they simply carried by the corners a large black velvet cloth with religious symbols embroidered on it. [This is one of the societies mentioned in Chapter III; its members charge a fee for their services at the funerals of well-to-do people, like this one, and use the proceeds to pay the expenses of poor peoples' funerals.]

An automobile with an ornate wooden coffin sticking out of the trunk behind, screeched to a halt in front of the alley, and the coffin (the ceremonial outer one which is not buried) was carried inside.

After about five minutes, several women dressed in stylish black appeared. Evidently the major mourners, they showed little emotion. Soon thereafter, a gray-bearded priest, wearing a large pectoral cross and various red accessories, and a younger priest, wearing a draped hat, appeared. [They were the Maronite bishop and an Orthodox archimandrite. Priests of different sects often attend the same funeral.] A couple of monks dressed in white and several more priests joined them, and then rather abruptly, it seemed, the coffin was carried out by an assortment of men.

The procession formed quickly, and the order of march was:

1. Crucifer, priest, and nuns.
2. Flower girls in two columns.
3. Man with religious banner.
4. The major mourners.
5. The burial society men with their cloth.
6. The bishop and most of the other priests.
7. The coffin carried by rapidly changing pallbearers about thirty to forty men.
8. About twenty women.
9. A pickup truck with an ornate black and silver back — the hearse which later took the body from the church to the cemetery.

There were no wailing women. Besides the shuffling of feet, the only sounds were the alternating chants of various priests. They moved fairly slowly across the Boulevard, but even so, someone had to run up to the head to tell the leaders to slow down so that the procession would not get separated. They went right through the busiest part of the Tal and Sahit Saraya 'Adimi, and northward on Shari' Kinayis to the Maronite church, then disappeared into it. The carrying of the coffin from the home to the church is also done in villages. [It is not always done in Tripoli, but it is considered to be a special honor to the deceased.]

The police did nothing to stop the traffic, and yet no cars barged into the procession. In fact, all along the way, people stopped what they were doing and stood silently watching it pass. However, as soon as the rear of it cleared the Tal, the cars which had in fact become congested behind it began honking furiously at each other.

Somewhat later, at the height of rush hour (4:20 to 5:00 P.M.), there was a major traffic jam at Sahit Saraya 'Adimi. Four streets meet here, two from the Tal, while the other two lead to two big Catholic schools as well as being on the main route from Bab al-Tibbani to Bab al-Raml. The normal traffic of cars, buses, and trucks is augmented at this hour by school buses and the cars of parents chauffeuring their children home from school (several children could easily walk to school but do not). Cars, trucks, buses, even carts, were trying to go in every direction, including northward on Shari' Kinayis, which was completely blocked with traffic coming the other way. Half a dozen policemen were at times doing their best — urging along cars which insisted on stopping in such a way as to block traffic further. However, one of them lost his temper outrageously, began cuffing pedestrians, and nearly came to blows with a man who had remonstrated with him. Nor could they systematically manage to stop one direction of flow to let another move for a while. In fact, they did not seem very well coordinated with each other. However, they did persuade a number of cars not to try to force their way north on Shari' Kinayis, down which, crowded among trucks and carts, the flower-bedecked hearse was inching its way toward the cemetery in Abu Samra.

NEIGHBORHOODS AND QUARTERS

Domestic Concealment

Although it may not be so well protected, legally, against government search and seizure, the Tripolitan's home is psychologically at least as much his castle as is the Englishman's. This is immediately apparent from the physical exteriors of the houses in the Old City. Those with storefronts in the street floors have no readily observable entries. One must look for, or inquire about, the front door. The windows above are high, shuttered, and often barred. In the dead-end streets and alleys where there are fewer storefronts, one is often faced by the blank walls of the street floors, in which the doors are small and heavy. There are no numbers and no nameplates — no ways in which one can deduce the identity of the inhabitants except by inquiry and eventual enlightenment by someone who knows them. A cross, carved or painted over a door, will of course suggest sectarian identity, but there are very few of these. More frequently (but still only in a minority of cases) one will see a pious Muslim phrase, such as "May God forgive the sins of the Faithful," painted over doorways, but this does not really help very much to identify the occupants.

To find a Tripolitan in his house in the Old City, one must either know him personally or locate him through someone else who does. And the latter, if he chooses, can easily warn the person one seeks in advance of one's finding him.

The exterior surfaces of these old houses are characteristically marred and defaced, and it is very difficult to deduce from them the socioeconomic status of the occupants. Within, there may equally well be (1) dark, dirty, crumbling, overcrowded rooms or (2) sumptuously furnished, carefully scrubbed and polished rooms around a small courtyard. I have seen both within equally battered exteriors.

These domestic arrangements, which very much assist the Tripolitan householder in concealing his identity and private circumstances from strangers, also bespeak the intensely personal and family-centered life he leads. I have already considered several aspects of that life. I must now add that besides the man's business activities and the woman's shopping, there is, ordinarily, relatively little social life outside of their own (or friends' or relatives') private homes. The chief exceptions are (for men) sitting in cafés or coffeehouses; for married couples or family groups, going to the movies or taking promenades; and for men and women separately, spending some leisure hours in one of the hammams.

Apart from these exceptions, and apart from children's play groups seen and heard outdoors, neighborhood activities consist primarily of visits within people's private homes. Consequently, neighborhood activities are very difficult to observe. This is probably one of the reasons why the I.R.F.E.D. Report stated that there was little or no "community spirit" in the quarters of Tripoli sampled (see Appendix A). Another reason for this judgment, I assume, was that there are few group interests apart from the familial, the sectarian, and the commercial.

So far in this section, I have referred only to houses, and by implication, neighborhoods, in the Old City. All that I have said, however, applies almost equally as well to the newer parts of the city. This is a very important matter. The wider streets and the modernistic architecture, with its conspicuous balconies and large glass windows, do not seem to accompany any less private or less secluded attitudes toward the family. The exteriors, foyers, and stairways of new apartment buildings quickly become scarred and scrawled upon. There may well be banks of tenants' letterboxes in the foyer, but only some of them are labeled, as are only some of the doors of the apartments themselves. To find someone's home in Abu Samra, Hayy Mutran, or any of the new sections, one must first locate his building, which will probably be known by the name of its owner and will never have a street number. The best way of doing this is to inquire in the small shops (mostly groceries, cleaners, hairdressers, barbers, and sellers of household furnishings) which typically occupy the ground floors of the modern apartment buildings. When one finds the building, one will probably have to ask the concierge for the specific apartment. Some highly westernized people have labels outside their doors — handwritten signs or calling cards — and some dignitaries (for example, the Mufti and the Presbyterian minister) even have brass nameplates, but these are extremely rare.

Neighborhood Stability

Many people who have moved from houses in the Old City to apartments in newer sections have mixed feelings about the move. As against the greater prestige of living in an apartment in a new section, there are some inconveniences, such as not having exclusive rights to the roof, noisy neighbors overhead, and western-style toilets on which one has to sit. (Modern fixtures designed for the squatting position are available but are not always installed in the new buildings.) To some extent, however, the balcony substitutes for the old roof as a place for drying laundry and fruit, for keeping potted plants, lounging, shouting to neighbors, and watching the activities in the street. Although there is a word for apartment or flat (*sha'i*) it does not seem to be used very much, and certainly not as much as the hallowed word *bayt*, which not only literally means house, but also "home" and kinfolk.

However, I was not able to get adequate information on any regrets at losing neighbors as a result of moving. Perhaps for those who moved voluntarily, there either were none or there were adequate compensations. Once established in new quarters, people tend to remain for a long time in the same place and thus to form ties with their new neighbors, if they did not know them already. Among the AUB Sample, the median and modal length of time lived in the same apartment had been seven years. All members of the sample knew, at least slightly, all or nearly all of the other families living in their building. However, the median number of families per building was only six (the range was 2 to 42). Each knew who owned the building in which he lived, and half of the owners were either relatives or friends. Very few of the really close friends of members of the sample lived in the same building or in nearby buildings — a situation similar to that revealed by a number of studies of modern North American cities. Other, older informants conveyed the same impressions: that they had lived in their present abodes for a long time, as had their friends in theirs, that they knew most of the other families in their own building as well as some of those in adjoining buildings, but that the dwellings of their best friends and relatives were widely scattered. None of these informants, however, participated in the sectarian, regional, and kinship clusters. Such clusters occur sporadically in both the Old City and the various newer parts of Tripoli.

The Hara Model and Tripoli

The composite description by Gibb and Bowen of eighteenth-century Middle Eastern cities provides us with a model of them on the eve of the onset of westernization. An important feature of this model is the division of the city into *harat*, or quarters, each with its shaykh, markets, mosques, and baths and a distinct kinship, sectarian, or regional identity of its own.[18] As Sjoberg shows, such a *"barrio* system" was characteristic of preindustrial cities in a rather wide variety of cultures.

The question is, however, to what extent modern Tripoli is the outgrowth of the effects of partial westernization on such a system of multiple, self-contained quarters. Probably eighteenth-century

Tripoli had nothing so full-blown as what Gibb and Bowen describe. The most important consideration here is comparative size. In the eighteenth century, Cairo and Aleppo had 263,000 and 150,000 people, respectively, according to Gibb and Bowen, who use these cities in their primary examples. In 1784, Tripoli had only 4,000 or 5,000 people. Cairo had 53 quarters as described above, with an average population, it follows, of roughly 4,500 people. In other words, the whole of Tripoli was about the same size as one of Cairo's average quarters.

Under such circumstances, it is very difficult to conceive of eighteenth-century Tripoli's having been divided into a large number of compartmentalized quarters, each with its own mosque, baths, and markets. In fact, the available evidence points to the probability that apart from having a distinctive Christian quarter with its Jewish appendage, old Tripoli consisted of houses with a single market system and one grand mosque plus a number of lesser ones. There are still a number of arched-over sections of streets, but none of them showed any trace of pivots or sockets for the hinged gates which would have closed off one quarter from another, as indeed was done in the larger Arab cities. Four sections of Tripoli include the word *bab* (gate) in their names. However, three of them (Bab al-Tibbani, Bab al-Raml, and Bab Hadadin) could have referred originally to gates or entrances on the edges of town, rather than to gates internally dividing the town. The fourth, Bab Hadid, is in the center of the Old City near the most upstream bridge, but one informant said he thought that the gate in question had actually been a framework of iron bars close enough together to prevent the passage of large animals but not of people.

If old Tripoli did not have compartmentalized, semiautonomous subcommunities (*harat*), it did have a number of different sections or neighborhoods. The present-day Old City still has such named sections. Appendix A describes each of these, and I have previously made a number of references to them. At this point, it seems advisable to recapitulate the names and to discuss some additional ideas concerning these neighborhoods and small quarters.

The Quarters of Tripoli

As one studies the map closely, one gets the impression that they seem to fall into three categories. Some seem to consist of a primary street with subsidiary alleys or streets. Others seem to consist of a network of streets or alleys without any one being primary. The third category consists of sections which include open spaces, all of which were on the edges of old Tripoli before the twentieth-century growth began.

Many of these names are generally familiar to those Tripolitans to whom I talked. This is particularly true, however, of the specialized or strongly commercial areas. It is not so true of the less commercial and more heavily residential areas. In the latter cases, many informants could not locate the sections and sometimes were not even familiar with the names. This seems to be a reflection of the home-centered aspect of the whole matter of neighborhoods and quarters, wherein many names are evolved and primarily used by the residents themselves. Such names are of no interest or use to outsiders unless they have business in the quarter concerned, and this is most likely to occur only in the case of commercially specialized quarters.

THE QUARTERS OF THE OLD CITY

1. Primary streets (primarily commercial) with offshoots (primarily residential).
    Bazarkan (cloth sellers)
    Kindarjiyyin (shoe sellers)
    Nahhasiyyin (coppersmiths)
    Khayyatin (tailors)
    Sagha (general food shops, originally named for goldsmiths)
    Nuri (named for the Nuri Hammam; includes the actual street of goldsmiths)
    'Attarin (originally named for perfume sellers; actually a segment of Sagha)
    Swayqah
    Suq al-Qamih } (food markets, east bank of river)

2. Networks of streets
    Rifa'iyyi (named for a family, primarily residential)
    Bab Hadadin (named either for a family or for formerly resident blacksmiths. Primarily residential except for the part which is the southern continuation of Sagha and 'Attarin)
    Ahwi Hitti (Hitti's coffeehouse. Southern end of Sagha-'Attarin-Bab Hadadin main street)
    Rimani (mostly residential, but with some shoemakers, adjoining Kindarjiyyi)
    Tirbi'a (furniture makers and residential)
    Hayy Nasara and Har Yihud (Christian and Jewish quarters.

These names are going out of use and are being replaced either by Tirbi'a or Shari' Kinayis)

Birkat al-Millaha ⎫ (Salty well. Shoe and leather workers. Suq al-
Suq al-Haraj ⎭ Haraj is a single, covered intersection of streets)

Bab Hadid (food stores and residential)

Tal'a al-Zahir (residential, on slope below al-Qubbah)

'Uqbi al-Mufti (residential, on slope below al-Qubbah)

3. Old Peripheral

Mawlawiyyi (begins with houses near Bab Hadid and becomes a path between the citadel and the river, leading to the Tikkiyah of the Mawlawi dervishes)

Bab al-Raml (includes large cemetery and used to be the main exit toward Beirut)

Sahit Saraya 'Adimi (site of the nineteenth-century Saraya which was city hall, provincial capitol, and governor's residence and was, like its two successors, built on the edge of the town; commercial and residential)

Dibbagha (tanners, area on river downstream from main old settlement; commercial except for crowded tenements in Khan al-Askar)

Bab al-Tibbani (Hay gate, main exit to Syria; wholesale foodstuffs and some residential)

Some Problems of Names and Terminology. Hassan el-Hajjé includes in his monograph on the Tripoli dialect a description of Tripoli in French with a parallel text in Tripoli Arabic transliterated into romanized phonetic characters. El-Hajjé is a native of Tripoli, and so one cannot disregard what he says about it. Nevertheless, his rather crude map places some quarters in accordance with my findings, but shows Rimani (a rather small and obscure quarter) as actually straddling the river. However, he mentions two names of quarters in the Old City, al-'Adsi (Lentils) and Jisrayn (Two Bridges), which I did not encounter at all; yet some Tripolitans may well use them. Al-'Adsi might loosely refer to some shops which sell lentils (just as some people refer to Suq al-Samak [Fish Market], meaning several shops more or less close together in the Old City), or it could be the name of an actual section. As to Jisrayn, the unanswered question is, *which* two bridges?

These and a number of other considerations lead to the idea that, although the section names are the primary location labels in the city, there is considerable lack of standardization in their use, and only some of them are widely known. Natives of Tripoli did not know some of the section names, and an informant who had been a member of the police force did not know where some of them were located. It was members of the post office department who were the most helpful in supplying the names. There probably exist many section names I never learned.

Home-centeredness is, I think, part of the explanation for this situation. More of it may be made clearer by listing, categorizing, and discussing the names of the newer sections of Tripoli. First, it must be understood that there are several words used for the idea of section or quarter itself. They are: *har* or *hara* (plural *harat*); *hayy* (plural *ahya'*); *shari'* (plural *shuwari'*); *muhalla* (plural *muhallat*). *Muhalla* is a rather generalized word meaning "district" or "place." I did not hear it in Tripoli, but el-Hajjé uses it, though apparently interchangeably with *hayy*. The root meaning of *hayy* is that of "living." *Shari'* means "street," but when coupled with a name it very frequently does not refer to a single thoroughfare but to a network of them (a section).

Lebanese friends and colleagues discussed at length the connotations and denotations of *har*, *hayy*, and *shari'*. It was admitted that all three are used to mean section or quarter. However, it was suggested that *har* originally meant a compound of buildings and therefore implies a small, tightly knit neighborhood, whereas *hayy* implies a somewhat larger and looser district but not so much so as *shari'*. But we had to agree, citing specific cases, that the actual usages do not consistently follow this logic. In Tripoli, *har* is used only rarely, but two instances are Har Yihud (an actual compound of buildings) and Harat al-Ramli (one of the new sections of the Mina). *Hayy* is used somewhat more frequently, but for places of different ages, such as Hayy Nasara (in Old City), Hayy Jadid (New Quarter, an early twentieth-century development in al-Qubbah), and Hayy Mutran, a very new section. *Shari'*, however, is used the most frequently of all, and it may refer to parts of the Old City (Shari' Bazarkan or Shari' Sagha) or to newer parts, where it may refer either to whole sections ('Azmi, Latifi, Qubbah, Abu Samra, and Tal) or to what are in fact very nearly just single thoroughfares (Sintral, Yazbik, and Rahbat).

These statements are based partly on my experiences of living in Tripoli and partly on study of the telephone directory, whose subscribers supplied their own addresses. If one seeks someone who lives on Shari' X, there is no way of knowing beforehand whether X is a specific street or a section. One can only inquire in the manner described earlier. Officially every thoroughfare has its own name, but most of these are known "only by the electric company," one amused informant told me. Only a few major streets have name signs, they are not posted at every intersection, and the official name may be entirely different from the name that most people actually use. However, the whole matter of official, specific names and signs is new, and in some cases it *is* affecting public usage. For example, the segment of Shari' al-Mina directly west of the Tal is officially Shari' Riad al-Sulh (a former premier of Lebanon), and some residents use this name, but no one, as far as I know, refers to Shari' Zahriyyah as Shari' al-Istiqlal (Independence Street) though that is what its sign says. The posting of some of the official names has simply added more possible alternatives to an already ambiguous situation. But if one knows where one's friends, relatives, and customers live, and if one is not eager to make it easy for strangers to find one's own home, these confusions may well not be considered a serious inconvenience. This seems to be exactly what most Tripolitans (and other Lebanese) do feel, at least unconsciously, and there is little difference in this regard between people who live in the Old City and those who live in one of the newer parts.

The names of the sections of the newer parts of Tripoli also seem to fall into categories, but they are slightly different from those of the Old City.

THE QUARTERS OF THE NEW CITY

1. Primary quarters (networks of streets). Most of them are located on Map 3.

    Shari' al-Tal (commercial and residential)
    Shari' 'Azmi (residential and household commercial)
    Shari' Latifi (residential and household commercial)
    Shari' al-Qubbah (residential and household commercial)
    Shari' Zahriyyah (commercial and residential)
    Shari' Abu Samra (residential and household commercial)
    Hayy (or Shari') Mutran (residential and household commercial)
    Hayy Ghuraba (commercial and residential, adjoining Zahriyyah)
    Shari' Madaris (residential and commercial)
    Karm Qullah (residential and commercial)

157

Shari' 'Uqbi al-Himrawi (residential, adjoining Qubbah)
Shari' Zihr al-Maghar (residential, adjoining Qubbah)
Ba'l Saraqbi (very poor residential, including bidonville)

2. Primary thoroughfares with no, or only a few, adjoining streets identified with them. All residential and commercial.
   Al-Bulifar (the Boulevard)
   Shari' Sintral (south of Tal)
   Shari' Yazbik (south from Tal)
   Shari' al-Mina (alias Riad al-Sulh — Muslim name)
   Shari' al-Ajam (between Yazbik and Bab al-Raml)
   Shari' Kinayis ⎫
   Shari' Rahbat ⎬ (both part of western border of Old City)
   Shari' 'Izz-al-Din (Tal to Sahit Saraya 'Adimi)
   Shari' Jamayzat (south of Riad al-Sulh)

3. Primary intersections and adjoining buildings. Commercial and residential.
   Sahit Kura (alias Husayni)
   Sahit Nijmi (literally: Place d'Etoile)
   Sahit Kiyali (adjoins Boulevard north of park)
   Suq al-Khudra (part of Bab al-Tibbani)

4. Peripheral
   Shari' Maluli (along road to Syria)
   Shari' Khanaq al-Himaru (along old Beirut road, bidonville adjoins)
   Shari' Mitayn (northern border of Shari' 'Azmi)

Despite all the "streets" in the names in this list, it is not, except partially in the case of category two, a list of individual thoroughfares, or streets in the western sense of the word. Rather, it is a list of sections or quarters which vary in size partly, it is true, because of the pattern of thoroughfares within them. The thoroughfares are much wider, straighter, and more conspicuous in the newer parts of the city than they are in the old. Nevertheless, the AUB Sample, mostly residents of the former, seemed to think in terms of quarters rather than of individual thoroughfares.[19]

THE QUARTERS OF THE MINA

Similar patterns on a smaller scale, seem to obtain in the Mina:

Old Town

1. Primary streets and offshoots
   Shari' al-Gumruk (customs; waterfront)

Suq al-Kharab (Christian commercial)
Suq al-Muslimiyyah (Muslim commercial)

2. Networks of streets
    Hayy Mar Ilyas (Christian residential)
    Sahit Tirb (Christian residential-commercial)
    Zawqaq al-Na'ura (Muslim residential)
    Shari' Nuss Birtawshi (Muslim residential)
    Buwwabi (Muslim residential)

New Town

1. Primary quarters
    Fawq al-Rih
    Hammam Maqlub
    Harat al-Ramli
    Qabr al-Zayni
    Abu Fraydu

2. Primary thoroughfares
    Shari' Mar Ilyas, alias Shari' Port Said (Christian and Muslim names of the new boulevard separating the new and old parts of the Mina)
    Shari' al-Mahatta (street connecting town with railroad station and new docks)

A Psychology of Quarters

In conclusion, there is in Tripoli, in both the Old City and the newer parts, a "psychology of quarters." It rests apparently on two highly valued considerations: the domestic privacy and the commercial convenience of the inhabitants. However, neither the new nor the old quarters fit all the specifications of the eighteenth-century model hara as analyzed by Gibb and Bowen.

A characteristic of the prewesternized model of the Arab city was that the merchants and craftsmen lived very close to their shops, if not on the same premises. Thus, to the extent that certain crafts were monopolized by certain groups of kinsmen or endogamous sect groups, the physical clustering of those crafts and of the kinship and sectarian groups would tend to coincide.

There are still tendencies for even the westernized businessmen to prefer to live as close as possible to their businesses. On the whole, there is no "zoning mentality" — no generalized objection to juxtaposing business establishments and residences — and there is, of necessity, considerable reliance on being able to walk to work. As opposed to these factors, which would tend to encourage people to have as little distance as possible between their homes and their places of business, there is the desire to live in a prestigeful or fashionable area. Of the latter, Abu Samra is one of the best examples, and it is comparatively isolated (by its elevation and location on an edge of the city). People who choose to live in Abu Samra will most likely also be choosing not to live close to their place of business.

The Tripoli telephone directory yields a subsample of 581 persons who had both business and residential telephones at different addresses. Such people are presumably even more prosperous, on the whole, than the people with only one telephone. Consequently, this subsample is especially biased in favor of people in the upper income brackets and/or among the relatively highly westernized elements in the population.

Table 35 illustrates the tendencies to which I referred above. The

TABLE 35. DEGREE OF ADJACENCY OF SUBSCRIBERS' BUSINESS
AND RESIDENTIAL TELEPHONES

Location of residential telephones	Tal		Zahriy-yah		Bab al-Tibbani		Tirbi'a		Sagha		Bazar-kan	
	No.	%	No.	%	No.	%	No.	%	No.	%	No.	%
In business quarter	7	8.5	8	26.7	9	14.1	0	0.0	0	0.0	0	0.0
Adjacent to business quarter	46	56.1	10	33.3	20	30.9	3	32.5	7	43.7	1	3.8
Not adjacent to business quarter: in Abu Samra	8	9.8	1	3.3	6	9.4	1	12.5	3	18.8	13	50.0
not in Abu Samra	17	20.7	11	36.7	27	42.2	4	55.0	6	37.5	12	46.2
Not located	4	4.9			2	3.4						
Total	82	100.0	30	100.0	64	100.0	8	100.0	16	100.0	26	100.0

tendency to live adjacent to, or in an adjacent quarter to, one's place of business is well illustrated in the Tal and in Zahriyyah. The tendency for prosperous people working in old parts of the city to live elsewhere is illustrated in Tirbi'a, Sagha, and especially Bazarkan. In Bab al-Tibbani, these two tendencies seem to be nearer to a sort of balance. The meaning of Table 35 can be clarified by discussing one of the columns. Eighty-two persons have business telephones in the

Tal quarter and also have home telephones. Of the home telephones, 8.5 per cent are in the Tal itself (and therefore could be on the same premises as the business), 56.1 per cent are in an adjacent quarter, 9.8 per cent are in Abu Samra, and 20.7 per cent are in some other nonadjacent quarter.

The objection can certainly be raised that since Tripoli is so small, some adjacency of domiciles and business places is simply inevitable. There may be some truth in this, but as a matter of fact there is relatively little overlap among the residential quarters adjacent to each of the six business quarters on which the analysis is based. (See Table IV, Appendix B.) In other words, there is some internal differentiation in this matter, suggesting people's deliberate choices within an admittedly crowded situation.

As to the criteria of adjacency, they are subjective judgments on my part. My judgments are based on my knowledge of the city and on my estimates as to the likelihood of locations in two quarters being within a short easy walk of each other, a long but otherwise easy walk, a difficult walk (involving climbing), or whether an automobile would most likely be employed. Obviously, then, my criteria are only approximate, for other peoples' judgments may differ from mine. Also, there is the problem posed by the fact that there is considerable margin for error in precisely locating business places and domiciles within the larger quarters. Linear distance, of course, is not the only criterion, but rather, distance with relative ease of travel taken into account. Abu Samra and Zihr al-Maghar are quite close to each other, but they are probably the least mutually accessible quarters in the city. In order to get from one to the other, one can walk or ride in an automobile. One must walk all the way down to the bridge between Bab Hadid and Swayqah and then climb up the steep slopes of each quarter. By car, one must go all the way around through Bab al-Tibbani. This is an extreme example, but it illustrates the type of factor I tried to take into account. In Appendix B there are some additional tables showing precisely what quarters were ‘judged to be adjacent or not adjacent to each of the six business quarters.

This analysis reveals nothing directly about the great majority of Tripolitans who have no telephone at all, let alone two. It certainly must not be misconstrued as showing that *in general* people living in the old parts of the city do not live adjacent to their places of work, for it only shows this tendency with respect to a very biased sample. On the contrary, considering the biases of the sample, the analysis indicates the considerable importance of home-business place adjacency among relatively wealthy or westernized people, which therefore implies an even greater importance of it among the relatively less wealthy or less westernized people.

FESTIVITIES AND AMUSEMENTS

Coffeehouse, Balcony, and Promenade

In the first section of Chapter V, I discussed the coffeehouses of Tripoli with particular reference to the ways in which they are connected with the means of transportation in and out of the city. This was related, in turn, to the way in which they are used as meeting places for business and friendship and in the interest of familial, sectarian, and local solidarity.

To these considerations it must now be added that coffeehouse life is also part of a complex of public leisure-time activities. A man sits for hours in a coffeehouse not only for the various reasons I have mentioned, but also simply to watch what is going on in the street. Sexually segregated, the coffeehouse gives him the opportunity to see and be seen away from the privacy of his home.

The distinction between this type of coffeehouse (*'ahwi*), preferably out of doors, and the sweet shop or small restaurant is definite though subtle. The latter serves more food, may admit women in company with their male relatives, and is more likely to be wholly indoors. As for the full-fledged restaurant (*mat'am*), where men and women may go out to dinner, there are very few in Tripoli, and those few are concentrated along the waterfront in the Mina. This is one of the ways in which Beirut offers many more facilities than Tripoli. One reason for it may be the supposedly greater relative strength of the home-centered tradition in Tripoli.

Women do not have at their disposal any close equivalent of the men's coffeehouse. However, those whose homes have balconies make ample use of them for lounging and watching the passing scene. There is also a good deal of sitting on chairs or stools on the sidewalk just outside the front door.

At any given moment during a normal day (except when the weather is very bad) the public face of Tripoli is double: the idle watchers and the busy watched. However, the same individual can and does easily shift from one role to the other.

Toward the end of every afternoon, but especially Friday and Sunday afternoons (closing days for most Muslim and Christian shops, respectively), family groups, male groups, and female groups sally forth in their best clothes for a promenade. They may walk around the streets, window shopping or chatting with friends they meet. Or they may walk to the nowhere-very-distant outskirts of town, where they can rest under olive or citrus trees before they return. The promenade may be concluded by going home, or to the movies or, for men, to a coffeehouse. It is a fairly formalized activity, in which the roles of watcher and watched are simultaneously combined.

Hammam and Cinema

The hammam, or public steam bath, is one of the classic institutions of the Islamic city. Indeed, it is a pre-Islamic phenomenon, for the Romans perfected it and bequeathed it to the Mediterranean area generally. Uncaring or unmindful of this ancestry, many travel accounts of the great Arab, Turkish, and Persian cities of the past have commented on the glories of their baths. More recent publications have been less kind, stressing the unwholesomeness of hammams, particularly because of the opportunities they provide for homosexual activities.

In 1961–62, there were four hammams in Tripoli, all in the Old City and all very old. The 'Izz al-Din Hammam, next to the Suq al-Khayyatin, was originally built during the last years of the thirteenth century (at the very beginning of the Mamluk period), and the Nuri Hammam, next to the Mansuri mosque, was originally built about 1330. I say "originally built" because these structures, both of which I visited, have obviously been repaired and redecorated many times in the interim. There are two other hammams, and before 1958 there had been six altogether. Two were severely damaged and went out of business between 1955 and 1958.

The four functioning hammams are owned as waqf dhurri, with commercial concessions to the actual operators. One of the latter, who ran the bath in collaboration with his wife, who was in charge during the women's hours, said that business was definitely not so good as it used to be. The main reason for the decline is that modern bathrooms in the new apartment buildings have greatly reduced many people's dependence on the public baths. The latter now cater primarily to poorer people still living in the Old City. The operator of the Nuri Hammam said that he had from one to about twenty-five customers a day. Women are apparently more regular customers than men, and the premises are reserved for them during certain hours of the day. A flag that features a white hand on a red field is hung over the entrance outside to warn away any men during women's hours. At one of the hammams, men who have had sexual intercourse during the previous night may wash themselves free of charge. In general, business is better in the winter, quite possibly because the hammam is a good place to get warm.

Like all the very old buildings in Tripoli, the Nuri and 'Izz al-Din hammams are very battered on the outside and also partially obscured by other structures. However, from appropriate vantage points one is readily impressed by their roofs, consisting of an assortment of domes of various sizes and shapes set with glass bottle-bottoms to admit daylight into the interior. Each hammam has a main salon where the bathers undress, and where they also can relax after their bath, lounging on couches in curtained compartments, eating oranges and drinking coffee. Each also has a hot steam room which has stone massage tables and cubicles with hot and cold running water for washing. There is, lastly, a third main room where the bathers cool off somewhat before returning to the salon.

The hammams were apparently very popular among the British troops billeted in Tripoli during World War II. One of them still has a sign saying "Turkish Base" surviving from that period. Similarly, there is a sign in the Tal saying "Moulin Rouge," which refers to a defunct wartime cabaret. These signs were made for foreigners, their usefulness has long since passed, and yet they remain, perhaps because no one really sees them.

In addition to some continuing use of the ancient baths, there is an establishment in Bab al-Raml where, in the evening, professional storytellers beguile their audiences. But this form of entertainment, evolved especially for illiterates, is of apparently minor importance now in comparison to the cinema, which is very popular. There were, in 1961–62, thirty-two movie theaters in Tripoli. They ranged from quite elaborate, 800-seat auditoriums to very small and ill-equipped establishments. The largest and most elaborate were in the Tal and along the boulevard, and most of the total were concentrated in these areas, although there was one in Bab al-Tibbani and at least two in Bab al-Raml.

Despite signs forbidding it, there is a good deal of smoking among Tripoli audiences. There was at least one fire as a result of this during the period of study.

Arabic and Euro-American films were shown in about equal proportions except during Ramadan, when the former seemed to be more numerous. The Arabic movies are mostly Egyptian, and my impressions of those I saw in Tripoli exemplify Landau's generalizations about the prevalence of slapstick, farce, melodrama, dancing, and music in Arabic movies.[20] On one occasion, I saw all of these, plus obvious advertising for an airline and a Beirut hotel, in one technicolor film of Lebanese manufacture.

The Euro-American films shown in Tripoli in 1961–62 seemed mostly to be American western and gangster pictures and Italian muscleman melodramas (Maciste, Hercules, Spartacus, Samson). Although the latter were in a certain general vogue at the time, I wonder if some significant selectivity may not have been at work in Tripoli. The strongman is a popular symbolic figure in the Arab world, and advertisements of muscleman contests and exhibitions are always among the posters on the walls of Tripoli's buildings. Among the audience reactions I noticed uproarious laughter at slapstick and verbal mannerisms, titters and hoots in response to what appeared to be effeminateness on the part of male characters, and rustlings of apparent disapproval at such actions as a woman drinking liquor or rejecting her children.

Organized Sports

Soccer and volleyball have some popularity in Lebanon, and there is even an amateur volleyball league. However, active interest is limited primarily to the secondary schools and to young adults with westernized educations, among whom there are some sport clubs. Mass spectatorism and professionalization of sports hardly exist.

In Tripoli there are a couple of sport clubs, and the YMCA and some of the schools encourage participation in sports. However, the municipal stadium, opened in 1958, has rarely been used. According to one informant, the authorities are fearful that athletic contests may transform themselves into ethnic, sectarian, or political riots, and he felt that their fears are justified. The school teams almost inevitably have sectarian identity, and the various western ideas concerning impersonal sportsmanship do not seem to be understood or accepted. There is no team, professional or amateur, which either in fact or in theory represents Tripoli, or any of its major sects, as a whole. For various reasons, the games tend to be intramural.

These are among the realities lying below the surface of publicity and propaganda in which there is much emphasis on physical fitness and on teams as aspects of modern nationalism.

Sectarian Festivals

Ramadan. The most important festival in Tripoli is the 28-day month of Ramadan, in which the Muslims fast during the daytime but indulge themselves during the nighttime. 'Id al-Fitr is the three-day closing observance of Ramadan. Second most important is 'Id al-Adha, which comes two months after 'Id al-Fitr and marks the ceremonies at Mount Arafat during the annual pilgrimage to Mecca. The exact dates of Muslim holy days are fixed according to a lunar calendar whose year is slightly shorter than the solar year. Consequently, they occur slightly earlier in each successive solar year and therefore, through the slow passage of time, occur at any season of the solar year.

In 1962, 'Id al-Fitr was early in March, and Ramadan, occurring in the winter, was not as irksome as it can be in the summer, when the prohibition on quenching one's thirst during the daytime can be a very severe trial. It also happened to overlap somewhat with Lent. This coincidence, coupled with very fresh memories of the abortive coup d'état of December 31, 1961, resulted in particularly strong protestations of unity and brotherhood among the Lebanese Christians and Muslims. The newspapers and magazines were full of feature stories and pictures on this subject. Great and approving attention was paid to the exchanges of ceremonial visits among the high dignitaries representing the different sects. For example, the Maronite president paid a visit to the Grand Mufti in Beirut at 'Id al-Fitr; the Sunni premier attended Easter mass at the Maronite cathedral in Tripoli; and the president and premier together attended Eastern Orthodox Easter ceremonies. However, these are only three highlights among many such activities of the notables and the basically similar activities of ordinary folk. The essential patterns are that Muslims exchange formal visits among themselves during Ramadan and also receive the formal calls of Christians. It is a particular honor to be a guest at an *iftar*, the first meal of the day at sundown. The Christians, in turn, exchange formal visits among themselves during Christmas week and at Easter and also receive the formal calls of Muslims. In other words, the Christians and Muslims reciprocate each others' formal calls and at the same time recognize each others' most important holy days. In all this, it is a moot question whether it is feelings of brotherliness or concerns about 'ayb and sharaf which are uppermost in peoples' motivations.

Between the Christian and Muslim observances there are some superficial similarities interwoven with some very different attitudes. Throughout Ramadan, the mosques are decorated with strings of electric light bulbs, and at night they are very reminiscent of the Christmastime decorations used in the industrial West. 'Id al-Fitr, at least as I observed it in Tripoli, is very similar in general atmosphere to the traditional Christian Carnival. Carnival, however, marks the temporary end of normal life and the beginning of a 40-day period of supposed meditation and penance marked by selective fasting which, in turn, ends with a festival of renewal. 'Id al-Fitr, on the other hand, marks the resumption of normal life at the end of a 28-day period during which oral deprivation and reduced work loads each day have alternated with oral and other indulgences each night, accompanied by various observances which seem to symbolize renewal. In comparing Lent and Ramadan, the Christians and the Muslims mutually accuse each other of being less rigorous and self-sacrificing.

In Tripoli, there are a number of quite noticeable differences in public life during Ramadan. To begin with, the normal pre-dawn call to prayer is accompanied by the crashing boom of a signal cannon located on one of the upper levels of the citadel, where there is a custodian's shack and also an air-raid warning siren. The early morning cannon is a warning, particularly to people who are asleep, that they have about one hour more in which to eat and drink before the fast begins. People who know larger cities like Beirut and Cairo have told me that the Ramadan cannon is often not readily audible there, but there is no problem in this regard in Tripoli.

During the day, the coffeehouses are almost, though not entirely, deserted. Gone are the water pipes, and none of the few customers drink coffee. Correspondingly, the coffee vendors and the sellers of various cold drinks and snacks are rarely seen. In fact, I was told that during Ramadan they must reorganize their whole procedure in order to stay in business.

I had the impression, too, that during Ramadan, fewer men were smoking cigarettes and more men were playing with *masbaha* (strings of beads, originally prayer beads) than normally.

As the afternoon wears on, and the usual traffic jam increases, one senses an additional tension during Ramadan. A quick look down a side alley here and there may reveal a man apparently catching a quick smoke or a woman hurriedly thrusting a flap of bread into the folds of her outer gown. Then . . . BOOM, the cannon crashes and rumbles over the city . . . once, and then a second time. But there is no rush of people anywhere in particular apart from the normal afternoon rush. Instead, that rush steadily subsides, rather than continuing, as normally, into the period of dusk. As a matter of fact, one notices that many small shops are already closed by the time of the signal. The reason is that many Muslims are either already at home waiting for the iftar, or they are making ready to go there without delay. While shops often close earlier than usual in the afternoon, they may also open somewhat later in the morning.

Sales, particularly of clothing, seem to be very frequent in Ramadan, and the food stores are stocked with special delicacies. For example, there are great piles of *ma'mul*, large, delicately sweet, nut-filled cookies which have been rolled in powdered sugar and are individually wrapped in wax paper. In general, Ramadan is a time for spending money on gifts, new clothes, special foods, and hospitality.

After people have had their iftars, and as dark descends on the city there is a partial resumption of some commercial activities. The coffeehouses and sweet shops are open and are doing a brisk business. The coffee vendors and hawkers of cold drinks, ka'k, and other food and drink, are very active in the streets. The cinemas seem to be unusually crowded, and there are customers in many of the clothing stores. It is during this time of the day, lasting about two to three hours, that Ramadan seems a period when daytime and nighttime activities are simply reversed.

'Id al-Fitr. 'Id al-Fitr is a three-day holiday which begins with the last cannon on the last afternoon of Ramadan. The following were my observations on March 6 and 7, 1962.

Though Tripoli seemed about as usual, everyone was actually in preparation for 'Id al-Fitr, which would begin at sunset. Even Christian shops tended to close, because most of their customers were Muslims. People in general had laid in three days' supply of what are normally fresh foods, since very little would be coming into the city, and that little would be unusually expensive. Eggs were already up from 9 per lira (33 cents) to 7 per lira. (Before the Point Four Program they had been 4 per lira.)

Many of the cinemas which normally run European films were this week running Egyptian ones, though there were still a couple of "westerns" in town and, as usual, the muscleman melodramas. All the cinemas had signs saying "Happy 'Id" to their customers.

Swings — crude, wooden platforms suspended from equally crude scaffolds made of posts and accommodating several small children at a time — were set up along the river at Swayqah, in the empty lot across the street from the cemetery entrance in Bab al-Raml, and in an empty lot near the citadel. At the Bab al-Tibbani and Bab al-Raml cemeteries, people were buying bunches of a small-leafed, densely foliaged green shrub and setting these and other floral items up on the graves. Quite a lot had been so decorated already. The sweet shops had piles of ma'mul (20 piasters, about 7 cents apiece), along with many other trays and piles of sweets, and the customers were many.

The cannon was fired several times at about 3 P.M. (the fourth prayer of the day). There was the usual bustle at 4:00 when the schools let out (no more school for the rest of the week), but the bustle did not subside as it had during the past month. At 5:30, the cannon fired again for the sunset prayer and the end of Ramadan.

About 6:00, the shops were all open in the Tal, busy but not crowded. Abu Samra seemed rather quiet, though there were many kitchen noises and smells. Seen from Abu Samra, the various lighted minarets resembled Christmas trees in shape, but the Mansuri mosque's lights, besides hanging down diagonally from the peak, also traced around its minaret's square corners and arched windows, making it reminiscent of a church steeple, which, of course, it originally was. At 8:45 P.M., all the clothing and food shops were doing very lively business. Most of them, normally, are closed at this time. Tripoli is usually very quiet after about 9:00, but on this night there was continued noise after this time, including more than one bunch of roistering young men walking along the street sounding as if they were drunk. Actually, the noise seemed to go on all night — cars as well as voices. It seemed that more lights were on than usual. Next morning, someone who lives in Bab Hadadin said that her neighbors had stayed up "all night," preparing food, taking baths, and such, so that they would have nothing to do during the 'Id.

The cannon fired at least once at about 3:30 A.M. Shortly thereafter, I began to be aware of increased activity in the street. By 4:45, there was a fairly steady stream of groups going by — mostly toward Bab al-Raml. I got up and joined the army of people going to the cemetery there. There was a large crowd both inside and outside of the cemetery, together with ka'k sellers and still-busy sellers of greenery for the graves. There was also a honking traffic jam and a real stream of people of all ages heading toward the cemetery. Those inside it seemed to be sitting or standing by the graves, supposedly saying special prayers for the dead.

In Bab Hadadin, the food shops and some clothing shops were open, but many shops were obviously closed. The Tal was not very busy, though it was certainly not deserted. Between the cemetery and the Mansuri mosque there was a heavy stream of people heading for the former, and there were at least a dozen beggars all along the way.

Outside the Mansuri mosque, at about 6 A.M., I found a platoon of soldiers lined up, with their backs to the old madrasahs, facing the mosque. Half were armed with rifles and half with band instruments, an officer with a sword in charge. There were a few civilians waiting around, but not many. As I was walking away, a large black Cadillac with a green flag on its left front fender drove up, and out got two shaykhs, one of whom was the Mufti of Tripoli. They received some snappy salutes and went into the mosque. This was about 6:15. There were people streaming through the street, mostly not stopping, on their way to the cemetery.

I returned at 6:30. The waiting crowd had increased, and a band of blue-uniformed boys, which I had seen on 'Ajam Street, was also lined up, at right angles to the soldiers. I stayed. After a few minutes, a Chevrolet Impala, preceded by two motorcycles and followed by four other cars and an army landrover, appeared and disgorged the president of the municipality, the Muhafiz, and the military commander of the north. They received a flourish from the soldiers and the national anthem from the boys, and went into the mosque. About 6:40, the cannon boomed, and I happened to look up at the minaret.

A red flag with a green rectangle bearing the Muslim credo in its center was being lowered from the staff. It got entangled in one of the wires holding the lights but finally came down. The soldiers were then moved over to the other side of the street with their backs now toward the mosque. The waiting crowd and the parked cars filled most of the space, although people still walked through — as many away from Bab al-Raml as toward it. At one point, a car actually pushed its way through the street as if the driver were oblivious to the ceremony in progress.

And so for about twenty minutes we all waited, and I counted veiled and unveiled women. Two impressions: (1) similarly dressed women of the same age, walking arm-in-arm (presumably close friends or relatives), one veiled and one not; (2) young married couples in each of which the wife was veiled and the husband was holding the baby. I stood right behind one such couple. Her veil had a fresh white tag which said "Made in France." The bands played a couple of numbers during this interval, and the flag was again raised to the peak.

At about 7:00, the cannon boomed, the flag was lowered, and the dignitaries reappeared. They stood more or less at attention while the national anthem was played, and then they walked rapidly to their cars, which were surrounded by people. The Mufti got a round of applause from some people near the door of his car, and the others stopped a couple of times to exchange a few words with individuals.

During the rest of the morning, while the various officials received formal calls, shops selling ready-made clothes and processed foods were open. This was a minority of the stores, but enough to give the impression of activity. They were also open in the Tal, Bazarkan, and Kindarjiyyi, but one noticed many closed shops in these same places, too. Conspicuous among the latter were the goldsmiths, greengrocers, butchers, and all where manual labor is involved, such as furniture making and automobile repair. However, some tailors were open, perhaps to make alterations in all the newly bought clothes.

By 9:30, the cemeteries were empty, but there was a great milling throng in the Tal. The cinemas were all open, and each had a large crowd outside. Then there were many petty salesmen — of key chains, plastic dolls and wallets, flashlights, paste jewelry, neckties. Also, a number of gambling games were in operation, some operated by the people who usually sell chocolate bars on the street. Miniature target ranges and various test-of-strength games were also available. Pushcarts selling bananas and sweets were frequent, as were the vendors of a drink made of carob molasses served from elaborate brass and tin containers. There were many more beggars than usual, for people are expected to give generously during the 'Id.

I had been told that the displays of extra finery in clothing would be conspicuous, but I did not find it so. There were armed guards on the alert in Bab al-Tibbani, but nothing seemed really unusual among the 'Alawite population there. Similarly, I could find nothing unusual along the waterfront in the Mina, although I had been told that it was a particularly favorite place on this occasion. Riding from the Mina back to Tripoli, I overheard, in fact, a father ask his children if they would prefer to go to the swings in the Swayqah or to those in Bab al-Raml. In another taxi, descending from the Qubbah, a man was cursing about the large number of children roaming about unattended in Bab al-Tibbani, while their mothers were off somewhere in the promenade. In the course of the latter, toward the middle of the afternoon, many people walked out along the boulevard, pausing to rest on the stones lying around outside the new, still unfinished mosque. Many women return from these walks carrying their high-heeled shoes rather than wearing them.

And so it went for two more days. Tripoli is quite transformed during 'Id al-Fitr, and similarly during 'Id al-Adha, but in Beirut, larger and more heterogeneous, the differences are not so easy to discern.

Dervish Zikrs. On the steep slopes of Abu Samra overlooking the river there is a compound of domed buildings. This is the Tikkiyah of the Mawlawi dervishes of Tripoli. There were once many dervish centers in the old Ottoman Empire, and this is one of the few that remains. In 1948, a zikr was performed here which has been beautifully described by Julian Huxley, for whose special benefit it may have been done. Huxley was especially impressed by the serenity of the men — most of them laymen with ordinary jobs — as they whirled around in their long white gowns and tall fezzes.[21] The shaykh wore a green cloth wrapped around his fez.[22]

By 1962, the Tikkiyah had apparently become a moribund institution. The shaykh lived there with his family, but I was unable to gain admittance, even though I was accompanied by a person who knew him. However, an American journalist was at about the same time able to get an interview with the shaykh, who is reported to have said bitterly that there were no longer enough people in Tripoli to have zikrs — at least twenty-five people, including musicians, are necessary — and that the last one had been about fifteen years previously.[23] Possibly this was the one attended by Huxley.

Christmas. While the above distinctively Islamic activity is dying out in Tripoli, some of the city's Muslims are adopting some of the superficial observances of Christmas. Trees and decorations are sold in the stores; some Muslims put trees in their homes; and I heard of one who invited friends to hear his children sing carols. This is perhaps the ultimate in the divorce of Christmas behavior from the supposed spiritual meaning of the occasion. For the latter surely has no significance to Muslims, and the imagery, even, is that of northern Europe and not of the Mediterranean. It is conceivable, of course, that Muslims could attach symbolisms of their own to a ceremonial green tree, but in all likelihood all this is but the adoption of a style which is thought to be fashionable among well-educated people with some prestige.

Fashionable Pleasures

Cultural Exchange. In 1958, the United States Information Service library and reading room in Tripoli was destroyed during the crisis. It has not been replaced.

However, there are French and German cultural missions there. In the spring of 1962, the former had an art exhibit which attracted the notables of the city, and at about the same time the Goethe Institute inaugurated its educational program in Tripoli. On 'Azmi Street, also, there is an art school staffed partly by Europeans, several of whom come specially from Beirut to teach their classes. The several European consulates in the Mina (Belgian, Danish, Italian) do not appear to contribute very much to the foreign-elite life of the city.

Touristic Festival. In May, 1962, there occurred for the first time a touristic festival. It was one of several sponsored by the government in each province. The posters for the Tripoli festival featured a photograph of a row of bathing beauties on water skis. Each had an Arabic letter on the front of her suit, and together they spelled Tripoli (T-R-A-B-L-S). When the great day arrived, there were water-skiing and fireworks exhibitions in the Mina. There was a parade of floats with symbols of the North: two fighting men for Zgharta, which is famous for its feuding factions; a block of soap for Tripoli; representations of *shanklish*, a type of cheese rolled in thyme, very popular in the North; and so on. I was told that this parade was subjected to abuse in Bab al-Tibbani. There was also a performance at the stadium, and some disorder occurred when elements in the audience tried to persuade a popular performer to sing a pro-Nasser song for which she was well known.

These negative incidents were not publicized, but the participation in the festival of important and fashionable (western-style) personages was. The whole concept of tourism, of course, is a new and alien one, and it emanates from Beirut.

Gambling. One of the old mansions in the Tal is occupied by an exclusive private club whose members belong to the upper class of the city. On Shariʿ al-Mina, there is another building which houses a sporting club whose membership apparently coincides very closely with the one in the Tal. The latter has a poor reputation among middle-class people who do not belong to it. They say that the main activity is gambling, that upperclass people gamble to excess; that, indeed, several old families have been ruined through gambling. They also conjure up the image of women who neglect their children, hide their gambling debts from their husbands, and are forced to borrow money from other men. Whatever the truth may really be, the club is definitely exclusive and private. Unlike the Greek Social Club of the Mina and the club for IPC employees, whose dinner parties were among those given some notice in the social sections of Beirut magazines, no publicity was ever attached to it.

Forbidden Pleasures

Liquor. Islam forbids the drinking of all alcoholic beverages. Lebanese Christians, however, have traditionally made and consumed wine and ʿaraq, and Lebanese Muslims have always at least been familiar with them.

Since World War II, especially, European and American distilled liquors have become generally available in Lebanon. In Tripoli, despite the predominantly Muslim population, bottles of scotch, gin, and brandy are openly on sale. Many of the bottles on display in shop windows looked somewhat dusty to me, but presumably there is some demand for them. Beer is also available, and two brands are brewed in Beirut itself.

There are, however, no bars in Tripoli, and no cabarets. From time to time, attempts have been made to start night clubs, but they have never been successful. One reason, I was told, was that respectable people did not dare patronize them, and therefore they became monopolized by vice-ridden elements in the population.

As far as vice itself is concerned, there is, according to the I.R.F.E.D. report, considerable traffic in narcotics. Complaints about this and about "smugglers," otherwise not described, were fairly common in the Tripoli newspapers.

Prostitution. Abu Fraydu, a shabby section of the Mina between the cemeteries and the rocky southern shore of the peninsula, is well known as the red-light district of Tripoli. In 1961, there were eight whorehouses and fifty licensed prostitutes there.[24] They were outlawed by the Muhafiz in December of 1961. However, the buses from Tripoli unloaded their passengers in what at that time happened to be the very center of Beirut's much larger red-light district, and the governor's decree, while it pleased the moralists of Tripoli, may not have seriously inconvenienced its patrons of the "oldest profession."

The Lure of Beirut

Beirut has more of everything that Tripoli has in the way of urban facilities. It also has facilities — from night clubs and first-class hotels to universities — which Tripoli does not have at all. Typical of most industrially underdeveloped nations, Lebanon is socially, politically, and economically dominated to a seemingly excessive degree by one major city, Beirut. Furthermore, Beirut has a newly acquired reputation for being a glamorous, exciting, international metropolis.

Tripoli's political and economic leaders can hardly compete with Beirut, and often they must take their cues from it. Personal reactions to this situation vary and may even be contradictory. Provincial rejection of the "big city," perhaps supported by sectarian resentments, is one. But in many ways Tripoli people are attracted to and by Beirut. Economic necessity is one of these ways. If one cannot find a job in Tripoli, Beirut is the place to look.

Social prestige is another way. There are several wealthy, fashionable Tripoli families which, in recent decades, have actually migrated to Beirut and become part of its "high society.'" More usually, however, there are young adults who have received university educations in Beirut and then must decide, as individuals, whether to stay in Beirut or to return to Tripoli to make a professional living. Some settle on one course, others on its alternative. Tripoli gains, but it also loses.

Short of migration to Beirut, there is continual travel to it by day — for business conferences, shopping sprees, and entertainment. Modern, rapid communications have augmented this and have also made it possible for outsiders who have business in Tripoli to conduct it by day, without spending the night. This, rather than any major tendency for businessmen to spend nights in the homes of friends or relatives, was cited as a major reason for the lack of first-class modern hotels in Tripoli, and this fact, of course, only adds impetus to the commuting trend.

At the end of Chapter II, I pointed out that Tripoli as it is today, a distinctive physical and social entity, is in very specific and concrete ways the product of a long succession of interacting exterior events and forces. But it is not a static "end product." Rather, it is, through its inhabitants, continually reacting and adapting to the world around it. Beirut, rather than Aleppo or Damascus as of old, is at the moment the most important single focal point of that world.

SECURITY, PRESTIGE, AND POWER

Security and Identity Groups

There are actual groupings of people in Tripoli who identify themselves in terms of kinship, sect, and village or region of origin. Some identify themselves simply in terms of one of these criteria. Others identify themselves in terms of more than one of them, and there are all possible combinations.

These groupings are, as I have discussed at some length, the basic units of social security in Lebanon and in Tripoli. I have also discussed the psychic costs which are, as it were, the price the Lebanese must pay for having ascribed memberships in such units. These "costs," such as intrafamilial jealousies, contribute to the instability of the groups.

"Social security" has defensive aspects and aggressive aspects. Among the former are the various forms of protection and camouflage which Lebanese social groups provide for their members. Among the aggressive, or at least active, aspects are the use of nepotistic "contacts" in the pursuit of one's ends.

Prestige and Power

However, prestige and power cannot be acquired and exercised only by means of the various units of social security. The *zu'ama* (political bosses), discussed in Chapter IV, rely on their kinship and sectarian ties and identities, but the most prestigeful of them also have influence which extends beyond these. Hence, in fact, their preeminent position.

Let us look at this whole situation from a different vantage point. The members of each of the major sects run the gamut of social recognition and prestige. So, too, do the members of each of the major clans. They are "major" in the first place because they have powerful and prestigeful members, but they also have members of the humblest sort. In Tripoli, although the Christians are in a small minority, there are prestigeful Christian individuals and families who are acknowledged as such by the Muslims, who, of course, have their own prestigeful individuals and families.

In other words, prestige requires more than particularly advantageous memberships in sect or family. These help, but they are not sufficient. Wealth is probably the single most important factor in prestige. This is, at any rate, what many Lebanese themselves think.[25] Certain types of occupation rather than others are also important, and so is the related factor of being highly educated (western-style), although this is not absolutely essential for every individual as long as there are close kinsmen who qualify in this regard. Political power, or at least influence, added to wealth, provides the basis for the highest prestige of all. Sect is an important element in this, but it is not an absolutely determining one, except for members of the smallest minor sects who are probably debarred from attaining the highest prestige in the society since they cannot count on anything but a small nucleus of followers.

The Most Prominent Families

In the spring of 1962, I asked the members of the AUB Sample to list the most prominent Muslim families and, separately, the most prominent Christian families of Tripoli. By dividing the members of

the sample themselves into Muslim and Christian groups, I obtained
four lists: the most prominent Muslim families according to Muslims
and according to Christians (see Table 36); and the most prominent.

TABLE 36. MOST PROMINENT MUSLIM FAMILIES
OF TRIPOLI

Muslim list		Christian list	
Families	Nominations	Families	Nominations
Karami	15	Karami	15
'Awayda	12	Muqaddim	10
'Adra	9	Zawq	8
Munla	9	'Awayda	7
Muqaddim	8	Ahdab	6
Ghandur	7	Ghandur	6
Zawq	6	Bisar	5
'Alam al-Din	5	Mir'ibi	5
Kabbara	5	Jisr	4
Jisr	4	Kabbara	4
Ahdab	4	Munla	4
Fattal	3	Hamza	4
Misqawi	3	Al-Umari	2
Husayni	3	Al-Rifa'i	2
Hamza	2	Sultan	2
Ra'd	1	Miqati	2
Minkara	1	'Abdul-Wahhab	2
Tubara	1	Misqawi	1
Safadi	1	Husayni	1
Zirayk	1	Qubtan	1
Majzub	1	Asafiri	1
Al-Sa'id	1	'Adra	1
Hula	1	'Abdul-Razzak	1
Ma'sarani	1	'Alam al-Din	1
Miqati	1	Ra'd	1
Al-Rifa'i	1		

Christian families according to Muslims and according to Christians
(see Table 37).

One of the most striking things about these lists is the high degree
of agreement between the Christians and the Muslims as to the identities of the top-ranking Muslim families. Of the eleven most often
nominated, the two groups of respondents agreed on nine. The most
glaring discrepancy is the fact that the Christians included among
the eleven most frequently mentioned families two which none of the

TABLE 37. MOST PROMINENT CHRISTIAN FAMILIES OF TRIPOLI

Muslim list		Christian list	
Families	Nominations	Families	Nominations
Burt	10	Burt	15
Khlat	8	Nahhas	11
Nawfal	3	Ghurayyib	6
Shammas	3	Nini	5
Nahhas	2	Bulus	5
Khuri	1	Khlat	4
Dib	1	Nawfal	3
Hammam	1	Shammas	3
Karam	1	Milki	2
Dirani	1	Yanni	2
'Arida	1	Fadil	2
'Abdul-Wahhab	1	'Arida	1
Sawaya	1	'Abdullah	1
Georges	1	Dahir	1
Bulus	1	Shidrawi	1
Franjiyah	1	Kayruz	1
Sarraf	1	Hajj	1
Ghurayyib	1	Franjiyah	1
'Abdul-Nur	1	'Abdul-Nur	1
		Karam	1
		Halabi	1
		Sarraf	1
		Battash	1

Muslims mentioned at all, the Mir'ibi and Bisar families. Other informants explained the discrepancy in this manner: the Mir'ibi family was, at the time, very much in the news owing to the marriage of one of its members to a Saudi Arabian shaykh of fabulous wealth. This probably led the Christians to mention the family as often as they did, disregarding the fact that it is not actually from Tripoli, but from the Akkar. The Bisars, though eminently respectable, are small in number and are felt to have lost the influence they had in the 1930's when they were involved in rivalry with the Karamis. To balance these two, the Muslim list includes two families in the top eleven who are mentioned by only one Christian apiece. In the case of the 'Adras, it was suggested that the Christians associated them more with Beirut (where many of them do indeed live), coupled with the fact that they are not politically active in Tripoli.

Leaving aside these two sets of discrepancies, the nine families mentioned most often by both Christians and Muslims were also felt by other informants to be undoubtedly among the most prominent Muslims in the city. Seven of them have, for at least several generations, had a firm economic base in land ownership. In most recent times, members of each have become qualified in modern professions, such as medicine, law, and engineering. Many are also in business in other ways than managing their lands. "Old family," wealth, and participation in prestigeful occupations (which require superior, westernized educations) — these are the main criteria of these families' high status in the city. The prestige is actually maintained, however, by certain specific individuals, for there are many members of these groups (which are actually clans or lineages) who are admittedly quite undistinguished. Families can, and do, in fact, fall from top status when there are too few individuals to provide reality for the claim. Similarly, families can rise to prominence by the efforts of a single man, but whether they remain in such a position for long depends on whether there is anyone else to consolidate it. Two of the nine most frequently mentioned Muslim families are definitely *nouveaux riches*, having begun in very humble circumstances after World War I. There are other such families farther down on the lists.

Political prominence is an additional factor in general prestige. The Muslim list contains the families of the premier of Lebanon (who is also a deputy in the national parliament), the mufti, the president of the municipality, and the three other parliamentary deputies. In the first case, actual political power plus prominence, plus the other prestigeful criteria, combine to make the Karamis the top family. At the other end of the scale, two of the families would probably not be on the list at all except for the fact that their members include parliamentary deputies.

Subtleties of Mobility and Distance. The criteria of social prestige are really quite clear and limited in number. The subtle difficulties encountered in placing individuals and groups in some sort of hierarchy are not due to lack of clarity as to what is and is not prestigeful, but to the different permutations of the criteria and to the problem of determining the extent to which a group's prestige can be "carried" by a small number of individuals. There is an element of precariousness in all this which is quite striking, as evidenced by the fact that the lists provided by the AUB Sample contain not only the names of *nouveaux* but also of respectable has-beens.

Compared to the western industrial, the Latin Mediterranean, and the Latin American urban cultures, the upper class people of Tripoli do not appear to display their wealth so conspicuously. According to some Islamic traditions, such display connotes sinful pride. True, early in the twentieth century, as described in Chapter II, a number of mansions were built, but only one or two of them have survived as mansions. Their glory was brief. At present, Tripoli's "millionaires," like almost everyone else, live in apartment buildings whose exteriors give only a very rough idea of the socioeconomic status of the occupants. And squatters' shacks sometimes immediately adjoin such buildings. Yet social distance is very definitely maintained, and sensitivity to what is and is not respectable is very marked indeed.

While sectarian identities tend to keep people of different sects apart, similar positions in the socioeconomic hierarchy give them something in common. Thus, there seems to be a certain amount of Muslim-Christian fraternization among upper class people, as evidenced in the Rotary and Lions clubs. As to the AUB Sample, its Christian and Muslim members seemed to be about equally knowledgeable in regard to the most prominent Muslim families. This is perhaps understandable considering the fact that the Muslims are predominant. When it came to naming Tripoli's most prominent Christian families, however, the discrepancies between the Christian and Muslim respondents were quite marked. Five of the Muslims, in fact, refused to answer the question at all, indicating that they did not know anything about the subject. Nevertheless, of the ten most frequently mentioned, the Christian and Muslim respondents agreed on five. Of these five, three definitely were considered by other informants to be among the most prominent Christian families.

The Burt family has built its fortune since World War I, and one member is a deputy in parliament, this probably being a major factor in its being mentioned by more respondents than any other. There are two other families on both lists which have recently acquired prestige. Two more which appear high on both lists are definitely old but still powerful families. Another two have definitely fallen from their positions of prestige, but in contrast to them, only the Christian respondents mentioned two which have very recently achieved prominence through the professional activities of single individuals. The upward and downward directions of mobility perhaps seem more clear-cut among these Christian families than among the Muslim ones. The most prominent Christian families appearing on both lists are all Eastern Orthodox, but some Maronites are also mentioned.

The complications of sect and class identities are clearly revealed among the Eastern Orthodox of Tripoli. The aristocrats among them, like many of the upper class Muslims, have been prominent for at least several generations — well back into Ottoman times. Other similarities are that while they have no village ties, they do have family connections in other cities of the eastern Mediterranean, such as Alexandria and Latakia. Such interaction as there is between the Christians and Muslims at this social level, however, seems to consist of the recently introduced business clubs and of university alumni and alumnae meetings. Intermarriage is virtually out of the question.

The Eastern Orthodox aristocrats also seem to maintain great distance between themselves and the other Eastern Orthodox. This cleavage is particularly sharp between them and the many people of Tripoli from the Kura district whose immediate forebears were peasants, but who, in the twentieth century, have been in the forefront of westernized professional achievements. They maintain their village ties, often being landowners, and sometimes commute on a daily basis. Typically, they have nonprofessional relatives both in the villages and in Tripoli, but they do not cluster together in any particular part of Tripoli.

The Sunni and the Orthodox sects of Tripoli are each subdivided into a full range of socioeconomic classes. But the 'Alawites, according to the others, are all lower-class people, while the Maronites appear to be represented by all levels except the very top. (The 'Aridas are Maronite upper class, but their social life is centered in Beirut, not in Tripoli.) It is among the 'Alawites and Maronites that physical clustering by sect in the city is noticeable — at least to some extent — very possibly a reflection of their greater dependence on this means of mutual support.

At various points in this spectrum, there are what look like social class groups as such — the Eastern Orthodox aristocrats, for example. But on the whole, the social classes of Tripoli are constructs in the minds of observers, each construct being a composite of qualities in various combinations, each level of prestige being a product of a particular combination. It is not surprising that when I asked the members of the AUB Sample to list what they thought were the social classes of Tripoli, no two answers were identical, although there was a general theme of high-middle-low with economic overtones.

Social prestige is a vital concern among these people, as has been indicated previously, but there are in the culture itself no systematic prestige categories apart from the very rough one of "rich, middle, and poor," generally correlated with "honored, respectable, and looked-down-upon."

Criteria of Prestige Classes

As I observed life in Tripoli, there seemed to be certain combinations of certain qualities to which people reacted in terms of differential social prestige. These were as follows:

1. Rich, professional, old family, politically prominent and powerful
2. Rich, professional, old family, politically prominent
3. Rich, professional, old family
4. Rich, professional, and/or politically prominent
5. Rich, nonprofessional
6. Middle, professional, old family
7. Middle, nonprofessional, old family
8. Middle, professional
9. Middle, nonprofessional, and/or artisan
10. Poor, nonprofessional, and/or artisan
11. Poor, semiskilled, illiterate
12. Poor, unskilled, illiterate

None of these constitutes an organized group, although some organized groups may have memberships which are relatively homogeneous in regard to them. High prestige is, to a considerable extent, a product of possessing several positively regarded qualities. Low prestige is a product of possessing negatively regarded qualities. In this connection, "professional" refers to some modern profession (such as law, medicine, engineering, or teaching) which implies a high degree of westernized education, and I try to indicate that this is not merely a middle class phenomenon. True, attainment of such professional standing has been a means of attaining middle class status, but in Tripoli it is also frequently essential for helping to maintain upper class standing as well. Rich, nonprofessional families are almost certain to be *nouveaux riches*, and they will not long maintain their prestige unless they acquire some professional members, or marry into an old family, or attain political influence, or, preferably, all three. People will go to great lengths to achieve such ends. For example, a *nouveau riche*, nonprofessional, politically ambitious man provided free refreshments for all comers in Tripoli's coffeehouses on the occasion of the birth of his first son. Anxiously upward-mobile families may also pay for flattering profiles of individual members which are printed in the local newspapers. These newspapers on their own initiative also print glowing descriptions of, for example, the new clinic of a young physician just going into practice. The young physician responds with a subscription and perhaps further contributions. Many of these newspapers are available only through the subscriptions of such people and are apparently supported by their contributions. Another kind of feature they print has the general refrain, "there are certain people in this city who seem to be fine, upstanding people, but they are not what they seem to be."

As far as actual income is concerned, the I.R.F.E.D. study made certain estimates expressed as five levels. Table 38 links these estimates with the estimated socioeconomic profiles of selected parts of Tripoli referred to in Appendix A.

TABLE 38. LEVELS OF PER CAPITA ANNUAL INCOME IN LEBANON AND SELECTED SECTIONS OF TRIPOLI

	Lebanon (figs. in Lebanese pounds)			Tripoli (% by quarter)				
Level	Av. income	Max. income	%	Ba'l	Bab al-Tibbani	Mina	Old City	Mutran
Very poor	1,000	1,200	8.8	10	..	6	5	..
Poor	2,000	2,500	41.2	75	90	60	40	10
Middle	3,500	5,000	32.0	14	10	30	50	78
Well-off	10,000	15,000	14.0	1	..	2	3	10
Rich	40,000	Over 40,000	4.0	..	..	2	2	2

SOURCES: *Le Commerce du Levant*, 9:20 (1961), I.R.F.E.D. report; I.R.F.E.D., 1961.

According to another source, in 1962 there were 30,000 workers in Beirut, Saida, and Tripoli who earned less than 2,500 Lebanese pounds a year, including such important people as bakery workers.[26]

While amount of income is an important element in social prestige, it is not the only element. It would be foolish to conclude from the I.R.F.E.D. estimates that there are five social classes in Tripoli. It would be almost as foolish to conclude from my remarks that there are necessarily twelve. Each of the twelve categories listed above is a complex standard whereby Tripolitans evaluate themselves as to social prestige.

Applications of such evaluations in the course of daily life result in various types of social behavior, but none of the standards in itself is "a group." Since social scientists have great difficulty in distinguishing a social class as an objective group from a social class as a mental construct, I have preferred to keep the expression "social class" out of my discussion as much as possible. Previous references to "upper class," "middle class," and the like, are related roughly, but only roughly, to the "rich" and "middle" categories noted above.

Chapter VII

TRIPOLI AND THE WORLD

THERE ARE THREE characteristics of twentieth-century mankind to which this study of Tripoli is particularly relevant. The first is great increase in population. The second is great increase in the number and size of cities, a complex of processes often simply labeled as "urbanization." The third is the intensification of mankind's involvement with industrial technology. The degree and quality of this intensification vary from place to place. Generally speaking, at or near the centers of origin of industrial technology the day-to-day problems of the intensification are talked of in such terms as "automation," "computerization," and the like. But elsewhere, especially in the technologically underdeveloped areas of the world, such problems are more likely to be summarized under the more general label of "industrialization."

Most of this concluding chapter will consider in more detail the extent to which Tripoli may be taken as a microcosm of mankind with respect to these three twentieth-century characteristics in particular. Some consideration will be given, too, to the proposition that, insofar as Tripoli *can* be taken as a microcosm, something of general usefulness may be learned from a study of it.

Although Tripoli has industry, the social relationships of its inhabitants are far from being "impersonal" in the manner so frequently assumed to be intrinsic to western industrial urbanism. This assumption itself is open to serious question.

By way of introduction to these matters, it is necessary to be explicit about what seems to be the prevailing intellectual mood of the times in which this study has been done.

URBAN RESEARCH AND THE PROBLEM OF INTELLECTUAL HYPOCHONDRIA

At the beginning of this book, I mentioned some of the intellectual problems created by the careless use of terms like "urbanization" and "industrialization." They are, in fact, so imprecise and so connotation-laden that they have become too treacherous for use in unambiguous discourse. Throughout this book, I have as much as possible avoided them and terms like them, and have never depended upon them for description or for argument. Elsewhere,[1] I have made the point that expressions like "industrial urbanism" are hopelessly ambiguous with reference to the western culture in terms of which they were initially used, and that therefore they are equally hopeless as tools for systematic thought on the characteristics and problems of cities in other cultures. Many social scientists, including the growing number of anthropologists doing research on cities,[2] would, I think, agree in principle on this matter.

We need a fresh start. But where and how? One possibility is the comparison of "a large number of cross-cultural urban studies the findings of which should be presented as free as possible from existing ambiguous and/or dogmatic concepts."[3] Yet many scholars may not have the inclination or patience to wait until such a "large number" of studies becomes available before trying to reformulate existing information into new hypotheses. Some may employ in this process some application of game theory and high-speed computer simulation of a large number of hypothetical situations.

However, regardless of whether the procedures consist of acting-out games, or of programming computers, or of reading, field work, and thinking, assumptions and conclusions will be screened through the individual scholar's essential orientation to himself and to human beings in general, and unless he makes conscious efforts to prevent it, that orientation will determine his assumptions and subjectively distort his conclusions. Furthermore, the social scientist must not only recognize his essential orientation toward human beings and make allowances for it, but he must also recognize the limits beyond which he is unable to make allowances. The fresh start we need must begin at a deeper level than the mere setting of new research problems.

The most prominent urban theories to date appear to have been formulated by city haters. At any rate, their vision of city life was unrelentingly pessimistic. The negative aspects of city life were emphasized, while its objectively obvious attractions and rewards were belittled or ignored. Awareness of, and making allowance for, personal preferences and emotional states might have lessened this imbalance and thereby increased the approximation of theory to reality, but it did not in fact do so.

At the present time, though the specific issue of country versus city seems to have gone out of focus among most intellectuals, many of the same spiritual problems remain in focus, and the tendency to rationalize emotional reactions in terms of either/or propositions appears to be as strong as ever. Take, for example, existentialism as a reflection of the troubles of the present-day world. It is "tinged with nostalgia for the supernatural [and] sees man as a fallen angel . . . caught between two worlds in neither of which he can be at home." [4] In this artificially created vacuum several rationalizations find room. One is that since "God is dead," purposeless destructiveness and hostility must be the prime movers in human behavior. Various wishful interpretations of Freudian id theory can be used to bolster this notion, too. From it follow the conclusions that (1) nothing can be done about the evil of human nature and (2) the source of that evil is beyond discovery or analysis.

Such despairing reactions seem evident in the writings of many contemporary intellectuals, including some social scientists. Their pessimism only accentuates the actual problems and, ironically for the social scientist, it seems to render absurd all his inquiries into the nature of human behavior. [5]

As with the old anticity urban theories, examples of actual behavior can easily be found which fit the case (but do not, therefore, prove its validity). Destructiveness and cruelty have indeed occurred on a greater numerical scale in the present century than perhaps ever before. But this is not necessarily an indication of the primacy of evil in human nature. Destructiveness and cruelty are nothing new in human behavior, and their enormousness in the twentieth century is due to the use of new technological devices and to the existence of more people than ever before. However, the *belief* that these destructive impulses are occupying a larger and larger amount of individuals' energy may itself intensify them. For example, there is some evidence that simulated violence in the mass media of communication evokes actual violence;[6] there is less evidence that it relieves or harmlessly deflects violent feelings. As to the actual violence and brutality of various spectator sports and other public spectacles, it is obvious that they stimulate violent feelings; although there is no evidence that they dissipate or alleviate them, this is one of the justifications that has been seriously suggested for them.

In other words, a one-sided theoretical view of human nature can help to exaggerate certain kinds of actual behavior, destructive ones in this case. Yet a slightly less one-sided view of the twentieth-century scene recognizes that acts of compassion and altruism have also occurred, and on a larger numerical scale than ever before. Again, the larger scale is not necessarily due to any greater motivation in individual persons, but to the availability of modern technological devices. But, as in the case of the destructive motivations, the constructive ones can be accentuated and augmented by conscious effort. The pessimistic social scientist who recognizes the existence of his pessimistic bias and makes some allowance for it in his thinking may, if he chooses, flexibly include in his formulations all the objectively observable, often contradictory, aspects of human behavior. His colleague who does not so recognize his biases (whether pessimistic or optimistic) is, on the other hand, often forced to rationalize away those aspects whose reality he would prefer not to admit.

This was the problem many earlier urban theorists failed to solve. The point of these observations is that it still is a problem and that it will not be solved by present or future urban theorists unless they make a conscious effort to do so.

TRIPOLI'S SIZE AND PHYSICAL NATURE

In Chapter II, the great growth of Tripoli's population was discussed — perhaps as much as a 600 per cent increase in fifty years. In this respect, it is certainly representative of many cities in the world. I also mentioned the density of its population, which is very high and continues to be very high in contrast to some other rapidly growing Arab cities (for example, Cairo and Baghdad), and in even more contrast to the highly industrialized cities of North America. Actually, there are several ways in which Tripoli can be contrasted with comparable cities in the United States, all of which are related to high population density: compactness, lack of single houses with corresponding predominance of apartment buildings, lack of suburbs, and relative lack of distinctiveness between commercial and residential sections. Whether these contrasts constitute differences of degree or of kind depends on various interpretations. Whatever the latter may be, some of the facts of the differences are fairly clear.

Table 39 compares Tripoli with the six United States cities closest to it in population according to the 1960 U.S. census. These cities were the 67th through the 72nd in size in the country.

TABLE 39. POPULATION DENSITIES OF TRIPOLI AND
NORTH AMERICAN CITIES

City	Population	Area (sq. mi.)	Population (sq. mi.)
Austin, Texas	186,545	49.0	3,776
Spokane, Wash.	181,608	43.0	4,223
St. Petersburg, Fla.	181,298	54.0	3,357
Tripoli	180,000	1.5	120,000
Gary, Ind.	178,320	42.0	4,287
Grand Rapids, Mich.	177,313	24.0	7,267
Springfield, Mass.	174,463	33.0	5,271

The figures for the American cities do not include suburban areas outside city limits, and Tripoli has no suburbs, so there is some comparability on that score. Tripoli's municipal borders do not, on the other hand, include all of the *de facto* city (Abu Samra, for example, is not included) and so my Tripoli figures are not quite comparable in a legal sense to the American ones. Also, at least some of the territories of the American cities probably lie outside of the built-up sections. But even with these qualifications, Tripoli's high density is very striking. Even if one used the minimum current estimate of Tripoli's population (125,000) instead of 180,000, its density would still be higher than that of the Borough of Manhattan, which has the highest density (76,156 persons per square mile) of any American city with over 100,000 people.

The main reasons for Tripoli's high density are the predominance of multistoried apartment houses, an average household size which may be about twice that of the United States (6 persons versus 3), and its very small area. Of the United States cities with over 100,000 people, the smallest in area is Cambridge, Massachusetts, which covers

6 square miles, has 107,716 people and a population density of 17,098 people per square mile, the highest density of any United States city of over 100,000 people outside of the New York metropolitan area.

On the outskirts of Beirut, there are some slight suggestions of suburban developments in the sense of settlements of detached one-household dwellings, served by shopping centers, whose inhabitants work in the main city. These are insignificant compared to what one would expect in the United States. On the outskirts of Tripoli, there are no such developments at all. The city has grown steadily outwards, and no new satellite residential settlements have been established. One effect of this is that there are really no transitional or peripheral areas; the densely packed city begins and ends abruptly. There are probably many reasons for the absence of suburbia, but I can be specific concerning only two possible ones. The first is that there are only about one-tenth the number of motor vehicles per person in Lebanon as there are in the United States. The second is that commuting patterns are beginning to develop between Tripoli and a number of peasant villages in the hinterland which can be reached fairly quickly by car, a sort of "exurban" development without any intervening suburban one.

As to the relative lack of distinctiveness between commercial and residential sections, very few people live in Bahsas, and no one, so far as I know, lives in the area surrounding the railroad station. These are almost completely commercial areas. In Tripoli proper there are only a few such areas. One is the section between Qbur Yihud and the Bab al-Tibbani bridge, and another is between Bazarkan and Dibbagha, but these are tiny areas. On the other hand, there are sections which are predominantly residential: Bab Hadadin, 'Uqbi al-Mufti, and Tal'a al-Zahir in the Old City and Mutran, 'Azmi, Abu Samra, and al-Qubbah among the new sections. Yet some commercial activities can be found in all of them. As for the Tal, it resembles, up to a point, the American downtown business district, and Zahriyyah with its workshops forms an axis between the Tal and Bab al-Tibbani, the wholesale food market area. Surely these are the commercial centers of Tripoli. They are, but they are also residential, and the residents of the Tal and Zahriyyah appear to include as well a large proportion of prosperous middle class people. Bab al-Tibbani is residential, but, as described in Appendix A, most of its inhabitants are poor. The figures concerning telephones in Table 40 may throw some additional light on this matter.

TABLE 40. FREQUENCY OF RESIDENTIAL AND BUSINESS
TELEPHONES IN VARIOUS SECTIONS OF TRIPOLI

Section	Home phones		Business phones		Total	
	No.	%	No.	%	No.	%
Tal	46	24.2	143	75.8	189	100.0
Zahriyyah	171	62.1	106	37.9	277	100.0
Bab al-Tibbani	28	10.1	241	89.9	269	100.0
Abu Samra	280	94.3	17	5.7	297	100.0
Mutran	217	90.1	24	9.9	241	100.0
al-Qubbah	178	86.3	28	13.7	204	100.0
Bab Hadadin	22	75.9	7	24.1	29	100.0
Bazarkan	3	6.0	47	94.0	50	100.0

There are about 3,400 telephones in Tripoli, of which 45 per cent are business telephones. The home telephones are concentrated in new areas where well-to-do people are also concentrated, and there is good reason to believe that it is almost entirely such people who have telephones in their homes. (There is a nonreturnable installation fee of about $80 and a returnable deposit of about $25.) Probably, therefore, the table greatly underrepresents the residential character of Bab al-Tibbani and Bazarkan, but it also brings into very high relief the residential character of the Tal and Zahriyyah.

My supposition on this subject is that the Tripolitans (and the Lebanese generally) do not have a "zoning" mentality, and that they are committed to a laissez-faire economic policy as far as land use (and everything else) is concerned. As discussed in Chapter VI, there are clear-cut social and architectural techniques whereby the household can and does barricade itself against the outside world. Beyond that, whatever other people do in and to the outside world is of little concern. High population density — which is traditional and not something new — may possibly be a contributory factor in the continuance of these reactions, which seem to consist of the desire for "noninvolvement" and for protection of privacy.

OTHER COMPONENTS OF TRIPOLITAN URBANISM

The Government

The industrialization of Tripoli began with the introduction of electricity and the opening of a cotton mill and a petroleum terminal — all in the period from about 1927 to 1932. At about the same time, Tripoli's government became more complex in structure and more active in the provision of social services. Governments that have more or less elaborate bureaucracies and provide services for the people are often identified with industrialized cultures, but it would be a mistake in Tripoli's case to think in terms of its having an "industrialized government."

The French mandate regime of Lebanon encouraged both industrialization and changes in the government, but they, in turn, did not cause each other. The services the government provides, however, are dependent in large measure on industrial technology or its products. This is conspicuously true in regard to education, public health, and sanitation. The majority of Tripoli's people are probably literate, owing in large measure to the public school system, and a literate majority is often associated with "industrialized culture."

Yet in other respects industrialization is irrelevant to the structure of Tripoli's government and the various activities connected with it. The great concentration of power in the national ministries and the minimal degree of formal public participation in the making of decisions and the appointment of officials are continuations of preindustrial Ottoman patterns, subsequently reinforced by French ones (see Chapter IV). The widespread practice of nepotism in the operations of the bureaucracy and the widespread public belief that nepotism and corruption are typical of the government are also continuations of practices and feelings which arose under preindustrial conditions. They are closely related to the attitude that the government is essentially a predator whose activities are to be evaded.

Ironically, the conditions which inspire peoples' cynicism are perpetuated by the people themselves, who believe that the only nonviolent way of having any impact on the government is through the exertion of pressures on or by relatives or cosectarian friends who are officials. Such attitudes and activities are specimens of that personal, nonanonymous orientation to life whose supposed absence from industrialized cultures is so often deplored, though not usually in the political sphere. In Lebanon, the political expression of this orientation is but one facet of a cultural complex which, historically speaking, is preindustrial. It is continuing on into a period of industrialization, but it cannot, simply because it is preindustrial in origin, be assumed somehow to be nonindustrial in theory. Personal "pull" and nepotism are practiced in the politics of fully industrialized cultures and, though they are generally deplored on ethical grounds and may

well have a harmful effect on both public services and public attitudes, they are obviously not "nonindustrial." It should be added that
political attitudes contrary to nepotistic ones and epitomized under
the principle of "equal protection of the law" are also preindustrial,
not intrinsically "industrial." They are, however, specific to a particular culture which is not the same as the Arab-Mediterranean one
to which Tripoli belongs.

The involvement of private citizens in the government of Tripoli
is not really "public involvement" at all. It is a series of individual
or small-group delegations to officials either on behalf of individuals
or on behalf of a group which is likely to be either a sectarian or a
kinship unit. Elections are few and far between. There are no municipal elections per se at all, and the election campaigns for the national
Chamber of Deputies are tightly interwoven with sectarian group
interests. Comments on public behavior and related governmental
operations (largely critical, sometimes satirical, and apparently not
intended to serve any special group interests) are to be found quite
frequently in some of the Beirut newspapers, and even some of the
Tripoli ones. These may have some effect and therefore constitute
a form of genuine public involvement. Between 1962 and 1965,
for example, obvious efforts were made to improve traffic behavior
through education and enforcement of existing laws. The newspapers,
through feature stories and letters to the editor, certainly make it
clear that some private citizens feel an urgent need for reform, but
it is not easy to show that they actually marshal much sense of public involvement. The tone of most of the comments is that the
government "ought to do something." There is very little suggestion
that people in general ought to do something — such as altering their
attitudes in regard to public responsibility. As to student demonstrations, they have a tendency either to become destructive or not to be
taken seriously.

Social responsibility in Tripoli continues to be focused primarily
within identity groups of long standing in the culture. The attitude
of "let the government do it" may reflect recent changes in the direction of more government services, but it is also consistent with the
traditionally passive, distant reaction to the government, and whatever the government "does," it must not conflict with the interests
of sect and kin group.

Identity Groups and the Individual

The structure and activities of sects and kin groups in Tripoli were discussed at length in Chapters III and VI. An important theme of those discussions was that the individual's involvement with his sect and his kinsmen is not a simple matter of unquestioning loyalty in return for unquestioning support. Rather, it is a matter of deep and sometimes stressful emotional conflict.

Socially, the individual is a member of a particular sect and a particular family. If he fails to demonstrate these identities, he is diminished as an individual. Whether one calls this demonstration "honor" (traditional *sharaf*) or "mask," [7] it can be maintained only at considerable emotional cost. It will be remembered, for example, that siblings are expected automatically to be mutually loyal and supportive, and yet other elements in the culture often lead to their hating each other. The same is true, to a less intense degree perhaps, among more distant relatives and among coreligionaries. Required by one set of values always to be "available," the individual nevertheless craves privacy and even concealment. Expected to share his good fortune, whether in the form of money or other social advantage, he also craves individual accomplishment and prestige, a craving that is, perhaps, symbolized by the muscleman as hero.

Such conflicts, such alienations of the person from his "true self," are the stuff of much contemporary western literature and social theory. Characteristically, these phenomena are attributed to the baleful influence of industrial technology and the anonymous city. However, as far as Tripoli is concerned, it is simply not valid to make such an attribution. The various conflicting elements are traditional — definitely preindustrial — and they are not exclusively urban, for Lebanese village life, too, is rife with them.

Tripoli has an industrializing economic base. However, its people characteristically are enmeshed in networks of personal obligations and identities which involve them in emotional conflicts and contradictory behavioral patterns. Their lives are intensely personal, and also beset by conflicting values and demands not caused by industrialization or any influences of modern technology.

In short, the Tripolitans do not fit the usual stereotype of "industrial man"; nor do they fit the equally deceptive stereotypes of "preindustrial man" or of the "folk community." I believe that the Tripolitans are in no way anomalous in this matter.

Another overworked abstraction in western thinking is "sense of community." There is little for Tripoli as a whole, but this is not because of any "loss of community" due to industrialization. There is no evidence that there ever was any more (or even as much) in preindustrial times, when Tripoli was far smaller. What "sense of community" there is occurs within the memberships of sects and kinship groups, and, as I have pointed out, it occurs at considerable cost. This cost involves strained interpersonal relationships, and it may also involve the retreat of many individuals from taking on any new social responsibilities or any responsibilities other than those which they cannot possibly avoid.

Martin Buber's dichotomy between I-Thou and I-It relationships has received much attention. The I-Thou relationship is one of total mutual commitment of persons to each other, and it is presumably the kind of relationship which is sought by the many who yearn for "sense of community." Harvey Cox has recently questioned the applicability of Buber's formulation to the nature and problems of the fully industrialized western city. Cox points out that no one can possibly form I-Thou relationships with everyone he encounters, and that Buber's formulation leaves him no other alternative than to treat all other persons as mere objects.[8] The latter alternative is, of course, the essence of the nightmare city of anonymity and alienation. Cox, citing Jane Jacobs[9] for support, points out vividly that many relationships in modern cities are between Buber's two extremes, and that it is on this kind of relationship that effective patterns of social responsibility must considerably depend.

The internal structure of the Tripolitan identity groups — particularly the family — is an illustration of what can develop when all relationships are expected ideally to be of the I-Thou type. The expectation is simply too much; everyone is bound to fail and, in the absence of positive alternatives, the results are as I have depicted them. The Tripolitans (and the Lebanese and the Arabs in general) arrived at this situation without industrialization. They may not even perceive it as a problem, and it would be inappropriate of me to prescribe for them.

However, the Tripolitan situation can serve as an object lesson for those inclined to look for panaceas for the various forms of malaise in western urban life. Specifically, it demonstrates that reinforcement of, and reliance on, social units of ascribed membership (kinship groups, sectarian groups for everyone except converts, racial groups, and "ethnic" groups) would by no means necessarily result either in greater social responsibility or in greater "integration" of the individual personality.

CONCLUSION

If one insists on group identity, one will necessarily exclude other human beings. If one wants "community," one cannot practice segregation. If one wants social "roots" and personal ties, one will necessarily incur obligations, some of which will be onerous. If one wants "freedom," one must accept a certain degree of rootlessness. If one wants social responsibility, one must accept some limitations on one's impulses for freedom. If one wants all of these things simultaneously, as many inhabitants of modern cities apparently do, then one must be able to accommodate the variously conflicting consequences.

Some of these implications, as well as the predicaments which result from failing to accept them, are illustrated in the life of Tripoli.

The existing dichotomous categorizations of human behavior do not really clarify the nature of those predicaments — in fact, they often becloud it by confusing so many of the relevant issues. These points, too, have been illustrated in this study. They could also, presumably, be illustrated by sufficiently detailed studies of any city. In all these respects Tripoli is assuredly one with the world.

Appendix A. Physical Description of Tripoli in 1961-62, with Emphasis on Ecological and Architectural Patterns

IT WOULD BE logical to begin a description of Tripoli with the Old City and then work outward to the newer parts. However, in view of the material in Chapter II, this procedure would be somewhat repetitious, and it would also be artificial. One cannot visit the Old City without first passing through newer sections. In fact, the traffic routes are such that a transient visitor may enter the city and leave it again without ever seeing the Old City at all. I prefer to use an order of presentation which is realistic in terms of transportation facilities and could actually be followed *in situ*. I will begin as if we were approaching Tripoli by car from the south (see Map 3). After lingering first in Bahsas, we go along the new boulevard and turn right into the Tal. From there, beginning at the city hall (building 31) we go along Shari' Zahriyyah, past the Orthodox and Presbyterian girls' schools (buildings 42 and 43), and across the bridge into Bab al-Tibbani. Turning left at the new mosque there (building 17), we proceed toward the outskirts of town and reach, on the right, the street which winds in sharp turns up past the Presbyterian boys' school (building 44) and into al-Qubbah, through which we pass until we reach the edge of the city on the road to Zgharta. From there we double back south of the Christian cemetery, and prepare to descend the steep slope to the river and the Old City. So far, our main means of transportation could have been an automobile, but from this point we can only go on foot. We cross the river on the bridge which leads into Bab Hadid (see Map 5), whence we turn right, or north, and go in a generally counterclockwise fashion through the Old City until we reach the citadel. From there, we go through Abu Samra, down to the large Muslim cemetery in Bab al-Raml, to Sahit Nijmi (the traffic circle just south of building 41, Map 3), thence through the Tal again, across the Boulevard and into the Mutran and 'Azmi sections. From there, in turn, we will go to the Mina. This is the sequence I shall employ, but the descriptions will not be limited to what they would be if they were literal reports of what was seen from a moving car or during a single walk. The present tense is generally used in order to simplify matters, but it must not be forgotten that I am describing Tripoli as it was in 1961–62. Conditions which were clearly temporary at that time are described in the past tense.

THE APPROACH FROM THE SOUTH

Tripoli's wholesale vegetable marketing area extends as far south as the small town of Batrun (see Map 1), but subjectively one does not feel really in Tripoli's orbit until one emerges from the tunnel in the great headland at Shikka. From there the lights of the city can first be seen at night, as can the highest parts of Mount Lebanon by day. The tall chimneys of the two cement factories at and just north of the settlement of Shikka belch forth chalky smoke, dusting the rocky landscape. The factory laborers live mostly in neighboring villages, but many of the executives and office personnel commute from Tripoli.

BAHSAS

Beyond Shikka, the highway runs right along the shore and is often closely overshadowed on the inland side by the escarpment of the coastal plateau. Bahsas is located at a point where the escarpment is cut through by a minor stream whose rocky bed is dry in summer and is followed by a road leading inland to Kura. At this point, also, the alluvial plain of Tripoli is beginning to open out westward. Bahsas is outside the city limits, and the consequent tax advantages are a major reason why modern industries began and have expanded there. Easy access to the plain of Kura, from whose villages many of the laborers come by day, is probably another reason; and the intersection of the main highway and the railroad is also helpful. On the outskirts of Bahsas is an electric power plant which was still under construction in 1962. This is followed by a series of large buildings along both sides of the highway for about three hundred yards. Except for the compound of structures which house the cotton mill, opened in 1930, these buildings are all very new. Set behind fences of concrete block and wire mesh, they look "natural" and ordinary to anyone familiar with western industrial plants in whose construction glass, reinforced concrete, and concrete block are featured. Very unwestern, or at least non-American, however, is the almost complete absence of identifying signs or advertising. The identity of these plants can only be ascertained by inquiry; and this reveals that, except for the cotton mill, they are all owned by residents of Tripoli. They consist of a construction company, a bottling plant, a refrigerated warehouse, a plywood factory, a cottonseed oil mill, a sugar refinery, and a scrap iron reduction plant. The largest structure in Bahsas is a long, five-story reinforced concrete building which stood unfinished in 1961–62 but was nevertheless used for the storage of new orange crates. Its owners, one of the most important entrepreneurial families of Tripoli, had not made known what the ultimate purpose of the building was, and there were many rumors about it. Above Bahsas, on the crest of the escarpment overlooking the stream, is a compound of houses built and owned by the Iraq Petroleum Company and inhabited by European members of its staff.

The road from Kura joins the main highway at the bridge over the stream, at which point the industrial development ends abruptly. Almost immediately the highway forks. To the right is the old main road which skirts the base of Abu Samra and also gives access to a road which winds up to Abu Samra, whose bright new apartment buildings jut upwards from the olive trees. Below these, however, on the slope itself, is a true bidonville of about fifty ramshackle huts made of boards and sheet metal. Along the road itself, before it passes by the cemetery and enters Bab al-Raml, are small apartment buildings with storefronts, mostly built since 1945. This section is called Khanaq al-Himaru (Chokes-his-Donkey).

THE BOULEVARD

The left-hand highway just north of the bridge at Bahsas is the Boulevard (al-bulifar), the new main entrance to the city. Opened in the late 1950's, it has fluorescent lights, four traffic lanes, and a paved median strip, but many details of the paving and curbing were not yet finished in 1962. The Boulevard passes through olive groves until it reaches a private school and the new Saraya on the left (buildings 46 and 30) and the new mosque on the right (building 12). The latter, surrounded in 1962 by the detritus of stonemasons still at work on it, has a round dome and a tall octagonal minaret whose conical top was painted bright kelly green during the period of study. The school building is severely rectangular in design, finished in yellow stucco, typical of Lebanese institutional buildings of the interwar period. The new Saraya, on the other hand, is a stylish, modernistic affair of glass, stone, and concrete. These buildings stand in groves of trees, but only about one hundred yards separate them from the densely built-up city, which begins suddenly with apartment buildings on the left and a huge, white, almost windowless, refrigerated warehouse on the right. These buildings face onto a wide traffic circle, as does a curved row of unfinished storefronts whose roofline is lower in the center to permit an unimpeded view from the Karami mansion of a rectangular pedestal in the center of the circle. In 1962, it was rumored that a statue of 'Abdul-Hamid Karami would be erected on this pedestal. More apartments and an automobile service station also face on the circle.

Between the circle and Shari' Mitayn, the Boulevard is almost completely built up on both sides by five-story to seven-story buildings with storefronts or cinema entrances on their street floors and balconies on their upper floors. The balconies belong either to private apartments (as indicated by clotheslines, chattering maids, and loungers looking at what is going on in the street) or to physicians' or lawyers' offices as indicated by painted signs. These professional signs are usually in Arabic plus English and/or French. They proclaim where the individual studied as well as his identity. The cinemas have neon signs, and many of the European-style stores and cafés do also. There are service stations on some of the corners, and auto repair shops in some of the stores, as well as banks and stationery stores. In 1962 the Boulevard was used by some cars for access into the Latifi section via a muddy side road, but beyond that, out in the orange groves, it was only partly paved, and was unused because there was no bridge to carry it across the Abu 'Ali.

THE TAL

The Tal consists of the pentagonal park, with a central fountain surrounded by an ornamental fence and sidewalks, where feathery-leaved, pollarded zinzilakht trees grow; the streets which encircle the park on all five sides; and the immediately adjacent streets and block. If pressed for the identity of Tal Street (Shari' al-Tal) as opposed to the Tal section, a Tripolitan would probably designate the eastward continuation of Shari' al-Mina which crosses the Boulevard, defines the southern edge of the park, and ends at Sahit Saraya 'Adimi. Turning into this street from the Boulevard, one sees one of the turn-of-the-century mansions whose upper floor is occupied by a private club for Iraq Petroleum Company employees and whose street floor is occupied by a sweet shop and the station of the major bus line to Beirut. On the right are a large indoor café, a cinema, and the Banque de Syrie et du Liban. The last is unusual in that it occupies its own special building rather than quarters in a multi-purpose building. Despite its name, which is a legacy from the French mandate, this institution is the official currency-issuing agency of the Lebanese government, and armed guards stand at its entrance.

Continuing along the right-hand side of the street, across from the park, are shops selling ready-made, European-style clothes, jewelry and cosmetics, electrical appliances; barbers and hairdressers; sweet shops; and cinemas. The upper floors of the five-story to six-story buildings here contain professional offices and also private apartments. Yazbik Street, which extends southward from the clocktower, has a particularly heavy concentration of lawyers' offices, with apartments on the upper floors. This is probably because the adjacent old Saraya housed the law courts until 1961, when they were moved to the new Saraya on the Boulevard.

Advertisements for movies, painted on long strips of cloth held up by ropes, flap overhead in the wide paved area in front of the old Saraya. Close by are three old hotels whose lobbies are on their second floors since the street floors are devoted to shops or cafés. One of the latter has an interior part for bad weather and an outdoor part which has a small fountain and in good weather is crowded with men at the very small tables. As Tal Street continues toward Sahit Saraya 'Adimi, the character of its storefronts remains about the same, while the buildings themselves range from converted mansions to "Turkish Victorian" hotels to modern, balconied structures of reinforced concrete. Among the stores is a branch of a Beirut concern which, when it was first opened after World War II, was remarkable for its wide variety of goods and its labeled, fixed prices. In layout and merchandise, the Tripoli branch is rather like an American dime store. The several sweet shops, often combined with the kitchens in which the products are made, are equipped with small tables where customers can enjoy their purchases. Tripoli is, in fact, well known for this specialty, and in 1962 one of the manufacturers opened a branch in Ras Beirut.

East of the park, several flights of steps lead from the street to the top of the Tal itself, where there is a very large open-air café which extends, also, down to the street. Other structures on the Tal itself are apartment houses, a hospital known (as usual) simply by the name of its proprietor, and a mosque whose minaret is made of a wooden framework covered with red and white tiles, checkerboard fashion. This curious structure adjoins more conventional buildings housing the offices of the Department of Awqaf, which administers the Muslim-endowed properties of the city. To the north of the park are more apartment buildings, a mansion containing the quarters of an upper class gambling club, and the municipal building or city hall (al-Baladiyyi), which houses the offices of the council and the engineering and sanitation departments. North of the city hall is Shari' Madaris (Schools Street) named for the fact that on it is one of the very few government schools built before World War II. The name has been extended to include the whole section north of the city hall, most of which is very new.

ZAHRIYYAH

Through traffic heading north proceeds from the city hall eastward to the Zahriyyah section, where some new building had occurred prior to World War I (as mentioned in Chapter I). Its main street, being the major traffic artery, is jammed with heavy traffic of all kinds. The buildings include some pre-World War I mansions, many interwar apartment buildings, the two girls' schools (as mentioned earlier) protected behind walls and fences, and some post-World War II apartment buildings (some of which have replaced older buildings). Groceries, pharmacies, laundries, and other household-service shops fill the street floors of these buildings, but there are also workshops, particularly those of furniture-makers and carpenters. These are also concentrated in the older side streets to the south and are even found in the newer streets to the north in the Latifi section. Between Zahriyyah Street and the large cemetery just west of the river is a section of new apartment buildings which have carpentry shops below. This is Hayy Ghuraba (Strangers' Quarter), named for the cemetery where, traditionally, strangers who died in Tripoli were buried. Across Zahriyyah Street from Hayy Ghuraba is a small lumberyard surrounded by a board fence. Until recently, there were Jewish graves here, which accounts for a name of the location still in use, Qbur Yihud. When the last remaining Jews departed Tripoli for Beirut or Israel (informants were not sure which), they took the graves with them. Between Qbur Yihud and the bridge, apartment buildings give way to a refrigerated warehouse and rows of one-story workshops (furniture and soapmaking and ironwork). A major product of the ironworkers is ornamental railings, which surmount the concrete block parapets of the new apartment building balconies, and gates which are also used in modern construction.

BAB AL-TIBBANI

The new mosque in Bab al-Tibbani was, like the one on the Boulevard, under construction in 1961–62. Its minaret, too, had a kelly green peak surmounted by a gleaming aluminum crescent. Unlike the other mosque, it is made of reinforced concrete (not dressed stone), has two domes of unequal size, and storefronts in its street floor.

To the through traffic at Bab al-Tibbani are added the trucks and carts serving the wholesale vegetable markets typical of the section, and the buses to and from the Akkar and Syria, which use Bab al-Tibbani as a terminus. The section consists, essentially, of the cemetery just east of the bridge and two or three blocks all around it. The vegetable markets are concentrated in and near the main intersection which is at the foot of the escarpment. South of the cemetery, Bab al-Tibbani gives way to Suq al-Qamih, a narrow street of very cluttered retail food and clothing shops. The 1955 flood did great damage here, and some of the shops are actually merely temporary booths facing away from the new course of the river and the empty, barren ground on both sides of it. The northern part of Bab al-Tibbani consists of relatively new three-story to four-story apartment buildings. To the east, the tall nineteenth-century houses ascend the slope, reached by flights of steps where, in good weather, urchins play and their elders sit on chairs and stools gossiping. Gray stucco with incised designs (crescents, stars, rectangles, and lozenges) is a surface finish, particularly noticeable in older houses in this area, although not limited to it.

Bab al-Tibbani is one of the four sections of Tripoli selected for particular attention in 1960 by the Institut de Recherches et de Formation en Vue de Développement (I.R.F.E.D.). This research group, headed by a French priest, had been commissioned by President Fuad Shihab to evaluate the socioeconomic resources and needs of all of Lebanon. Its report on Bab al-Tibbani says that 90 per cent of the inhabitants are lower class (French "populaire") and 10 per cent middle class. Though on the whole relatively recent in construction, it is generally dirty and in bad repair, with poorly drained streets and insufficient police protection, only two schools and one cinema. There are several soapmaking and candymaking establishments, and the import and distribution of eggs from Syria is important. Connected with the bus traffic to and from Syria are a number of lower class cafés and small hotels which are "quite shabby" ("assez miteux"). Seventy-five per cent of the inhabitants are 'Alawite immigrants from Syria. Few people older than twenty years have had more than a primary education. Among the lower class majority, domestic hygiene is generally very bad, and alcoholism is a frequent problem. There are "intense neighborhood relations" but little interest in initiating public improvements.[1]

North of Bab al-Tibbani there are two new sections which constitute the outer edge of Tripoli in this sector. East of the main road, and built on the slope, is Maluli; it has a mosque and includes among its apartment buildings the only government-financed housing in the city. Across the main road is Ba'al Saraqbi which includes apartment buildings and shacks.

[1] I.R.F.E.D., *Etude préliminaire sur les besoins et les possibilités de développement au Liban, 1959–60* (1962), pp. 5–6.

APPENDIX A

The I.R.F.E.D. investigators consider Ba'al Saraqbi, with its true bidon-ville, to be acutely in need of improvement, although their social class evaluation makes it sound more varied than Bab al-Tibbani: 10 per cent destitute, 75 per cent lower class, and 15 per cent average or well off. Half of its population, immediately adjoining Bab al-Tibbani, is 'Alawite. Forty per cent work in the wholesale food markets. The unemployment rate is 25 per cent, alcoholism and drug addiction (morphine and opium) are serious problems, less than half of the children have received even the first part of elementary schooling, and about 80 per cent of the people over fifteen years of age are illiterate. There are "intense neighborhood activities," unspecified except that they involve "political, social, and ethnic tensions." [2] The president of the municipal council told me that there are in Tripoli about 20,000 immigrants from Syria who do the kinds of work no one else is willing to do, and it is reasonable to guess that most of them live in Bab al-Tibbani and Ba'al Saraqbi. Among middle class Tripolitans, these sections have the reputation of being tough, dangerous, and unwholesome, and the concentration of 'Alawites in them is a generally known fact. Otherwise I am not able to comment usefully on the I.R.F.E.D. evaluations.

AL-QUBBAH

Al-Qubbah (locally pronounced al-'Ibbi), which means a natural prom-ontory, is on the crest of the escarpment. Between it and the river — that is, on the actual slopes — are networks of paved paths and steps which connect buildings either belonging to the Old City or, like Hayy Jadid (New Quarter) below building 44, representing the earliest growth beyond the Old City. 'Uqbi al-Mufti and Tal'a al-Zahir are two of the Old City sections here. In order to visit them, one must go on foot and climb up and down, and their names are actually unfamiliar to Tripoli-tans who have never had any business in them.

Al-Qubbah can be reached by steps from Swayqah (see Map 5) or from Bab al-Tibbani. It can also be reached by a paved street winding up from the northern edge of Bab al-Tibbani, and by a new road which starts outside the city beyond Maluli and follows the contours of a dry stream bed gradually upward. In 1962, most of this road was outside the built-up parts of the city, although there already was a new army camp and a government hospital east of it at the point where it makes an acute turn. These structures are not shown on the maps, but they are directly north of the building compound (item 2, Map 3) which was originally French army barracks and is now IPC headquarters. Most of the buildings in al-Qubbah are new, and there still are some vacant areas

[2] *Ibid.*, pp. 3–5.

1. Boulevard, looking north, cinema at left adjoining typical 1920's building

2. New buildings on the Boulevard, near al-Tal

3. *New buildings on left, garden wall of early 20th century mansion (near traffic circle on Boulevard) on right*

4. *The clocktower in al-Tal*

5. *Shari' al-Mina, looking west from al-Tal, near intersection of the Boulevard*

6. *Early 20th century mansion in al-Tal, IPC club above, bus station below*

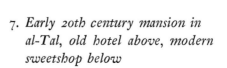

7. *Early 20th century mansion in al-Tal, old hotel above, modern sweetshop below*

8. *Shariʿ al-Tal, looking east toward Sahit Saraya ʾAdimi, modern shops below, professional offices and apartments above, arcaded early 20th century mansion right of center*

9. *Café in al-Tal*

10. Shops in al-Tal

11. Outdoor coffeehouse in al-Tal, rugs for sale on fence, early 20th century hotels in rear

12. Central fountain in park

13. Sahit Nijmi, looking toward Sahit Kura

*14. Shariʿ Rahbat, looking from Sahit Saraya ʾAdimi
toward Sahit Nijmi, National Evangelical Church
(Presbyterian) on left*

15. *Sahit Saraya 'Adimi, view from Kindarjiyyi*

16. *Sahit Saraya 'Adimi, looking toward Shari' Kinayis*

17. *Grocery in apartment house, bicycle for home deliveries, ka'k vendor at left with tripod*

18. Coffee vendors in al-Tal

*19. Pushcarts and small shops in the Old City,
apartments on upper floors*

20. Making of furniture

21. *Nahhasiyyin: stamping designs into tray for tourist market*

22. *Locally made and imported kitchenware for sale*

23. *Making kitchenware for local market*

24. Quiltmakers

25. Bedsprings, mattresses, and quilts for sale. Note protective hand stenciled on pillar and photos of Shihab and Nasser on wall.

26. Foodstores in Rifa 'iyah

27. *Seated man selling national lottery tickets, man on left carrying live chicken by feet*

28. *Bazarkan*

29. *Houses near Sagha*

30. *Minaret of Mansuri mosque (originally a Crusader belfry), 20th century addition to mosque in foreground*

31. *'Izz al-Din Hammam (14th century) surrounded by later structures*

32. *The citadel, seen from the river, from upstream*

33. Abu Samra, seen from Taylan mosque

34. Maronite cathedral in Hayy Mutran

35. *Apartment building in Shariʿ ʿAzmi*

36. Shariʿ ʿAzmi, ungraded street in foreground

37. Zihr al-Maghar and Mount Lebanon

38. Zihr al-Maghar

surrounded by buildings. Just north of the cemetery, however, is a section which was mostly built up between 1900 and 1945. It is inhabited by over a thousand people who are associated with the Maronite village of Hadchite high in the mountains. There is a Maronite church in this section whose typical open belfry is now overshadowed by tall apartment buildings. Before they were built, however, the minaret of a nearby mosque was heightened so as to be taller than the belfry.

The main thoroughfare of al-Qubbah runs crookedly from the Presbyterian boys' school to this Hadchite section, where it curves decidedly to the east and leads to the fork near IPC headquarters. It is lined with small shops. South of this eastward segment of the street is a newly built-up area extending to the crest of the escarpment, where one can look across the river to Abu Samra on the other side. The traffic circle and segment of concentric streets here can be clearly seen in Map 3. They reflect the new street plan mentioned in Chapter I. This is an area of two-story or three-story modern apartment buildings whose roofs bristle with reinforced concrete pillars intended eventually to support additional stories. Such unfinished but inhabited buildings are particularly common here and in Abu Samra, but they occur elsewhere in Tripoli and are, in fact, widely encountered all over Lebanon. Many streets in this new section are unpaved or partially paved, and the traffic circle is not yet functional. Its curbs and those of the radiating streets are set, but the actual roadway runs directly across it, and olive groves impinge directly on it to the south. On the crest, and partly down the slope until it becomes too steep, are apartment buildings of from three to seven stories, facing similar buildings in Abu Samra. All this is the most recent outgrowth of al-Qubbah, and some people know it by its own name, Zihr al-Maghar.

THE SLOPES OF THE RIVER

On both sides of the river at this point, the slopes are steep and rough with pockmarked, striated, weathered limestone. Lower down, paths follow the contours. On the Zihr al-Maghar side, a path leads to a small bidonville, and on the Abu Samra side one leads to the Mawlawi Tikki-yah (building 14, Map 3) and an old mill still in use, followed by a row of new, low apartment houses. In the narrow bottomland of the river grow tall reeds, and some orange trees and palms. The main stream of the river has a pebbly bottom, but there is also a canal on the left side (looking downstream) with a concrete wall; the canal was once used to carry water intended for domestic purposes. Farther upstream are the ruins of an aqueduct which once crossed the river.

Another new section, 'Uqbi al-Himrawi, is built on the steep slopes opposite the citadel. From this vantage point the citadel looks very impressive, rising above old houses whose walls come progressively closer to the river as one looks downstream until, at the first bridge, it actually washes them. This pedestrian bridge is a temporary construction of steel girders and boards to replace an old masonry bridge that was destroyed by the 1955 flood. To the north of the bridge, before one crosses it, runs Swayqah (little Suq) which is simply a continuation of Suq al-Qamih and is very similar to it. This bridge and the next one downstream are heavily used, for they are the most convenient means of access to Swayqah and to the houses on the slopes above it.

The sheer masonry walls rising from the river on its west bank are punctured by heavily barred, sometimes overhanging windows, and tufts of weeds sprout here and there. An occasional dome or minaret relieves the roof line, and one can get some perspective on some of the really old houses so as to gain an idea of the style. The roof is either entirely flat or else part of it is hipped and red-tiled. The houses are usually three stories high, with a few barred and shuttered windows. Very frequently there are round or six-cornered portholes above the windows to help ventilate the high-ceilinged rooms in summer. None of Tripoli's old houses has the elaborately carved and latticed *haramlik* bays seen near al-Azhar in Cairo, and preserved in various museums of Islamic art; but in some instances semicylindrical wooden projections serve the same purpose: a view of the street in all directions without the viewer's being seen. There are good photographs of some of these houses in the UNESCO volume cited in Chapter II. They commonly have interior courts — often no more spacious than air shafts — no hint of whose existence is to be seen outside. The ground floors of many of these houses are vaulted, and in some cases the arches, with their projecting supports, are allowed to show on the exterior of the building, giving a medieval effect.

THE OLD CITY

The I.R.F.E.D. report describes the Old City as if it were an internally undifferentiated unit. This is an inaccurate view, but I suspect that it is an "image" of whose accuracy many Tripolitans have convinced themselves. The report says that the Old City dates from about 1650. This is obviously not true for the Mamluk and early Ottoman monuments, but it may be intended to mean that most of the houses date from not earlier than about 1650, and this may be true. Certainly many of them are newer, and there was a serious earthquake in the seventeenth century which did great damage. In February of 1962, demolition crews discovered in a subterranean wall a box of gold coins minted in 1526. With reference to the inhabitants of the Old City, the report says that 5 per cent are rich, 50 per cent are middle class, 40 per cent lower class, and 5 per cent destitute, and that in general they have a strongly traditional-ist mentality. There is some alcoholism among the older people and hashish smoking among the younger. About one-third of the children have finished primary school. There is "lively neighborhood life." [3]

Crossing the bridge into the Old City, one enters the Bab Hadid (Iron Gate) section and quickly arrives at building 5 (Map 5). Here is an open area from which streets and alleys go off in several directions. Up toward the castle goes a new street wide enough for automobiles. In fact, in 1962, demolition was taking place for the further extension of this street into the Old City. One informant said that this process had already de-stroyed an old concentration at this location of shops specializing in cheesemaking. To the north and south run narrow alleys on which there are relatively few shops. The one to the north is at one point arched over by two stories of rooms, a type of construction of which there were still several examples in 1962. The specimen illustrated in the UNESCO volume [4] was destroyed by the 1955 flood. The alley leading to the south into the Mawlawiyyi section is at times virtually a tunnel between the heavy front doors and under the rooms of old houses.

Building 5 is partly a cluster of domes which cover the 'Izz-al-Din Hammam and the adjoining Suq al-Khayyatin (Tailors' Bazaar) both of which are Mamluk structures still fully in use. The tailors' suq is, in effect, a single short street, arched over and nearly closed at the top, with shops on each side and tailors busily working at sewing machines outside the shops. The effect is as much that of a long hall-like workshop as it is that of a street. The tailors here specialize in the custom-making of clothing of traditional style such as *shirwal*, the very baggy men's trousers still very much favored, especially among men of all ages from the Akkar. This tailors' suq is actually a part of Bazarkan, the street of small cloth shops extending to the south for a short way and to the north until the shops' goods change to clothes and shoes and then to leather. A small square with a fountain in the middle (Birkat al-Millaha) and a covered intersection of alleys (Suq al-Haraj) are two features of this clothes-shoes-leather section which adjoins Dibbagha, the tradi-tional section of tanneries already mentioned. Many of the shops here are in one-story structures, but most of the shops in the Old City actually comprise the street floors of buildings whose upper floors contain private homes. Most of the old mosques are similarly obscured by the shops on

[3] *Ibid.*, pp. 6–8.
[4] UNESCO, *Lebanon* (Paris, 1954), plate 31.

their street floors, and only the sharp eye is likely, on first acquaintance, to discover the mosques' entrances, which may provide pleasing glimpses of clean, smooth, uncluttered floors, in marked contrast with the dirty confusion outside.

Tirbi'a is a network of alleys where furnituremakers are concentrated. In these small shops European-style chairs, sofas, tables, and cabinets are fashioned out of wood. Some shops specialize in modernistic designs, but a large number produce late Victorian and Edwardian scrollwork. The reek of varnish, the scrape of sandpaper, and the whir of various electric tools fill the air here. Shops making iron bedspring frames mark the transition from Tirbi'a to Nahhasiyyin, where men and boys hammer out brass and copper trays for the Beirut tourist market and various copper and brass utensils for conservative Lebanese and Syrian housekeepers. Also sold here are European ready-made tinned or aluminum kitchen utensils, such as kettles, baking trays, and coffee beakers of various sizes.

Between Sahit Saraya 'Adimi and Khan al-Sabun (building 3, Map 5) runs Kindarjiyyi, an alley whose shops specialize in ready-made clothes, such as socks, scarves, and underwear, and especially shoes, slippers, and sandals. Khan al-Sabun (Soap Khan) is used for the curing and storage of the old-fashioned soap for which Tripoli is well known. Running between it and the Nuri Hammam (building 6) is a single street on which there are about forty small goldsmiths' shops. Thin bangles with rather standardized, incised decorations are made and sold on the premises. Also sold are rings and gold coins, either plain or set in filigree work. The majority of goldsmiths are Christians, but their clientele consists mostly of Muslim peasants who come here to invest their free capital in the one precious metal in which they have firm trust. The goldsmiths' prices are determined very largely by weight and are linked to the fluctuations of the uncontrolled Beirut gold market.

Pushcarts, as well as shoppers, fill all these alleys in the daytime, but at night the carts are gone, and the shops are closed tight either by metal barricades or by wooden doors which, when open, may support display cases and racks. Because of the disappearance of the latter at night, the commercial alleys of the Old City are actually considerably wider at night than they are in the daytime.

Between the Nuri Hammam and the Mansuri mosque (building 1, Map 5) runs an alley which becomes a tunnel before it emerges on 'Attarin and Sagha, two names of a single narrow street extending southward and leading eventually into Bab al-Raml. The shops on this long street do not give a superficial impression of homogeneity, but groceries, butcher shops, and fishmongers do seem to predominate, although there are some stationery shops, small cafés, and other retailers. This gives the impression of being the main street of the Old City. It varies from about fifteen to twenty feet in width, with a sidewalk on each side and a roadway just wide enough for pushcarts. Dead-end streets and steps lead off from it up the slopes of Abu Samra. On the opposite side, it gives access to the sections I have already described and to Bab Hadadin (Smiths' Gate) which, like the dead-end streets, is primarily residential. There are some, but very few, storefronts in the street floors of its houses, and the bottom parts of the house walls are usually blank, pierced only by the rather small and very heavy doors. Most of the windows are in the upper stories, usually have wooden shutters, and often have iron or wooden bars.

URBAN RENEWAL

As Map 5 indicates, a new street has been cut into the Old City from Sahit Nijmi, which passes by the low, rather featureless southern façade of the Mansuri mosque, and provides automobile access to Abu Samra. Another street, parallel to it, has been cut into Bab Hadadin, effectively destroying what had been a triangular cul-de-sac of old alleys. Another new street has been cut from Sahit Saraya 'Adimi to the Mansuri mosque. A typical quality of these new streets is that they look as if the wreckers who cleared them arbitrarily ignored anything not standing directly in their path. At many points these new streets pass between the broken arches and even whole ground-floor rooms of buildings which were otherwise destroyed, and peddlers frequently set up booths in these ruins where they afford some shelter. American urban renewal projects often produce such a blitzed effect, but, as in the case of the West End project in Boston, there is much public complaint about it: many people care. Do many Tripolitans care? Although I heard many complaints about the city from its residents, none touched on this subject, and there are general indications of lack of concern for the exterior appearance of buildings.

A street of steps leads from 'Attarin up the slope to the citadel, the bottom of which is at eye level with the roofs of the nearest buildings. The huge bulk of the citadel is deserted inside except for restoration work crews, whose rather desultory efforts are supported by the Lebanese Ministry of Antiquities with financial assistance from the United States. The great massive iron-sheathed wooden gate is closed most of the time. Children play in the stony rubble around the building, pedestrians on errands down in the Old City frequently pass by, and an occasional automobile ventures down from Abu Samra to Bab Hadid where, in 1962, it could only turn around and return the way it came.

APPENDIX A

ABU SAMRA

Almost all of the buildings in Abu Samra have been built since 1945, and most of the streets have been laid out since then, too. As in Zihr al-Maghar, there are the outlines of traffic circles which have not yet been fully realized. Some of the streets are paved; others are partially paved, with whole sections consisting of fist-sized stones which have been broken by hand labor and may wait for some time before they are further crushed by rollers and asphalted. Then there are a few blocks in Abu Samra where buildings have been erected in anticipation of planned streets; these have yet even to be graded and are simply rough, weedy ground where goats occasionally graze. A road leaves Abu Samra toward the southeast, but it is not heavily used as a thoroughfare to the hinterland, and the police conduct road tests on it for people seeking drivers' licenses. From here there is a clean-sweep view across the olive groves of the plateau and up the slopes of Mount Lebanon. From the buildings along the crest above the river, or from the few remaining gaps between them, there is a fine view of the citadel downstream and of Zihr al-Maghar across the way. But the streets and buildings have been built in such a way that it is not easy for the passerby to get these views.

THE NEW ARCHITECTURE

Most of the buildings in Abu Samra are apartment houses whose style is a definite type, though no two buildings are identical. The frame is reinforced concrete; maximum height is eight stories and average about six. The nonbearing walls are usually made of concrete block or, occasionally, stones from demolished buildings. Balconies, stacked, one above another with or without connecting pillars, are universal, and all apartments have at least one. The surface treatment is smooth stucco painted white or light gray, or a variety of pastel blues, greens, yellows, or pinks. Combinations such as colored walls and white trim around windows and balconies are common, but a building with, say, green walls and yellow or pink pillars is not unusual. Windows are never screened for flies, but they always have shutters, and these are of two kinds: one a set of hinged wooden panels with louvers, the other a screen of horizontal slats to be cranked up and down. There seems to be a general tendency to keep the shutters closed, even when the sun is not especially strong. The balconies and roofs are constantly used for drying laundry as well as for lounging.

Buildings of less than maximum height are, as I mentioned before, frequently unfinished, and have the vertical members of the frame on their roofs, each sprouting reinforcement rods, which may eventually support additional floors. The parapets of balconies-to-be may also break the roof line of such buildings. The roofs are easily reached by the main stairs. Inspection of additions to apartment houses thirty to forty years old in Tripoli shows that this practice of leaving buildings unfinished is nothing new and that many years may elapse before they are completed. Tax advantages and the unwillingness of builders to go into debt in order to complete a building were the reasons given me for this widespread practice.

In general style, these buildings are very similar to structures in present-day southern France, Italy, Greece, and many other Mediterranean countries. The lack of decoration, the emphasis on balconies, the frequent use of curved surfaces, and the pale colors all convey a more "modern" effect than is customary in North American cities of the same general size. Hand labor, however, is conspicuous in their construction. Concrete is mixed in the street, and large piles of sand and gravel are obstacles with which the pedestrian must learn to cope. The concrete is carried up on men's backs in 5-gallon cans. The workers often sing rhythmically at their tasks, and some of them camp out in the building while it is under construction. Shopkeepers, also, may set up business in the ground floor before any of the apartments are ready for occupancy.

There are some shops in Abu Samra, and all of them deal in household supplies, such as bottled gas, kerosene, packaged foods, bottled drinks, etc.

BAB AL-RAML

Descending from Abu Samra to Bab al-Raml (Sand Gate), one goes from newest Tripoli to middle-aged Tripoli. At the eastern corner of the large cemetery are several open-air cafés (as in the Tal) and a great variety of shops below the rather dingy apartments. Automobile repair shops, also, are particularly frequent here. The cemetery, with its many canopied graves, is partly surrounded by one-story buildings containing shops and partly by a wall. The main entrance in the latter consists of two gates, side by side, above each of which is a sign. One says, in Arabic, "men" and the other "women," but usually only one of the gates was open, and members of both sexes used it.

The main street at Bab al-Raml, which bends at the corner I have just mentioned, is a segment of what was until recently the main road out of Tripoli to Beirut. This route continues on into the Tal past the northern corner of the cemetery. Just north of this corner, across the street from greasy machine shops, is a row of several early twentieth-century mansions, one of which had a garden and cypress trees behind an ornamental wall.

Additional stories have subsequently been built, each floor repeating the original pattern of central ornamental windows and French doors behind pillars supporting balconies. At first the homes of notables, these buildings now house apartments and physicians' offices. The Karami mansion is very close, though it is surrounded by a high wall and has a barren area to its south and east where there are some shacks and tents of squatters.

Between this area and the Tal are a mixture of twentieth-century buildings from the earliest to the latest. The ground floors are all commercial, but there are no workshops except for automobile repair. The upper floors are apartments. Sahit Kura is a major intersection here; from it a new straight street runs directly to Sahit Nijmi. Hardware stores and the establishments of plumbers and electricians are common here. Taxis and buses which make regular runs to the Christian villages of al-Kura park in the middle of the square (hence its name), and there are also several coffeehouses here, frequented by some rather rough customers. The Tripoli jail (at the rear of the old Saraya) is at one corner of Sahit Kura, and one block west of this, parallel to Shari' al-Tal, is Shari' Sintral (French: "centrale") which is named for the telephone exchange building on it. The shopfronts in these streets are like those in the Tal, containing businesses which cater to middle-class people with Europeanized tastes: electrical appliances, automobiles, optical equipment, insurance, banks, and "nouveautés" (ladies' accessories of the latest European fashion). Among the electrical appliances in 1962 were television sets even though Tripoli did not yet receive television signals. Some of the businesses in the one-room street floor shops are very high-risk enterprises. For example, one shop was lit by a naked electric light bulb and furnished solely with a desk, two chairs, and a telephone. It appeared to be a one-man loan company.

HAYY MUTRAN AND THE OTHER
NEW WESTERN QUARTERS

The main westward street in Hayy Mutran is Shari' al-Mina, along which some of the earliest twentieth-century growth took place. Some of the buildings on it are large, red-tiled houses; others are apartment houses of the 1920's, and there are some newer structures. In general, this main thoroughfare is more battered and old-fashioned in appearance than are the adjacent blocks on each side of it, where most of the buildings are very new. Buildings extend, with some gaps, out along Shari' al-Mina about as far as Duktura Rifa'i's hospital (building 52, Map 3), but solid-block build-up does not extend beyond the area between building 48 (a Catholic school) and the new Maronite cathedral (building 20). There is a similar extension along Shari' 'Azmi, but there are no buildings on Shari' Mitayn beyond the municipal stadium (building 5). Duktur Nini's new hospital (building 51) stands in a clearing in the orange trees, and there are only scattered buildings on the street which approaches it. The street connecting Shari' al-Mina and Shari' 'Azmi has no buildings on it except at each corner (building 50 is Duktur Munla's hospital). This mostly unpaved street passes through dense orange groves, views of which are frequently blocked off by high screens of reeds separating the groves of different owners. Black water flows sluggishly in the drainage ditches; many of these now run through covered conduits under the pavements of Hayy Mutran. Scattered among the trees are the huts of grove laborers and watchmen, who often may be seen roasting corn over outdoor braziers.

Shari' al-Mina and Shari' Mitayn have only recently been widened, straightened, and provided with median strips. In 1961–62, the paving and curbing of these avenues was only partially completed. Also, throughout the period of my study, open ditches, piles of earth, stacks of pipes, and whiffs of sewer gas were noticeable features of the new, western parts of Tripoli where improvements in the sewer system were under way.

Hayy Mutran (Bishop's Quarter) takes its name from the Maronite bishop's residence, built in the 1920's on the northeastern side of the large triangular block which is unmistakable in Map 3. The street defining this side of the block is Shari' Mutran. Some people call the whole section, not just this street, Shari' Mutran, but others have adopted the more general term Hayy, while still others sometimes call the whole section "Shari' al-Mina." When building was first begun here early in the century, the area was called Hayy Saqah (Ditches) after the drainage canals which had to be covered as orange trees were cut down and streets were laid out.

The newest apartment houses in Hayy Mutran are of the same style as those in Abu Samra, although there seem to be fewer partly finished buildings. There also seem to be more street-floor shops — chiefly groceries, cleaners, and laundries. The older apartment buildings are of several styles, two deserving of mention. The first of these is an adaptation of the early twentieth-century Lebanese mansion. Its rectangular floor plan consists of a central hall and formal parlor, with the other rooms opening off from it on both sides. At each end of the hall is a set of ornamental, arched-top windows with French doors and a veranda outside. The apartment adaptation of this consists essentially of stacking four or five such floors on top of each other, putting an exterior staircase on one side and supporting the verandas on columns. The other type of old apartment building dispenses with the symmetrical floor plan, the verandas and columns, and provides a single balcony for each window. Both types of building have considerable ornamentation of a generalized Italian or specifically Venetian sort.

The I.R.F.E.D. report says that the settlement of Hayy Mutran began about 1920 and has developed rapidly since 1940. This is accurate unless one includes in the section Shari' al-Mina, which had been built up before World War I. The report goes on to say that Hayy Mutran was originally occupied by foreigners, diplomats, and the rich. IPC did commission and/or supervise a number of buildings here, some of which still have the window screens the company required. However, aside from IPC personnel, the foreign population of Tripoli has been very small indeed. Fifty per cent of the present population of Hayy Mutran are said originally to have come from northern Mount Lebanon and 10 per cent from the Akkar, and these people include merchants, lawyers, officials, physicians, engineers, and property owners. Ten per cent of the inhabitants are said to be poor or lower class, 78 per cent middle class, 10 per cent well off, and 2 per cent rich. Despite the relatively high standard of living here, there is little neighborhood life and there is a kind of individualism inimical to mutual aid activities and to actions which might improve the quarter.[5]

The two major landmarks of Hayy Mutran are the Maronite bishop's cruciform yellow stucco residence, partly hidden behind a wall and surrounded by large trees; and the new Maronite cathedral, with a single steeple, a hexagonal cupola, small gothic windows, and a thoroughly non-Mediterranean look about it. Made of light gray stone, it stands starkly by itself. These landmarks are among several indications that the relative strength of the Maronites in Tripoli has been increasing in recent decades.

Shari' 'Azmi is the name of the section between the street of that name and Shari' Mitayn. Like Abu Samra, it has some elegant modernistic buildings and also some unfinished streets, some auto repair shops along Shari' Mitayn, and a large refrigerated warehouse.

THE MINA

The regular route of the *service* taxis between Tripoli and the Mina runs along Shari' 'Azmi and returns to Tripoli along Shari' al-Mina. In

[5] I.R.F.E.D., *Etude préliminaire*, pp. 9–10.

1962, the segment of Shari' Mitayn between the stadium and the railroad station was too rough for ordinary traffic. The last building in Tripoli on 'Azmi Street is about six hundred yards from the station, and it is unique. It is the only free-standing modern villa in the city. Financial difficulties prevented its owner from living in it, and it was converted into a hotel. In 1962 it was the only hotel in the city meeting modern European standards.

The railroad station is surrounded by warehouses, small freight cars on sidings, and lumber yards piled with huge unmilled logs. North of the station is the recently expanded dock area, not yet fully developed. (See Map 2 for details of the Mina.) West of the station is a "zone franche" where, as in Beirut, goods in transit may be stored without payment of customs duties; and west of this are repair facilities for small vessels on the site of the old seaplane base.

The Mina itself (Map 2) appears to be divided in two by a wide avenue, an extension of Shari' al-Mina. Called Shari' Mar Ilyas (St. Elias Street) by the Christians and Shari' Port Said (in memory of the 1956 Suez crisis) by the Muslims, it is entirely new. It was laid out in an area which was only sparsely built up, and many people still think of the entrance to the Mina as being via the smaller streets to the north. As the street patterns indicate, the old parts of the Mina are generally north of Shari' Mar Ilyas/Port Said, and some new automobile streets have been cut into them from the new avenue. Except along the western shoreline and scattered here and there east as far as the cemeteries, the buildings south of the avenue are mostly very new. Whereas there are several separate new parts of Tripoli, there is really only one in the Mina.

The I.R.F.E.D. investigators estimate that two-thirds of the Mina's population live north of Mar Ilyas/Port Said avenue, and that the greater part of the houses there may be as old as three hundred years. The new section south of the avenue has been developing rapidly since 1952. I.R.F.E.D.'s socioeconomic estimate of the Mina's population is 6 per cent destitute, 60 per cent lower class (or poor), 30 per cent middle class, 2 per cent well off, and 2 per cent rich. On these estimates, its population is more similar to that of the Old City of Tripoli than to the other sections — but is in general poorer. The report cites problems of drug addiction and alcoholism, the presence of intense neighborhood relations, and, as in all the other sections in the sample, no sense of community.[6]

Architecturally, the Mina is very similar to Tripoli except that it has no Mamluk period buildings, fewer mosques, and more churches. Also, one is more aware of single, private houses; a number of these have

[6] *Ibid.*, pp. 8–9.

walled yards and gardens. None of them is new. They are noticeable in Fawq al-Rih and Mar Ilyas (the two main sections west of the traffic circle on the new avenue) as well as along the avenue on what were the outskirts of the old town. The commercial life of the latter is centered along the northern waterfront, where there are the customs house, an old khan serving as a tenement, offices of shipping companies, a few European consulates, a large number of cafés and restaurants, and fishermen's nets drying on racks. There are also a few streets resembling Sagha and 'Attarin in Tripoli, notably Suq al-Kharab (mostly Christian) and Suq al-Muslimiyyah. Sahit Tirb (the main open area near the center of the old town) has a large church on it and is the site of a graveyard which was moved away in the recent past. It marks the general boundary between the Christian part of the old Mina (west) and the Muslim part (east). The mainly residential sections of the latter are Zuqaq Na'ura, Nuss Birtawshi and Buwwabi, and they are reminiscent of Bab Hadadin. The area south of the avenue has several built-up sections interspersed with empty wastelands. From west to east they are: Fawq al-Rih and Hammam Maqlub, respectively north and south of the small half-moon bay; Harat al-Ramli and Qabr al-Zayni, mostly new and relatively prosperous in appearance, although the apartment buildings are generally not as tall as those in Tripoli; and Abu Fraydu, adjoining the large Christian cemetery and notorious for its brothels.

The Mina is the traditional port of Tripoli, and the port, despite its current problems, contributes much to the welfare of the people through jobs and a portion of the customs duties received. Tripoli depends on the Mina, and the Mina people certainly depend on Tripoli for a wider variety of job opportunities than are to be found in their own town. Yet the Mina is actually a separate municipality, and many of its people are somewhat jealously conscious of their being distinct from Tripoli. The Mina is generally thought of as being poorer and more Christian, and these are probably more important elements in such feelings than is its being a separate municipality.

THE IPC TERMINAL

There is, finally, another port of Tripoli, the Iraq Petroleum Company's terminal, on the shore about a mile beyond al-Biddawi. Here is received and stored the oil which flows through pipelines from Kirkuk in northern Iraq. The tanks are on the slopes of Mount Turbul, and from them the oil flows to the beach; there it is distributed by underwater pipes to four mooring stations about a mile offshore. These facilities have recently been enlarged to accommodate supertankers, and many of the operations are being automated. The terminal compound, very carefully guarded, includes an office building and villas for the top supervisory personnel. Royalties paid by IPC to the Lebanese government are an important item in the budget of the Tripoli municipality, although the terminal is not within its borders.

Tripoli, the Mina, Bahsas, al-Biddawi, and the IPC terminal are physically and in other respects separate entities, but they are so interrelated socioeconomically that most outsiders think of them all together as constituting Tripoli. This is a legitimate point of view, and in general in this book I have concentrated my discussions on Tripoli proper, treating the other locations as subsidiary to it.

POSTSCRIPT 1965

At the time of the writing of this book, three years after the completion of the field study, some changes are already observable in Tripoli.

Most conspicuous to the visitor are the embellishments along the Boulevard. The center strip has lawn and flowerbeds, and there is a fountain at the intersection of the Boulevard and Tal Street. A bronze statue of 'Abdul-Hamid Karami (slim, bareheaded, dressed in a western business suit, and striding forward with one arm raised as if in greeting) stands in the circle next to the Karami mansion, facing south toward Beirut. The roadway of the Boulevard has been completed across the river so that through traffic can now bypass most of the city.

The sides and center strip of Shari' al-Mina have likewise been beautified with grass and flowers all the way to the Mina, and there are signs admonishing people to care for the plantings, but there are only a few new buildings along this and the two parallel avenues. There is no sign of the proposed international fair except for a development office on Shari' 'Azmi.

There seems to have been additional building in Maluli, along the roads leading out of town eastward from al-Qubbah, and in Zihr al-Maghar. There is a second new mosque, with slender Turkish style minaret, in Bab al-Tibbani, and the one nearing completion in 1962 now already looks somewhat worn. The bright green of the peak of its minaret, as well as that of the minaret of the new mosque on the Boulevard, has been replaced with a more neutral color.

Destruction and construction continue in the Old City. The concrete course of the river now extends upstream almost to the Bab Hadid footbridge, and there is a swath of demolition on both sides of it. Water flows through it, and the old, curved segment of the river is being filled in with earth and rubble. The empty area between the old course and the new one is, however, still empty.

APPENDIX A

Suq Nahhasiyyin has been replaced by a wider, paved street which runs from the 'Izz al-Din Hammam to Shari' Kinayis. It is therefore now possible to drive an automobile down from Abu Samra, past the citadel, through Bab Hadid, and thence to Shari' Kinayis. The coppersmiths and brassworkers have retreated into Tirbi'a and apparently are no longer clustered. Half the buildings along Kindarjiyyi have been torn down, presumably in order to facilitate the widening of the street. There has also been some demolition of old buildings between Sahit Nijmi and Bab al-Raml, but otherwise the Old City seems very much as it was three years before.

In Bahsas, there is an additional compound of buildings on the southern outskirts, but there have been few other changes, and the large building which was unfinished in 1962 is still apparently unfinished, although some modifications have been made in its window openings.

PHOTOGRAPHS

The photographs in this book were taken by Mr. Jeff Farrell during a three-day period in January of 1962. It will be noticed that a number of people in the pictures are dressed for the chilly weather but that nevertheless many others are lightly clad. The caption of each photograph is intended to place the scene in terms which should already be familiar, and to illustrate various points in previous discussions. Some of these points will be reemphasized in what follows. The pictures themselves raise some additional points, to be discussed here as well.

The first three illustrations show the commercial character of the Boulevard, but it must be remembered that most of the upper floors are private apartments. The two seven-story structures in Figure 2 are actually the wings of a single building whose deeply recessed main entrance serves as the foyer for two cinemas. A bank and a café occupy most of the street floor, and professional offices and private apartments occupy the upper floors. This is a typical modern multipurpose building. Figure 3 contrasts the crowded contemporary constructions with the spacious elegance attempted by some of the notables of Tripoli on the outskirts of the city before World War I.

Figures 4 and 5 look westward along the same street, which begins as Shari' al-Tal and then becomes Shari' al-Mina. In terms of Map 3, we are here looking from building 4 (clocktower) to building 47 (the Catholic school, seen in the distance in Figure 5). The building in Figure 4, in use below but only partly finished on the upper floors, is but the first example of this pattern. The trees on each side of the clocktower grow in the sidewalk along the southern edge of the park; when the picture was taken they had not yet been pollarded, as many of their companions on other sides of the park had been.

Figure 6 could very nearly be attached to the right of Figure 5, and the roofline of this old house can be seen in Figure 4 beyond the trees to the left of the tower. Figure 6 also shows the way in which newer structures adhere to older ones, eventually sometimes, though not yet in this case, obscuring the form of the latter. Figures 6 and 7 show two versions of the triple-arch motif so popular in Lebanese architecture before World War I. The row of buildings in Figure 8 mask the actual Tal, or hillock, from which the section gets its name.

Figures 9 and 10 further illustrate the shopfronts of the Tal section. The café in Figure 9 is owned and frequented by Christians. Taxis park near it, and like many cafés it serves travelers to certain villages not only as an eating place but also as a message center and temporary depository for packages. The advertisements pasted on its walls have nothing to do with the café and are representative of the uncontrolled posting of bills, characteristic not only of Tripoli but of all Lebanese communities.

The coffeehouse shown in Figure 11 is directly across the street from the café in Figure 9 and is frequented by Muslims except during the daytime in Ramadan, the month of fasting, when it is deserted. The building in the right-hand background of Figure 11 illustrates what I have previously called the Turkish Victorian style, but note the cinema entrance on its street floor. The street floor of the other old building contains the indoor part of the coffeehouse for use in inclement weather.

The park, Figure 12, dates from the 1920's and is much frequented except in bad weather and at night, when its gates are shut and locked. Figures 13–16 show the streets along the western edge of the Old City from Sahit Nijmi to Shari' Kinayis. The street floors here contain a mixture of types of shop, but hardware dealers, electricians, and plumbers are numerous. The apartments on the upper floors are typically very spacious by American standards and inhabited mostly by middle class and even some quite wealthy families. The church in Figure 14 is building 21 (Map 3). The cypresses behind it grow in the yard of the gendarmerie (building 12, Map 5), which used to house one of the Presbyterian schools. Shari' Kinayis was cut through old buildings, remnants of some of which can be seen in Figure 16. In some of the pictures, the advertisements of certain European products are very much in evidence, signs obviously provided by the manufacturer.

Figure 17 shows a typical household-service establishment, in a 1920's apartment building in Hayy Mutran, whose street floor is not entirely commercialized. Coffee vendors in the Tal are shown in Figure 18. Figure

19 is a good example of the intensely commercial activity of the Old City, again combined with domestic households on the upper floors.

The furnituremakers in Figure 20 can be found in large numbers in Tirbi'a, Shari' Kinayis, and adjoining portions of Zahriyyah. Their products are largely a response to demands created by the boom in modern apartment building. Whereas the physical concentration of the workshops and their small size seems traditional, the tools and products of these men are strictly modern.

The craftsman in Figure 21 uses Belgian brass and copper sheets for making trays; these are sold in the tourist market centered in Beirut. His highly standardized designs, modifications of classic Islamic motifs, can be produced fairly rapidly. The two shops shown in Figure 22, however, sell specifically to the local market. The shiny, domelike objects in the window at the left are brass charcoal braziers, used in formal parlors partly for warmth and partly for decoration. The pestles and mortars are of solid brass and are used to pulverize herbs, nuts, and seeds. Other brass objects include pots and grinders for Turkish coffee. The trays and shallow pans are locally made (see Figure 23), but the stacks of aluminum pots and buckets, the various strainers and other kitchen equipment, and (probably) the coffee beakers hanging overhead are all imported, probably from France or Italy. The cups and ceramic vases are also imported, probably from Germany or Czechoslovakia. These, the small workshops depicted in Figures 24 and 25, and the stores in Figures 26, 27, and 28 are very common in certain parts of the Old City, but they are not restricted to it. They are characteristic of the small, low-overhead businesses by which many people in Tripoli earn their living.

Figure 29 is a view of old houses where there are no shops. This phenomenon is unlikely to occur for more than a short block or so in any one place, but it does recur often enough to be noted as one type of neighborhood. The Mansuri mosque, the principal mosque of Tripoli, is a low structure with a large rectangular courtyard. Madrasahs adhere to it on the east side, and other buildings press so closely upon it that it is impossible to see it as a whole. Its only conspicuous feature is its minaret, originally a Crusader belfry; the Muslims have added a dark green lantern topped by a flagpole (see Figure 30). The 'Izz-al-Din Hammam (Figure 31) is even more obscured by shopfronts and houses. The citadel is conspicuous and impressive when viewed from the river (Figure 32), but it has been so surrounded by tall modern buildings on the other side that it can easily be overlooked from that angle.

Figure 33 gives a good idea of what the modern apartment buildings are like, *en masse*, but even in Abu Samra there are a few older buildings to contrast with them. There has been a tremendous increase in the number of government schools in Tripoli since 1943, but most of them use rented quarters in buildings designed for other purposes. The combination of apartments and commercial outlets in new buildings persists here too; but relatively uncommercialized new buildings are also found in Hayy Mutran (Figure 34). The new buildings designed without shopfronts, however, are not in the majority and are always interspersed with those which do have shopfronts, as along Shari' 'Azmi.

The considerable elegance of design seen in some buildings, as in Figure 35, is usually accompanied in the newest sections by unfinished streets and weedy lots (see Figure 36). Throughout the city one notes the abrupt change from buildings to orchards.

Finally, Figures 37 and 38 convey some idea of the splendid natural surroundings of Tripoli. The juxtaposition of poor shacks and fine modern buildings is illustrative of the frequent heterogeneity of the city's sections.

Appendix B. Supplementary Tables

APPENDIX B

TABLE I. DOUBLE TELEPHONE SUBSCRIBERS BY LOCATIONS OF BUSINESS AND RESIDENTIAL PHONES

Locations of residential phones	Locations of business phones					
	Tal (incl. Yazbik)	Zahriyyah	Bab al-Tibbani	Tirbi'a	Sagha	Bazarkan
Tal (incl. Yazbik)	11	1	3	1		3
Mitayn	1					
Mutran	14		2		1	
Boulevard	6		1		1	
Shari' al-Mina	5	2	2		1	
'Azmi	11	3	2	1	1	1
Sintral	1	1	1			
Jamayzat	1	1	1			1
Madaris	2	3	1			
Latifi	1	3	6		1	
Zahriyyah	3	8	4	2	3	
Ghuraba		1	1			
Suq al-Khudra			1			
Bab al-Tibbani	1	2	9			
Maluli			2			
Qubbah	3	2	12	2	1	3
Zihr al-Maghar	3		4			
Nijmi	2					
Karm Qullah					1	
'Ajam	3		1			1
Bab al-Raml	1				2	
Abu Samra	8	1	6	1	3	13
Tirbi'a			2			
Sagha				1		
Bazarkan				1		
Nuri						
Nahhasiyyin					1	
'Attarin					1	
Nasara		1				1
Rifa'iyyi						
Kindarjiyyi			1			
Bab Hadid			1			
Al-Mina	1	1				
Not located	4		2			
Total	82	30	64	8	16	26

SUPPLEMENTARY TABLES

TABLE II. NUMBER OF DOUBLE AND SINGLE TELEPHONE SUBSCRIBERS BY QUARTER

Quarter	Residential phones			Business phones		
	Double	Single	Total	Double	Single	Total
Tal (inc. Yazbik)	9	68	77	82	115	197
Zahriyyah	8	163	171	30	76	106
Bab al-Tibbani	9	19	28	64	177	241
Tirbi'a	0	24	24	8	12	20
Sagha	0	6	6	16	28	44
Bazarkan	0	3	3	26	21	47

TABLES IIIa–IIIf. DOUBLE TELEPHONE SUBSCRIBERS

(Location of business telephones by degree of adjacency of residential telephones)

Table IIIa. Al-Tal

Location of residential telephones	Business Telephones in al-Tal	
	No.	%
In al-Tal	7	8.5
Adjacent to Tal	46	56.1
Yazbik	4	
Zahriyyah	3	
Mutran	14	
Boulevard	6	
Shari' al-Mina	5	
'Azmi	11	
Sintral	1	
Madaris	2	
Not adjacent to Tal	25	30.5
Bab al-Tibbani	1	
Qubbah	3	
Zihr al-Maghar	3	
Jamayzat	1	
Mitayn	1	
Bab al-Raml	1	
'Ajam	3	
Nijmi	2	
Latifi	1	
Al-Mina	1	
Abu Samra	8	
Not located	4	4.9
Total	82	100.0

APPENDIX B

Table IIIb. Zahriyyah

Location of residential telephones	Business telephones in Zahriyyah		
	No.		%
In Zahriyyah	8		26.7
Adjacent to Zahriyyah	10		33.3
Tal		1	
Bab al-Tibbani		2	
Latifi		3	
Madaris		3	
Ghuraba		1	
Not adjacent to Zahriyyah	12		40.0
Shari' al-Mina		2	
'Azmi		3	
Qubbah		2	
Jamayzat		1	
Sintral		1	
Rifa'iyyi		1	
Al-Mina		1	
Abu Samra		1	
Total	30		100.0

SUPPLEMENTARY TABLES

Table IIIc. Bab al-Tibbani

Location of residential telephones	Business telephones in Bab al-Tibbani	
	No.	%
In Bab al-Tibbani	9	14.1
Adjacent to Bab al-Tibbani	20	30.9
Zahriyyah	4	
Qubbah	12	
Ghuraba	1	
Suq al-Khudra	1	
Maluli	2	
Not adjacent to Bab al-Tibbani	33	51.6
Latifi	6	
Tal	3	
Hayy Mutran	2	
Boulevard	1	
Sh. al-Mina	2	
Zihr al-Maghar	4	
'Azmi	1	
'Ajam	1	
Madaris	1	
Jamayzat	1	
Sintral	1	
Kindarjiyyi	1	
Bab Hadid	1	
Tirbi'a	2	
Abu Samra	6	
Not located	2	3.4
Total	64	100.0

APPENDIX B

Table IIId. Tirbiʻa

Location of residential telephones	Business telephones in Tirbiʻa		
	No.		%
In Tirbiʻa	0		0.0
Adjacent to Tirbiʻa	3		37.5
Nuri		1	
Zahriyyah		2	
Not adjacent to Tirbiʻa	5		62.5
ʻAzmi		1	
Qubbah		2	
Tal		1	
Abu Samra		1	
Total	8		100.0

Table IIIe. Sagha

Location of residential telephones	Business telephones in Sagha		
	No.		%
In Sagha	0		0.0
Adjacent to Sagha	7		43.7
Nahhasiyyin		1	
ʻAttarin		1	
Zahriyyah		3	
Bab al-Raml		2	
Not adjacent to Sagha	9		56.3
Hayy Mutran		1	
Sh. al-Mina		1	
ʻAzmi		1	
Qubbah		1	
Latifi		1	
Karm Qullah		1	
Abu Samra		3	
Total	16		100.0

Table IIIf. Bazarkan

Location of residential telephones	Business telephones in Bazarkan		
	No.		%
In Bazarkan	0		0.0
Adjacent to Bazarkan	1		3.8
Nasara		1	
Not adjacent to Bazarkan	25		96.2
Tal		3	
Boulevard		3	
'Azmi		1	
Qubbah		3	
Ajam		1	
Jamayzat		1	
Abu Samra		3	
Total	26		100.0

TABLE IV. ADJACENT QUARTERS WHERE SUBSCRIBERS HAVE RESIDENTIAL AND BUSINESS TELEPHONES

Quarters where residential telephones are located	Quarters where business telephones are located					
	Tal	Zahriyyah	Bab al-Tibbani	Tirbi'a	Sagha	Bazarkan
Tal	X	X				
Bab al-Tibbani		X	X			
Zahriyyah	X	X	X	X	X	
Tirbi'a						
Sagha						
Bazarkan						
Yazbik	X					
Hayy Mutran	X					
Boulevard	X					
Shari' al-Mina	X					
'Azmi	X					
Madaris	X	X				
Qubbah			X			
Ghuraba		X	X			
Suq al-Khudra			X			
Maluli			X			
Latifi		X				
Sintral	X					
Nuri				X		
Nahhasiyyin					X	
'Attarin					X	
Bab al-Raml					X	
Hayy Nasara						X

Bibliography

Abu-Lughod, Janet, "Migrant Adjustment to City Life: The Egyptian Case," *American Journal of Sociology*, 67:22–23 (1961).

Abu-Lughod, Janet and Ezz el-Din Attiya, *Cairo Fact Book*. Social Research Center, American University at Cairo, 1963.

Adib Pasha, Auguste, *Le Liban après la guerre*. Cairo: Imprimerie Paul Barbey, 1919.

Ammar, Hamed, *Growing Up in an Egyptian Village*. London: Routledge, Kegan Paul, 1954.

Annuaire des Professions au Liban, Edition 1961–62. Beirut: General Advertising House, 1962.

Baedeker, Karl, *Palestine and Syria*. Leipzig, 1912.

Bartlett, W. H., William Purser, et al., *Syria, the Holy Land, Asia Minor*. Illustrated with text by John Carne, 3 vols. London and Paris: Fisher & Son, 1836–37.

Basbous, Malek and Ismat Boulos, "La Pêche au Liban," *Le Commerce du Levant*, 11:26 (July 1961).

Benet, Francisco, "The Ideology of Islamic Civilization," *International Journal of Comparative Sociology*, 4:211–226 (1963).

Burckhardt, John Lewis, *Travels in Syria and the Holy Land*. London: John Murray, 1822.

Charles-Roux, Fr., *Les échelles de Syrie et de Palestine au XVIIIe siècle*. Paris: Librairie Orientale Paul Geuthner, 1928.

Chehabe ed-Dine, Said, *Géographie humaine de Beyrouth*. Beirut: Imprimerie Calfat, 1960.

Churchill, Charles W., *The City of Beirut: A Socio-Economic Survey*. Beirut: Dar el-Kitab, 1954.

Churchill, Charles W., "Village Life in the Central Beqa' Valley of Lebanon," *Middle East Economic Papers* (1959), pp. 1–48.

Cox, Harvey, *The Secular City*. New York: Macmillan Co., 1965.

Delprat, Rosie, "La libanaise et le travail: dans le milieu ouvrier," *L'Orient*, February 26, 1962, p. 4.

BIBLIOGRAPHY

——, "Suzanne, Leyla et les autres: sont-elles contentes de leur sort?" *L'Orient Littéraire* (Beirut) March 3, 1962. (English translation in *Middle East Forum*, 38:13–15 (April 1962).

Directory of Voluntary Welfare Societies in Lebanon. Beirut: Federation of Non-Governmental Organizations Publications, 1958.

Dussaud, R., P. Deschamps, and H. Seyrig, *La Syrie antique et médiévale illustrée*. Paris: Librarie Orientaliste Paul Geuthner, 1931.

Elliott, John L., "Report on a Survey of the Soap Industry in Lebanon and Syria." Beirut: Industry Institute, 1956. 21 pp., mimeographed.

Fetter, George C. "A Comparative Study of Attitudes of Christian and of Moslem Lebanese Villages," *Journal for the Scientific Study of Religion*, 4:48–59 (1964).

Feuer, Lewis, "What is Alienation? The Career of a Concept," in *Sociology on Trial*, ed. Maurice Stein and Arthur Vidich. Englewood Cliffs: Prentice Hall, 1963.

Frankel, Charles, *The Love of Anxiety and Other Essays*. New York: Harper and Row, 1965.

Geographical Handbook Series, B.R. 513, *Syria*. London: Naval Intelligence Division, 1943.

Ghandour, Leila H., "The Relationship of Attitude to Social Classes in Beirut, Lebanon." Unpublished M.A. thesis, Department of Sociology, American University of Beirut, 1960.

Gibb, H. A. R. and Harold Bowen, *Islamic Society and the West*, vol. I, part 1. London: Oxford University Press, 1950.

Glazer, Nathan and Daniel P. Moynihan, *Beyond the Melting Pot*. Cambridge, Mass.: Massachusetts Institute of Technology Press, 1964.

Gorton, William W., Miles Prescott, and Gabriel Najjar, *Village Survey: Kasmie Rural Improvement Project*. Beirut: Lebanese Ministry of National Economy, 1953.

Grunebaum, G. E. von, *Modern Islam: The Search for Identity*. Berkeley and Los Angeles: University of California Press, 1962.

Grunwald, Kurt, and Joachim O. Ronall, *Industrialization in the Middle East*. New York: Council for Middle Eastern Affairs Press, 1960.

Gulick, John, *Social Structure and Culture Change in a Lebanese Village*. New York: Viking Fund Publications in Anthropology, no. 21, 1955.

—— "Images of an Arab City," *Journal of the American Institute of Planners*, 29:179–198 (1963).

—— "Urban Anthropology: Its Present and Future," *Transactions of the New York Academy of Sciences*, ser. II, 25:445–458 (1963).

—— "Old Values and New Institutions in a Lebanese Arab City," in *Dimensions of Cultural Change in the Middle East*, ed. John Gulick, *Human Organization*, 24:49–52 (1965).

—— "The Religious Structure of Lebanese Culture" in *Internationales Jahrbuch für Religionssoziologie*, vol. I, ed. Joachim Matthes. Köln and Opladen: Westdeutscher Verlag, 1965, pp. 151–187.

Hacker, Jane M., *Modern Amman: A Social Study*. Department of Geography, Durham Colleges in the City of Durham, Research Papers Series, no. 3. Durham, 1960.

el-Hajjé, Hassan, *Le parler arabe de Tripoli (Liban)*. Paris: Librairie C. Klincksieck, 1954.

Heyd, W., *Histoire du commerce du Levant au moyen-âge*. 2 vols. Amsterdam: Adolf M. Hakkert, 1959. Originally published in 1878.

Hitti, Philip K., *Lebanon in History*. New York: Macmillan Co., 1957.

Hottinger, Arnold, "Zu'ama and Parties in the Lebanese Crisis of 1958," *Middle East Journal*, 15:127–140 (1961).

Huxley, Julian, *From an Antique Land*. New York: Crown Publishers, 1954.

I.F.D. (Institut de Formation en Vue du Développement), *Le Liban face à son développement*. Beirut, 1963.

I.R.F.E.D. (Institut de Recherches et de Formation en Vue du Développement), *Etude préliminaire sur les besoins et les possibilités de développement au Liban, 1959–60*, vol. III: *Le Nord du Liban*. 1962.

Jabra, Jabra I., *Hunters in a Narrow Street*. London: Heinemann, 1960.

Jacobs, Jane, *The Death and Life of Great American Cities*. New York: Vintage Press, 1963.

Jessup, Henry H., *Fifty-three Years in Syria*. 2 vols. London and Edinburgh: Fleming H. Revell Co., 1910.

Karam, Jihad, "Central-Local Government Relationships in Lebanon as Reflected through a Case Study of the Municipality of Tripoli." Unpublished M.A. thesis, Department of Political Studies and Public Administration, American University of Beirut, 1961.

Khalaf, Samir G., "Management's Attitude toward Human Relations in Lebanese Industry." Unpublished M.A. thesis, Department of Sociology, American University of Beirut, 1957.

——— "Managerial Ideology and Industrial Conflict in Lebanon." Unpublished diss., Department of Sociology, Princeton University, 1963.

——— *Prostitution in a Changing Society: A Sociological Survey of Legal Prostitution in Beirut*. Beirut: Khayats, 1965.

——— "Industrial Conflict in Lebanon," in *Dimensions of Cultural Change in the Middle East*, ed. John Gulick, *Human Organization*, 24:24–33 (1965).

Khatchadourian, Haig, "The Mask and the Face: A Study of 'Make-Believe' in Middle Eastern Society," *Middle East Forum*, 37:15–18 (1961).

——— "Moral Make-Believe in Arab Society," *Middle East Forum*, 38:16–20 (1962).

al-Khoury, Ignace Tannous, *Mustapha Barbar: Hakim Tarabulsi* (Governor of Tripoli). Beirut: Mitab'at al-Rahabaniyyat al-Lubnaniyyah, 1957.

Khoury, Leila, "Standards Implied in the Grants-in-Aid Program of the Ministry of Social Affairs in Lebanon, with Special Reference to Orphanages." Unpublished B.A. thesis, Beirut College for Women, 1959.

Klat, Paul J., "Waqf, or Mortmain, Property in Lebanon," *Middle East Economic Papers* (1961), pp. 34–44.

——— "Automobiles in Lebanon," *Middle East Express* (Beirut), no. 11 (May 14, 1962), pp. 3–4.

BIBLIOGRAPHY

Landau, Jacob M., *Studies in the Arab Theater and Cinema*. Philadelphia: University of Pennsylvania Press, 1958.

Langley, Kathleen M., *The Industrialization of Iraq*. Cambridge, Mass.: Center for Middle Eastern Studies, 1961.

Lewis, W. H., *Levantine Adventurer*. New York: Harcourt, Brace, World, 1963.

Longrigg, Stephen H., *Syria and Lebanon under French Mandate*. London: Oxford University Press, 1958.

—— *Oil in the Middle East*, 2nd ed. London: Oxford University Press, 1961.

Mahmasani, Subhi, *Al-Awda'u al-Tashri'yat fi dawwal al-Arabiyyatu* (Legal Systems in the Arab States), 2nd ed. Beirut: Dar al-'Ilm l-il-Malayin, 1962.

Patterson, James L., *Journal of a Tour in Egypt, Palestine, Syria and Greece*. London, 1852.

Planhol, Xavier de, *The World of Islam*. Ithaca: Cornell University Press, 1959.

Potter, Dalton, "The Bazaar Merchant," in *Social Forces in the Middle East*, ed. S. N. Fisher. Ithaca: Cornell University Press, 1955.

Prothro, E. Terry, *Child Rearing in the Lebanon*. Cambridge, Mass.: Center for Middle Eastern Studies, 1961.

Pye, Lucian W., *Politics, Personality, and Nation Building: Burma's Search for Identity*. New Haven and London: Yale University Press, 1962.

al-Qalqashandi, Ahmad Shihab al-Din, *Subh al-A'sha*, vol. IV. Cairo, 1914. Originally written about 1390.

Reissman, Leonard, *The Urban Process: Cities in Industrial Societies*. New York: Free Press of Glencoe, 1964.

Republic of Lebanon, *Industrial Census of Lebanon, 1955*. 2 vols. Beirut: Ministry of National Economy, 1957–58.

République Libanaise, *Annuaire officiel du téléphone au Liban*. Beirut: Ministère des P.T.T., 1961. There is also an Arabic edition.

Richard, Jean, *Le comté de Tripoli sous la dynastie Toulousaine (1102–1187)*. Paris: Librairie Orientaliste Paul Geuthner, 1945.

Ritsher, Walter H., *Municipal Government in the Lebanon*. Beirut: American Press, 1932.

Rondot, Pierre, *L'Islam et les musulmans d'aujourd'hui*. Paris: Editions de l'Orante, vol. II, 1960.

Rosenberg, Harold, "It Can Happen to Anyone" (Review of *Alienation*, ed. Gerald Sykes). *New York Times Book Review*, December 20, 1964, pp. 1, 8c, 14–15.

Rosenfeld, Henry, "Processes of Structural Change within the Arab Village Extended Family," *American Anthropologist*, 60:1127–1139 (1958).

Sjoberg, Gideon, *The Preindustrial City*. Glencoe: Free Press, 1960.

Sullivan, Thomas, "The Whirling Dervishes," *Middle East Forum*, 28:23–26 (1962).

Sweet, Louise E., *Tell Toqaan: A Syrian Village*. Anthropological Papers,

Museum of Anthropology, no. 15. Ann Arbor: University of Michigan Press, 1960.

Thomson, William M., *The Holy Land: Lebanon, Damascus and Beyond Jordan.* New York: Harper, 1886.

UNESCO, *Lebanon: Suggestions for the Plan of Tripoli and for the Surroundings of the Baalbek Acropolis.* Paris, 1954.

—— *The Effects of Television on Children and Adolescents.* Reports and Papers on Mass Communication, no. 43. Paris, 1964.

Verney, Noel and George Dambmann, *Les puissances étrangères dans le Levant, en Syrie, et en Palestine.* Paris and Lyon, 1900.

Volney, C. F. C., *Voyage en Egypt et en Syrie.* Paris and The Hague: Mouton and Co., 1959. Originally published in 1787.

Weulersse, Jacques, *Antioche: Essai de géographie urbaine.* Cairo: Bulletin d'Etudes Orientales de l'Institut Français de Damas, 4:27–79 (1935).

Yanni, Jurjis Effendi, *Tarikh Suriyyah* (History of Syria). Beirut: Al-Matba' al-Adabiyyah, 1881.

Yaukey, David, *Fertility Differences in a Modernizing Country.* Princeton: Princeton University Press, 1961.

Ziadeh, Nicola A., *Urban Life in Syria under the Early Mamluks.* Beirut: American University of Beirut, 1953.

Beirut Magazines Cited
 Le Commerce du Levant
 Magazine
 Middle East Express
 La Revue du Liban
 al-Usbu' al-'Arabi

Lebanese Newspapers Cited
 Beirut Weekly (Beirut)
 The Daily Star (Beirut)
 La Gazette (Beirut)
 al-Hadara (Tripoli)
 al-Insha' (Tripoli)
 al-Jarida (Beirut)
 L'Orient (Beirut)
 Al-Nahar (Beirut)
 Trablus (Tripoli)

Notes

Fuller information on publications cited is given
in the preceding Bibliography.

II. *The Growth of Tripoli*

1. Hitti, *Lebanon in History*, p. 153.
2. *Ibid.*, p. 170.
3. Yanni, *Tarikh Suriyyah*, p. 377; in Arabic.
4. Hitti, *Lebanon in History*, p. 185.
5. Burckhardt, *Travels in Syria and the Holy Land*, p. 166.
6. Hitti, *Lebanon in History*, pp. 278–279.
7. *Ibid.*, p. 289.
8. Heyd, *Histoire du commerce du Levant au moyen-âge*, I, 170.
9. *Ibid.*, pp. 177–179.
10. UNESCO, *Lebanon: Suggestions for the Plan of Tripoli*, p. 10.
11. Ziadeh, *Urban Life in Syria under the Early Mamluks*, p. 66.
12. *Ibid.*, p. 81.
13. Hitti, *Lebanon in History*, p. 331.
14. *Ibid.*, p. 327.
15. Ziadeh, *Urban Life in Syria*, p. 38.
16. UNESCO, *Lebanon*, p. 14.
17. Ziadeh, *Urban Life in Syria*, p. 97.
18. *Ibid.*, p. 83.
19. Hitti, *Lebanon in History*, p. 342.
20. Ziadeh, *Urban Life in Syria*, map facing p. 38.
21. UNESCO, *Lebanon*, p. 12.
22. Ziadeh, *Urban Life in Syria*, p. 93.
23. al-Qalqashandi, *Subh al-A'sha*, IV, 142–143.
24. Hitti, *Lebanon in History*, p. 337.
25. Ziadeh, *Urban Life in Syria*, p. 2.
26. *Ibid.*, pp. 105–106.
27. Hitti, *Lebanon in History*, p. 335.

28. *Ibid.*, pp. 338–339.

29. Charles-Roux, *Les échelles de Syrie et de Palestine au XVIIIe siècle*, p. 8.

30. Lewis, *Levantine Adventurer*, pp. 82–83.

31. Charles-Roux, *Les échelles*, pp. 2, 7.

32. Yanni, *Tarikh Suriyyah*, pp. 399–413.

33. Volney, *Voyage en Egypte et en Syrie*, pp. 282–284.

34. *Ibid.*, pp. 281–282, *et passim*.

35. *Ibid.*, p. 282.

36. *Ibid.*, p. 166.

37. *Ibid.*, p. 172.

38. Charles-Roux, *Les échelles*, plate XXIV.

39. *Ibid.*, plate XVII.

40. *Ibid.*

41. al-Khoury, *Mustapha Barbar*, p. 103.

42. *Ibid.*, p. 141.

43. Yanni, *Tarikh Suriyyah*, p. 415.

44. *Ibid.*, pp. 418–421.

45. Burckhardt, *Travels in Syria*, pp. 163–168.

46. Bartlett, et al., *Syria, the Holy Land, Asia Minor*, I, 22.

47. Bartlett, et al., II, 9.

48. Hitti, *Lebanon in History*, p. 426.

49. Patterson, *Journal of a Tour in Egypt, Palestine, Syria and Greece*, p. 323.

50. Hitti, *Lebanon in History*, p. 401.

51. Yanni, *Tarikh Suriyyah*, p. 411.

52. Jessup, *Fifty-three Years in Syria*, II, 165.

53. *Ibid.*, I, 614; II, 151.

54. *Ibid.*, I, 118.

55. *Ibid.*, II, 806.

56. *Ibid.*, I, 112.

57. *Ibid.*, I, 113–116.

58. *Ibid.*, II, 143.

59. *Ibid.*, II, 387.

60. Thomson, *The Holy Land: Lebanon, Damascus, and beyond Jordan*, pp. 275–277.

61. Baedeker, *Palestine and Syria*, p. 336.

62. *Ibid.*, pp. 336–338.

63. Longrigg, *Syria and Lebanon under French Mandate*, p. 201.

64. Churchill, *The City of Beirut: A Socio-Economic Survey*, p. 30.

65. Hacker, *Modern Amman: A Social Study*, p. 75.

66. Chehabe ed-Dine, *Géographie humaine de Beyrouth*, pp. 208–209.

67. Abu-Lughod and Attiya, *Cairo Fact Book*, p. 24.

68. I.F.D., *Le Liban face à son développement*, p. 212.

69. Dussaud, et al., *La Syrie antique et médiévale illustrée*, plate 112.

70. Geographical Handbook Series, *Syria*, p. 306.

71. Grunwald and Ronall, *Industrialization in the Middle East*, p. 298.
72. *Ibid.*, p. 315.
73. Longrigg, *Oil in the Middle East*, p. 89.
74. Al-Khoury, *Mustapha Barbar*, p. 18.
75. Longrigg, *Syria and Lebanon*, pp. 219–221.
76. *Ibid.*, p. 252.

III. *Sectarian Activities and Organizations*

1. Glazer and Moynihan, *Beyond the Melting Pot.*
2. Gulick, "The Religious Structure of Lebanese Culture," p. 166.
3. Sjoberg, *The Preindustrial City*, pp. 256ff.
4. Feuer, "What is Alienation? The Career of a Concept"; Rosenberg, "It Can Happen to Anyone."
5. Gulick, "The Religious Structure of Lebanese Culture," pp. 163–166.
6. Yaukey, *Fertility Differences in a Modernizing Country*, p. 45.
7. Jessup, *Fifty-three Years in Syria*, I, p. 144.
8. Mahmasani, *Legal Systems in the Arab States*, pp. 253–254.
9. Klat, "Waqf, or Mortmain, Property in Lebanon," p. 37.
10. *Al-Insha'*, January 31, 1962.
11. *Al-Hadara*, January 28, 1962.
12. Khoury, "Standards Implied in the Grants-in-Aid Program of the Ministry of Social Affairs in Lebanon, with Special Reference to Orphanages," p. 51.
13. *Ibid.*, pp. 52–53.

IV. *Governmental Administration and Services*

1. Benet, "The Ideology of Islamic Civilization," p. 226.
2. Grunebaum, *Modern Islam: The Search for Identity*, p. 137.
3. Ritsher, *Municipal Government in the Lebanon*, p. 1.
4. *Al-Jarida*, January 11, 1963.
5. Reissman, *The Urban Process: Cities in Industrial Societies*, p. 164.
6. Hottinger, "Zu'ama and Parties in the Lebanese Crisis of 1958."
7. Pye, *Politics, Personality, and Nation Building: Burma's Search for Identity*, pp. 16–19.
8. *Al-Jarida*, January 11, 1963.
9. Karam, "Central-Local Government Relationship in Lebanon as reflected through a Case Study of the Municipality of Tripoli," p. 40.
10. *Ibid.*, p. 43.
11. *Ibid.*, p. 66.
12. *Trablus*, December 13, 1961.
13. Karam, "Central-Local Government Relationships," pp. 62–64.
14. *Ibid.*, p. 145.
15. *Ibid.*, pp. 143–153.
16. *Ibid.*, p. 100.

17. *Ibid.*, pp. 95–96.

18. *Al-Nahar*, March 13, 1962.

19. *L'Orient*, January 19, 1962.

20. *The Daily Star*, November 24, 1961.

21. Mahmasani, *Legal Systems in the Arab States*, pp. 248–251.

22. *L'Orient*, January 19, 1962.

23. Klat, "Automobiles in Lebanon," p. 3.

24. *Al-Jarida*, January 11, 1963.

25. *Al-Hadara*, March 1, 1962.

26. *Al-Nahar*, March 18, 1962.

27. Fetter, "A Comparative Study of Attitudes of Christian and of Moslem Lebanese Villages," p. 59.

V. *Work and Commerce*

1. *Al-Hadara*, January 28, 1962.

2. *Le Commerce du Levant*, no. 15 (1961), pp. 24–25.

3. Abu-Lughod, "Migrant Adjustment to City Life: The Egyptian Case," p. 26.

4. el-Hajjé, *Le parler arabe de Tripoli (Liban)*, p. 182.

5. *Le Commerce du Levant*, no. 18 (1962), p. 29. Translation mine.

6. *L'Orient*, March 2, 1962. Translation mine.

7. *Le Commerce du Levant*, no. 18 (1962), pp. 28–29.

8. *La Revue du Liban*, April 21, 1962.

9. Elliott, "Report on a Survey of the Soap Indusrty in Lebanon and Syria," p. 2.

10. *Ibid.*, pp. 3–5.

11. *Ibid.*, pp. 20–21.

12. *Le Commerce du Levant*, no. 18 (1961), p. 67.

13. *Magazine*, no. 268 (February 8, 1962), pp. 26–29; *La Gazette*, no. 173 (June 1, 1962), pp. 1–2.

14. *L'Orient*, December 21, 1961.

15. *Beirut Weekly*, December 18, 1961.

16. Potter, "The Bazaar Merchant."

17. Weulersse, *Antioche: Essai de géographie urbaine*, p. 74.

18. République Libanaise, *Annuaire officiel du téléphone au Liban*.

19. *Annuaire des Professions au Liban*.

20. *Middle East Express*, no. 13 (May 28, 1962), p. 3.

21. Grunwald and Ronall, *Industrialization in the Middle East*, p. 298.

22. *Le Commerce du Levant*, no. 18 (February 1962), p. 67.

23. *Ibid.*, no. 8 (1961), p. 40.

24. Langley, *The Industrialization of Iraq*, pp. 89–90.

25. Khalaf, "Management's Attitude toward Human Relations in Lebanese Industry," pp. 39ff.

26. Khalaf, "Managerial Ideology and Industrial Conflict in Lebanon."

27. *Ibid.*, pp. 334–336.

VI. *Private Life and Public Face*

1. Gulick, *Social Structure and Culture Change in a Lebanese Village*, pp. 48–49.
2. Rosenfeld, "Processes of Structural Change within the Arab Village Extended Family."
3. Churchill, *The City of Beirut*; Hacker, *Modern Amman*.
4. Yaukey, *Fertility Differences*.
5. *Beirut Weekly*, November 6, 1961.
6. Rondot, *L'Islam et les musulmans d'aujourd'hui*, p. 161.
7. Khatchadourian, "The Mask and the Face: A Study of 'Make-Believe' in Middle Eastern Society," p. 16.
8. *Ibid.*, p. 17.
9. Ammar, *Growing Up in an Egyptian Village*.
10. Planhol, *The World of Islam*, p. 22.
11. *Ibid.*, p. 8.
12. *Al-Usbu' al-'Arabi*, January 29, 1962.
13. *The Daily Star*, May 16, 1952.
14. *Al-Hadara*, January 28, 1962.
15. *Middle East Forum* 38:13–15 (April 1962).
16. *L'Orient*, February 26, 1962, p. 4.
17. Jabra, *Hunters in a Narrow Street*, pp. 140–141.
18. Gibb and Bowen, *Islamic Society and the West*, pp. 279–280.
19. Gulick, "Images of an Arab City," p. 193.
20. Landau, *Studies in the Arab Theater and Cinema*, pp. 198ff.
21. Huxley, *From an Antique Land*, pp. 89–91.
22. Personal communication from Julian Huxley, March 15, 1965.
23. Sullivan, "The Whirling Dervishes," p. 26.
24. Khalaf, *Prostitution in a Changing Society: A Sociological Survey of Legal Prostitution in Beirut*, pp. 108–109.
25. Ghandour, "The Relationship of Attitude to Social Classes in Beirut, Lebanon," p. 96.
26. *La Gazette*, May 4, 1962.

VII. *Tripoli and the World*

1. Gulick, "Old Values and New Institutions," pp. 49–52.
2. Gulick, "Urban Anthropology: Its Present and Future."
3. Gulick, "Old Values and New Institutions," p. 50.
4. Frankel, *The Love of Anxiety and Other Essays*, p. 1.
5. *Ibid.*, "The Anti-Intellectualism of the Intellectuals," pp. 12–39.
6. UNESCO, *The Effects of Television on Children and Adolescents*, p. 14.
7. Katchadourian, "The Mask and the Face."
8. Cox, *The Secular City*, p. 48.
9. Jacobs, *The Death and Life of Great American Cities*.

Index

'Abdul-Wahhab, family of, residential cluster, 138
Abu-'Ali River, 6, new channel project, 9, 76, 219. *See also* Qadisha River
Abu Fraydu, 159, 175, 218
Abu Samra, 6–7, 9, 17, 114, 156–157, 161, 169, 190, 201, 207, 211–212, 215, 220, 222; cemetery, 149; growth, 32; home and business telephones, 160; informal dress, 145; movement of people to, 77; public telephone, 83; Sunni Muslims, 67; water tanks, 33
Administrative districts: degree of correspondence with quarters, 79; jurisdiction not extended to newest sections, 77; mukhtars, 77
'Adra, family of, 138, 179
Al-'Adsi, 155
Advertisements, posting of, 221
Ahwi Hitti, 154
Akkar, 10, 27, 179, 205, 216
'Alawites, 19, 27, 172, 182, 205–206; immigration, 43; kinship clusters, 139; residential cluster, 67
Aleppo, city, 16, 18, 27, 153, 176
Alexander the Great, 11
Alexandretta, annexation, 34
Alexandria, city, 182
Algeria, demonstration over, 87–88
Alienation, 196; ambiguity of, 41
'Alush, family of, 140
American University of Beirut, 23, 45; sample of Tripolitan students, 124
'Amman, city, average household size, 32
Anonymity: lack of, 71, 119–120; and industrialization, 109
Antioch, city, 16; suqs compared to Tripoli's, 103
Apartments, new: length of residence in, 152; related to household composition, 127
Apartment buildings, new: architecture, 212–213, 215–216; attitudes toward, 151; construction, 204; effects on population density, 32; shops in, 151
Arab countries, wood imports, 93
'Arida, family of, 182; cotton mill, 33, 100, 107, 110, 144

Aristocrats, 26; mansions, 28. *See also* Classes; Prestige; Upper class
Armenians, 44; Armenian benevolent society, 61; Armenian priest, clothing, 52
'Attarin, 2, 154, 210
Automation, 109
Automobile repair shops, 216; at transportation nodes, 92
Automobile service, increase of, 108
Automobiles, number in Tripoli, 82. *See also* Traffic, automotive
'Awayda, family of, residence cluster, 138
Awqaf, department, 45–49, 64, 203; familial, 139. *See also* Waqf
Al-Azhar, 47, 208
'Azmi Bey, 29

Bab Hadadin, 154, 170, 191, 211; as administrative district, 77; significance of name, 101, 153
Bab Hadid, 2, 155, 161, 209; as administrative district, 77; significance of name, 153
Bab al-Raml, 155, 171, 169, 201, 210, 213, 220; as center for southward travel, 91; graves, 56; police station, 76; professional storytellers, 164; public telephone, 83; significance of name, 153
Bab al-Tibbani, 1, 29, 80, 82, 114, 155, 161, 169, 172, 174, 191, 204–206; as agricultural-produce distribution center, 89; 'Alawites, 67, 139; as administrative district, 77; commercial specialization, 106; growth, 32; home and business telephones, 160; income levels, 184, 206; percentage of "merchants," 106; police station, 76; public telephone, 83; second new mosque, 219; significance of name, 153; Syrians, 90–91
Baghdad, city, 86, 145, 189; polygamy in, 129
Balkans, import of wood from, 93
Bahsas, 107, 220; as truck terminal, 91; beginnings as industrial area, 33; industrial plants, 200–201; lack of signs, 57, 119; new businesses, 108; new cottonseed-oil plant, 98; public telephones, 83

INDEX

Banks: names, 108–109; telephones, 120
Banque de Syrie et du Liban, 202
Banyas, expansion as petroleum terminal, 35
Bar Association of Tripoli, 79; number of Christians and Muslims, 114
Barbar, Mustapha, governor of Tripoli, 20–21
Barracks, 206
Barrio system, 152
Bashir II, 20
Baths, public. *See* Hammams
Batrun, 200; qada' of, 110
Bayt, 152
Bazarkan, 5, 154, 171, 191, 209; commercial specialization, 106; home and business telephones, 160; percentage of "merchants," 106. *See also* Cloth merchants
Ba'al Saraqbi, 158, 206; income levels, 184
Ba'lbaki, Layla, novels of, 142
Beauty-queen complex, 142
Bedouin, 136
Beirut, 3–4, 7, 10, 13, 16, 22, 27, 30, 33, 82–83, 89, 93, 107, 111–114, 142, 144, 162, 166–167, 172, 175, 179, 184, 203–204, 213, 217, 222; branch of Tripoli sweet shop, 97; competitive growth, 35; gold market, 210; household size, 32; highway traffic, 90; lawyers' strike, 80; polygamy, 129; population, 19; predominance, 175–176; press, 74; retail competition, 90; suburbs, 191
Beirut Bar Association, strike, 79
Beirut College for Women, 45, 143
Belly dancers, reactions to, 54
Benevolent associations: enumerated, 61–62; functions, 64; sectarian participation, 63–64
Al-Biddawi, 107, 218; public telephone, 83; sacred fish, 12
Bidonville, 158, 201, 207
Birkat al-Millaha, 155, 209; leather-goods shops, 100
Birth rates, differences in urban-rural, 125
Bisar, Dr. 'Abdul-Latif, political role, 34
Bisar, family of, 179
Blum, Léon, delegation to, 34
Boulevard, the, 114, 158, 201
Boys, percentage in schools compared to girls, 84
British troops, 30
Brothels. *See* Prostitution
Bsharri, 96

Buber, Martin, 196
Buildings, unfinished, 207, 213
Bureaucratization, 109
Bus transportation, 1, 3, 90, 202, 205
Burt, family of, 181
Businesses: adjacency to homes, 160, 162; infrequency of impersonal names, 119–120; number of employees, 108
Butcher shops, 2, 210
Buwwabi, 28, 138, 159, 218

Cabaret, defunct, 164
Cafés. *See* Coffeehouses
Cairo, 4, 167, 189, 208; 18th century population, 153; population density, 32; prestige, 47
California, 83
Cambridge, Mass., 190
Campaign, fund-raising, 68
Cement: factories, 9, 107, 110; products exported, 108
Cemeteries, 149, 213; decoration, 169
Census of 1932, 31, 41
Chamber of Commerce, 117
Children: illegitimate, 65; play groups, 150
Christians, 10, 26, 30, 140; as goldsmiths, 103; as lawyers, 79, 114; as members of service clubs, 116; attitudes toward family associations, 141; birth rate, 125; contrasted with Muslims, 135, 146, 177–180; Greek, 21, 24; movement from Tirbi'a, 101; nuclear family households among, 126; preference for non-government schools, 84; quarter, 154; relations with Muslims, 166–167; village ties, 126
Christmas, adaptations of Muslims to, 173
Churches, markers, 56
Cinemas, 1, 5, 54, 150, 168, 171, 202; audience reactions, 165; increase, 108; number and distribution, 164–165
Citadel, 6, 14, 167, 208, 211, 222
Citrus production. *See* Orchards
City Hall. *See* Municipality
City haters, influence of, 188
Civic responsibility: lack, 141; need, 143
Classes, social: summarized, 183; relation to sects, 66, 182. *See also* Aristocrats; Lower class; Middle class; Prestige; Upper class
Clinics, surgical, 113
Clocktower, 28, 220
Cloth merchants, 5, 100, 154, 209. *See also* Bazarkan

INDEX

Clothes, ready-made, 210

Clothing: and prestige, 145; identity-group significance, 51–52; winter, 9; women's styles, 53. *See also* Women

Clusters, residential: kin, 137; sectarian, 66–67

Coffee vendors, 1, 4, 168, 221

Coffeehouses, 150, 168, 184, 210, 221; at transportation nodes, 92; compared to British pubs, 92; compared to sweet shops and restaurants, 162; regional specialization, 92; sectarian specialization, 92

Commercial areas, compared with residential, 191

Community, lack of sense of, 67, 151, 196–197

Confectioners, number of employees, 97

Confessionalism, 40–41

Connecticut, traffic casualties compared, 81–83

Contraception, 126

Coppersmiths. *See* Nahhasiyyin

Cotton, 18

Courts: judicial, types of, 80; Shari'a, 45–46, 80

Crisis of 1958, 93, 173

Crusaders, 13–14, 222

Dabbusi, family association, 140

Damascus, 10, 16, 100–101, 128, 140, 176

"Dating," 143

Dentists, 104, 112

Demolition, effects, 209

Demonstrations: of 1936–37, 34; nonviolent, 86–88

Desegregation, sexual, 68

Dibbagha, 20, 25, 79, 100–101, 155, 191, 209

Druze, 23, 40, 44, 52, 73, 136, 140, 143

Eastern Orthodox Church, 44, 76, 92, 116, 166; archbishop, 48–49; cathedral, 25; churches, location, 49; class division, 182; distinguished from Greek Orthodox, 26; population, 29; priest, headgear, 51; Maronite funeral, 148; residence of members, 67; schools, location, 49; youth organization, 49, 68

Education: *baccalauréat, première partie,* 57, 59; examinations, attitudes toward, 59; *kulliyah,* 57; kuttabs, decline, 60; madrasahs, 16, 60; Ministry of, 59, 70, 85; teacher-parent relationship, 85; western, 127. *See also* Schools

Electric appliances, 214; increase of service for, 108

Electric power: introduction, 33; lack, 30; recency, 83

Engineers, 104, 112

Eminent domain, 139

Existentialism, 188

Exports, 27, 89

Exurban developments, 191

Factories: cement, 9, 107, 110; plywood, 108, 110

Families: associations, 140–141; Christian, most prestigeful, 177–180; Muslim, most prestigeful, 177–180; "old," lineages and clans, 137

Family, the: ambivalent feelings, 134; extended, 121, 123, 127, 136, 139; importance in Lebanese culture, 37–38; nuclear among Christians and Muslims, 126. *See also* Kin groups

Fawq al-Rih, 159, 218

Feuds, motives for, 132

Financing, national and international, 109

Fish market, 210

Fishing, commercial, 99

Flood of 1955, 9, 16, 25, 205, 208–209

Freighters, Tripoli-owned, 108

French, the, 18–19, 79

French cultural mission, 173

French mandate, 30, 193, 202

Frost, Robert, quoted, 38

Funerals, 146; Christian and Muslim compared, 147; notices of different sects, 56; Maronite procession, 147–149

Furniture makers, 5, 154, 204, 210, 222; increase, 108

Gambling, private club, 174

Gaza, 16

Girls, percentage in schools compared to boys, 84–85

Goethe Institute, 173

Gold, investment, 210

Goldsmiths, 5, 210; Christian majority, 103; suq, 101

Government: attitudes toward, 72–73, 193; centralization, 69–70; involvement, 71; increase of services, 57; image of good government, 73; "nonindustrial" nature, 193; schools, use of rented quarters, 223; services, Ottoman, 70; office telephones, 120

Grand Mufti of Lebanon, 166; statement concerning polygamy, 130

247

INDEX

Krak des Chevaliers, 13
Kura, 107, 182; as Eastern Orthodox stronghold, 95; olives, 95

Labor unions, 103, 117–119
Landlordism, 33
Latin County of Tripoli, 13
Latakia, 13, 19, 35, 182
Law: attitudes toward, 80; enforcement, 70, 74
Lawyers, 79, 113; offices, 114, 203
Lent, compared to Ramadan, 167
Library: of YMCA, 68; public, request for, 86
Lions Club. *See* Service clubs
Liquor, sale of, 174
Lottery, national, 4
Lower class, 144. *See also* Class; Prestige

Maluli, 158, 206; public housing, 205; increased building, 206
Mamluk, 208–209; towers, 14; period, 163
Manhattan, 190
Mansuri mosque, 16, 56, 101, 163, 169–170, 210–211, 222
Maronites, 10, 19, 22–23, 26, 29, 44, 92, 116, 143, 166, 182, 207; bishop, 49, 148, 215–216; cathedral, 215–216; clusters in Qubbah and Hayy Mutran, 67; connections with Vatican, 50; French orientation, 50; funeral, 147–149; presidency of Lebanon, 34; patriarch, 50; priest, costume, 51–52; schools, 50
Marriage between cousins, 135. *See also* Polygamy; Weddings
"Mask," 132, 195
Mass spectatorism, 165
Mawlawiyyi, 100, 155
Mecca, 19, 51, 166
Merchants, 68; traditional role defined, 106
Middle class, 59, 143, 174, 185; attitudes concerning Bab al-Tibbani, 206; attitudes toward labor, 144; attitudes toward upper class, 145; decreasing occurrence of extended family, 127; shops catering to, 214. *See also* Classes; Prestige; Upper class
Mihaytrah, as administrative district, 77
Mina, the, 2, 4, 6–7, 20–21, 27–28, 31, 49, 114, 156, 172–175, 216–218; age of houses, 217; as separate municipality, 75; as truck terminal, 91; Christian and Muslim parts, 218; compared to Old City and to Tripoli in general, 217–218; customs duties, 75; foreign con-

sulates, 173; income levels, 184, 217; new quarters, 159; old quarters, 158–159; port business, 92–93; public telephone, 83; seaplane base, 93
Minorities, Lebanese and U.S. attitudes compared, 73
Mir'ibi family, 179
Mongol invasions, 18
Mosques, 1; decorations, 167, 169; markers, 56; number in Tripoli, 47; storefronts in, 204
Mount Lebanon, 6–7, 10, 26, 200, 216; Mutaserifiyah, 30; view, 212
Mount Turbul, 6, 218
Mufti of Tripoli, 34, 45–46, 51, 170–171
Muhafazat al-Shamal, 10, 80; established, 34; municipal importance in Tripoli, 74
Muhafiz, 70–71, 73, 75, 87–88, 170, 175; as chief municipal authority, 71; as traditional good ruler, 74
Muhammad, 12; descendants, 51
Muhtasib, 17
Mujamalat, 132
Mukhtars of Tripoli, 77
Municipality: budget, 75–76; city hall, 76, 203; chartered, 70; council, 31, 75–76, 79; employees, 76; government, lack of interest in, 74–75; revenues, 76; traditional Muslim structure, 69
Muqaddim family, political activities, 34
Munsif, household composition, 122–123
Muscleman films, 165
Muslims, 10, 12, 23, 29, 92; aristocrats, 24; as members of service clubs, 116; as physicians, 114; attendance at Christian schools, 59; compared with Christians, 125, 177–180; family privacy, 121; frequency of nuclear family households, 126; hospital, 113; importance as officers of labor unions, 119; infrequency of village ties, 125; kulliyah, 47; participation in YMCA, 68; proportion in government schools, 85; relations with Christians, 166, 181; shaykhs, costume, 51
Muslims, Shi'a, 13, 27, 43, 140
Muslims, Sunni, 17, 72, 76, 143, 182; aristocrats, 26; majority in Tripoli, 43–44; organization in Tripoli, 45–48

Nahhasiyyin, suq, 5, 100, 154, 210; destruction, 220
Narcotics, 175
Nasser, President Gamal 'Abdul, 4, 87
Nationalism, 166

INDEX

Neighborhoods, 129, 150, 205–206, 209
New Jersey, 83
New York, 83
New York Times, mention of Tripoli, 86
North Carolina, 83
North Lebanon: labor force, 144; number of productive establishments, 109. *See also* Muhafazat
Nouveaux riches, 180–181, 184
Nuri, 154; as administrative district, 77
Nurseries, day-care, 145
Nuss Birtawshi, 159, 218

Occupations, sample, 104–105
Old City, 16, 20, 24, 27, 29, 114, 151, 153, 155, 163, 206, 208–211, 222; as potential tourist attraction, 94; attitudes of Tripolitans toward, 94, 208; compared to the Mina, 217–218; demolition, 219; effects of moving away from, 127; houses, 150; income levels, 184, 209; quarters, 154–155; residential clusters of lineages, 158; smallness of businesses, 112; veiled women, 55
Orchard laborers, demography of, 95
Orchards, 27; at Miniyah, 94; citrus, 25, 95, 97; fear of, 28; initial destruction for buildings, 33; olive, 95, 207; spraying, disagreements concerning, 97; threats to, 96
Orphanages, 65–66
Orphans, services at funeral, 147
Orthodox. *See* Eastern Orthodox Church
Ottoman Empire, 20, 28, 70, 172, 208; administration, 27; educational reforms, 60; government, 69, 193; municipal law of 1877, 70; pashalik of Tripoli, 18; Turks, 18, 30
Ownership, fragmentation, 139

Palestine war, 35
Palestinian refugees, 66–68
Paris, population density compared to Tripoli's, 32
Park, municipal, 4, 9, 220
Parliament of Lebanon, 72; Tripoli deputies in, 43
Parties, political, incomplete development, 71
Persians, 11
Personality: female, development according to vulnerable ego hypothesis, 133; integration, 197; male, development according to vulnerable ego hypothesis, 133–134
Pharmaceuticals, price problem, 114–115

Pharmacies: concentrations, 114; number, 113; number and population estimates, 114–115
Pharmacists, 104, 112
Phoenicians, 11
Physicians, 104, 112; location of offices, 114; Muslims among, 114; number, 113; women, 142
Planning projects, financing, 76–77
Plumbers, 108
Point IV program, 108
Police stations, locations, 76
Polygamy, 129–130. *See also* Marriage; Weddings
Population: density, 32, 189–191; estimates, 31, 114–115; growth, 32
Postal service, 82–83
Premiership of Lebanon, 72; Sunni Muslim in, 31
Presbyterians, 45, 116; American orientation, 50; assistance to Palestinian refugees, 66
Press, the, 4, 70, 73, 166, 194; complaints expressed in, 74, 114; court notices, 80
Prestige, 177; and sectarianism, 66, clothing and, 145; criteria, 183–184; familial, 180. *See also* Classes; Middle class; Upper class
Printing presses of Tripoli, 103
Productive establishments of North Lebanon and Tripoli, 109–110
Professionals, 68
Promenades, 150, 163, 172
Prostitution, 175, 218
Psychiatric service, 113–114

Qabr al-Zayni, 159, 218
Qada' of Tripoli, 75, 110
Qadi, 17, 45–46
Qadisha River, 6, 10. *See also* Abu-'Ali River
Qalawun, 14
Qbur Yihud, 191, 204
Quarter, Christian, 153. *See also* Hayy Nasara
Quarters, 152; commercial, 154; degrees of correspondence with administrative districts, 79; knowledge of names, 83, 155–156, 206; names, 154; network of streets pattern, 154; new, 157–158; old, 154–155; "psychology," 159; residential, 154. *See also* Har; Hara; Hayy; Shari'; Suqs
Al-Qubbah, 4, 6–7, 9, 17, 20, 49, 79, 114, 144, 156–157, 172, 191, 206–207; as administrative district, 77; as center of

INDEX

Social distance, 181
Social responsibility, 69, 197
Social solidarity, sectarian, 66
Social welfare services, 66
Sportsmanship, 165
Stadium, municipal, 165
Streets: lack of signs, 157; lack of paving, 207, 212; plans, 35; unfinished, 216; widening, effects, 211
Student Union of Tripoli, 85, 87
Suburbs, lack in Tripoli, 191
Sugar refinery, 108, 110
Suqs, 16, 100
Suq al-Haraj, 155, 209; leather workers, 100
Suq al-Kharab, 159, 218
Suq al-Khudra, 158
Suq al-Muslimiyyah, 159, 218
Suq al-Qamih, 154, 205, 208
Supreme Islamic Council of Lebanon, 46
Sur (Tyre), 22
Swayqah, 79, 154, 161, 206, 208; as administrative district, 77; children's swings, 169
Syria, 14; clothing, 3; customs barriers, 35, 96; customs duties, 33; rug sellers from, 3; separation from, 34; ties of Tripoli to, 34

Tabbikha, family association, 140
Tajir, traditional role, 103–104. *See also* Merchants
Tal, the, 1, 3, 7, 25, 28, 55, 79, 82, 118, 156–157, 169, 171, 191, 213, 221; as administrative district, 77; as Beirut bus terminal, 91; as truck terminal, 91; fashionable sweet shops, 97; house and business telephones, 160; municipal building, 76; park, 202; police station, 76; public telephone, 83
Tal'a al-Zahir, 155, 191, 206
Tanners, 209
Taxes, 76; collection, 70
Taxis: owners' and drivers' union, 118; number, 91; *service*, 91, 216
Telephones: number, 18; predominance of individualized-personal subscriptions, 120
Telephone directory: as source of information for occupations, 104; references to, 141
Telephone exchange, 83, 214. *See also* Shari' Sintral
Television, 214
Tel Toqaan, household composition, 122–123

Tikkiyah, of the Mawlawi dervishes, 155, 172, 207
Tirbi'a, 5, 79, 114, 154, 210, 222; concentration of iron workers, 101; emigration of Christians from, 101; home and business telephones, 160
Tourism: facilities, 94; festival, 173–174; market, 210–222
Trablus al-Sham, 10
Trade Fair, proposed, 94, 219
Traffic, automotive, 5; congestion, 75; drivers' behavior, 81; fatalities and technological change, 82; problems, 81; rush hour, 149; safety campaign, 81
Tramway, 27–28
Transportation nodes, 91–92
"Tribalism," 136
Tripolis, 11

'Ulama, 23, 45–46
Underdeveloped nations, 71
Uniate Catholics, 50
United States Information Service, 173
UNRWA, 68
Upper class, 59, 63, 174, 182, 185, 187; and service-club memberships, 116; decreasing occurrence of extended family households, 127; women's parties, 145. *See also* Aristocrats; Classes; Prestige
'Uqbi al-Himrawi, 158, 208
'Uqbi al-Mufti, 155, 191, 206
Urban renewal, attitudes toward, 211
Urbanization, ambiguity of, 187

Veiled women, percentage in Tripoli, 56
Vice, 175
Volleyball, 165
Voting: by men and by women, 144; rarity of occasion for, 81
Vulnerable ego, hypothesis, 133–134

Wali, 69, 71
Waqf, 20, 47; dhurri and khayri, 47–48. *See also* Awqaf
Warehouses, 108, 204
Water supply: polluted, 30; modern system, 83, 207
Weavers, silk, 13, 19, 21, 30; decline, 100
Weddings: belly dances at, 54; virginity of bride demonstrated at, 146
West Africa: emigration to, 34, 60; import of wood from, 93
West Germany, recognizes Israel, 86
Women: education, 142; employees in North Lebanon, 109; higher education

252

HARVARD MIDDLE EASTERN STUDIES

* Published jointly by the Center for International Affairs and the Center for Middle Eastern Studies.

† Published jointly by the Center for Middle Eastern Studies and the Joint Center for Urban Studies.

051099